William Cash read English at Cambridge and is the author of a Hollywood memoir and a biography of Graham Greene. During the 1990s, he worked in the US as West Coast correspondent of the *Times* and as US special correspondent for the *Daily Telegraph*. His play, *The Green Room*, about the English philosopher A. J. Ayer, was named as a Critics' Choice of the Edinburgh Festival by the *Observer*.

William is the founder of *Spear's* magazine and chairman of the *Catholic Herald*. He now writes for the *Sunday Times Magazine*, *Telegraph Magazine*, *New Statesman* and the *Times*, and appears regularly on TV and radio. A two-time winner of editor of the year at the PPA Independent Publisher awards, he campaigns for heritage causes and is a special adviser to English Heritage. He lives between Shropshire and London.

Praise for *Restoration Heart*

'I read most of it in one exciting sitting. It's brilliant, gripping and sad. The personal romantic memoir is terrific'

Harry Mount, editor of *The Oldie*

'It never fails to entertain, a compulsive and entertaining read'

Sir Roy Strong

'Hilarious . . . *Restoration Heart* conveys the transformative power of good architecture . . . this book is one to be treasured'

The New Criterion, critic's pick

'A funny and unexpectedly touching book'

Country Life

'A riotously colourful book'

Mail on Sunday

'Immensely readable . . . Laugh-out-loud funny, *Restoration Heart* is a delightful true story of love, hope and redemption by one of the foremost society writers of our day'

Tatler

'An excellent memoir'

Nicholas Coleridge

'Recommended . . . unexpected poignancy'

New Statesman

'*Restoration Heart* will cheer anyone who has reached mid-life without finding fame, success, fulfilment or love . . . This entertaining, often poignant book, is straight out of Waugh or Wodehouse'

Clare Asquith, *Catholic Herald*

'A touching, entertaining memoir which traces the twin track restoration of a broken heart and dilapidated Shropshire Manor'

Brendan Walsh, editor of *The Tablet*

'An endearing story of rebuilding and restoring'

You magazine

'Wittily recounted and moving . . . This book will surely give heart to anyone embarking on a seemingly Sisyphean restoration job, be it of the house or of the soul'

Mary Killen, *The Lady*

'Cash's transition from self-confessed failure into a blissful late parent with a proud home, children, and happy marriage, is genuinely endearing. In this wry account of repeated ruined romances and of "Money-Pit Manor", Cash evokes those gentle post-war Ealing comedies – though not so much *Passport to Pimlico* as a "Sonnet to Shropshire"'

Philippa Stockley, *The Art Newspaper*

'*Restoration Heart* beats with humour, longing, resilience and a love of history and William's place in the world. The love of language and the search for beauty and redemption are hardwired into our Cash genes, and William writes about his particular search with great eloquence, and with sad but wry observations of his journey. I loved *Restoration Heart* and I am certain that even those who are not 'cousins' will love it as well'

Rosanne Cash, Grammy Award-winning singer-songwriter and author, and daughter of Johnny Cash

'A good read'

Aasmah Mir, *Times* radio presenter

'A very amusing and candid memoir'

Jeremy Musson, architectural historian and broadcaster

'I'm very much enjoying *Restoration Heart*'

John Challis, aka 'Boycie' from *Only Fools and Horses*

Restoration Heart

A Memoir

William Cash

CONSTABLE

CONSTABLE

First published in Great Britain in 2019 by Constable
This paperback edition published in Great Britain in 2020 by Constable

1 3 5 7 9 10 8 6 4 2

Copyright © William Cash, 2019

The moral right of the author has been asserted.

A CIP catalogue record for this book
is available from the British Library.

ISBN: 978-1-47213-217-8

Typeset in Electra LT Std by SX Composing DTP, Rayleigh, Essex
Printed and bound in Great Britain by Clays Ltd, Elcograf S.p.A.

Papers used by Constable are from well-managed forests
and other responsible sources.

Constable
An imprint of
Little, Brown Book Group
Carmelite House
50 Victoria Embankment
London EC4Y 0DZ

An Hachette UK Company
www.hachette.co.uk

www.littlebrown.co.uk

To L.R.C

Contents

'My heart is by dejection, clay,
And by self-murder, red.'

'A Litany' (1609), John Donne

'A remote and beautiful place . . .'

Upton Cressett in *Shropshire: A Shell Guide*
by John Betjeman and John Piper (Faber, 1951)

JULY, 2010

Peering through the closed curtains of my Shropshire hideout, I could see a black Land Rover Defender circling the gravelled courtyard area outside. It was around 11 a.m. on Saturday, 17 July.

I was being doorstepped about a breaking British political sex scandal. A stocky man in a checked shirt, holding a motorised camera, stepped out, with a blonde woman in jeans. As the pair hovered outside, two dachshunds began yapping loudly, guarding my front door. I could hear voices outside.

'This is Upton Cressett,' the photographer said. 'I saw the signs.'

'But is William living here?' said the woman. 'The gates are locked. There's scaffolding up. Looks like a building site.'

'I can hear dogs. Somebody's in the cottage.'

There was a loud knock at the door. Then another. I froze.

'Maybe it's just a caretaker,' the man said.

I was not dressed for a Sunday tabloid interview. I was an unshaven forty-three-year-old publisher, feeling past his prime, wearing slippers and striped pyjamas that no longer fitted. The 'Wanted' look was completed by my uncombed hair and a moth-eaten grey cashmere dressing-gown. A Christmas present, in another life, from a former mother-in-law.

I had gone into hiding in a cottage – the Coach House – ever since a photo of my girlfriend had appeared on the front page of the *Sunday Mirror*, alongside that of a well-known British politician, touted as a future prime minister.

I stayed in the bedroom until I heard the Land Rover drive away.

Not long after, my mobile rang. It was a tabloid news desk.

'Hope you can help us,' a voice said. 'We've emailed you some questions that we'd appreciate your responses to. Before we go to print.'

'What questions?'

'Well, there's a report that your girlfriend was very popular at Edinburgh University and that while dancing at a James Bond party, got herself entangled . . . in a chandelier. She was dating some wealthy Dutchman . . . Do you know who he was?'

'We're no longer together,' I said. 'I haven't spoken to her for a week. You'll need to ask her or her lawyer.'

'Do you know about a wine cellar or a CCTV tape?'

'Fuck off,' I said, and hung up.

Our last lunch together had been at Motcombs wine bar in Belgravia only a week before. We had drunk two bottles of rosé in the sun and talked of marriage.

'Upton Cressett will be ready in a few months,' I'd said. 'We'll have children of our own. And then we'll look like any other family. Nobody will ask any questions. Marriage *isn't* just a piece of paper. It's important.'

She had ended our relationship on the day the tabloids showed up outside our London front door – and her mother's house in Folkestone. I was 'under accusation'.

After retreating to Shropshire to escape, I lay on the sofa in my darkened cottage trying to understand how my life had reached this abyss. A double-divorcé, without children, camping out in a former tack room. With another relationship behind me, and only two books in more than twenty years, I found myself thinking of Graham Greene's verdict: 'No man is a success to himself.'

Some hours after that phone call, I went for an early-evening walk with the dogs, heading towards the Norman church. In summers past, when I was growing up, my mother's garden would have been at its very best in July. Now the velvety Old English, crimson roses my mother had lovingly trained up the diapered brick walls had hardly bloomed for not being pruned. They had smelt of myrrh, old fruit and sweet anise.

The yew topiary in front of the house hadn't been clipped for several years. Weeds and dandelions grew along once neatly edged gravel paths. Two of the six huge Spanish chestnut trees that flanked the Gatehouse, planted to commemorate victory at Waterloo, were now dying. Their cracked and gnarled branches offered only a few green leaves – a symbol of my own stripped spirit.

The small church of St Michael's, with its twelfth-century weathered timber porch, had long been a sanctuary for me. If you stand by its studded oak door, and look towards the ancient manor of Upton Cressett, the view is as authentically Elizabethan as any you will see in England.

The house is wrapped in history. As the vermilion evening sky blazed across the mullioned windows, the diamond-shaped, leaded glass glinting, the towering stacks of twisted chimneys looked almost exactly as they would have done some 450 years earlier when priest-hunters had waited in the shadows of remote family chapels.

I went in and sat on a pew. Brushing away bat droppings, I thought about what the walls had witnessed: the gilded murals of golden archangels hurriedly whitewashed over in the Reformation; the black-cloaked, anti-papist Pursuivants, arriving on horseback in the reign of Elizabeth I to search the house and church. I imagined a terrified priest dashing through the crypt into the brick escape tunnel, emerging in a field by the medieval fish ponds, then running for his life into the woods.

The church's Norman font held special significance for me. As I ran my hand along its thick lead lining, burred and beaten with age, the moulded arch carvings felt like rough-stone cheekbones. For a moment, I forgot my despair. Upton Cressett – and its ancient spirit – was time's own survivor, which gave me a breath of hope. That others before me had been hunted down at Upton Cressett, I found strangely comforting.

As I closed the church door behind me and stepped outside into the darkening evening air, I almost felt as if I was on the run myself – from my past.

I started this memoir six years later, as the last weeks of a wet August fell away before I turned fifty. The floor of my office – a former pig shed – became a multi-coloured sea of letters, faxes, box files, photos, newspaper diary items and cuttings albums – all overflowing with the debris of a life at its half-century mark. The letters and diaries go back to my early school and teenage days. There are also several shelves of red cloth Binder Boxes, each containing love letters.

Retracing my history through this hoard has required an uneasy confrontation with my past. My red boxes are supplied by Ryder & Co, who hold a royal warrant and supply similar boxes to the British Museum. You cannot archive handwritten love letters, the ink sometimes smudged, in a school ring binder. One fat box for each failed relationship – the state papers of my heart.

My Binder Boxes are lined up in chronological order with my exes' initials on the spine. The chronology is not entirely accurate as the transitions sometimes involved a certain amount of what my female friends call 'ship-jumping'. Few lives are without conflicted emotions, and letting go of the past is something I have never found easy.

As I began sorting, I wondered what I might say in a speech at a birthday dinner in the Norman church where, it is said, Prince Rupert had knelt before battle during the Civil War. It was now used only for the occasional concert, history talk or guided tour. With only two slit windows on the main south wall, it has the feel of a dimly lit castle chamber. It suited my reflective mood perfectly.

I have been giving guided tours at Upton Cressett since I was in my early teens. That damp August, I had opened the front door on more than one occasion at 2.30 p.m. to find a solitary couple waiting patiently in the rain, huddled under an umbrella. I knew how it must feel to be an actor on tour playing to an all but empty house.

The tours always ended in the Great Hall dining room. Standing just inside the medieval fireplace, I'd relate how the eldest 'Prince in the Tower' – now King Edward V, after his father's death – had reputedly stayed at the timber manor of Hugh Cressett on his fateful journey in April 1483 from nearby Ludlow Castle to London. 'One can imagine the young king, tired after a day's ride,' I'd say, standing by the basket of logs, 'warming his cold hands as two hundred Yorkist soldiers guarded the moat.'

But this memoir is a very different sort of tour. It's an excavation – an archaeological memory dig – of house and heart. When I took over the house, both were in an advanced state of disrepair, in need of fixing up – and redemption.

The novelist Candia McWilliam has written movingly of her experience of being 'rescued by architecture', and of her 'capacity to be completely changed by a building, to be inhabited by it imaginatively and emotionally'. That was what I was hoping for when I took on Upton Cressett after my life had crashed in my forties. My second marriage had ended, after barely a year, in 2009. At forty-three, I was faced with the task of renovating the oldest dated brick manor house in Shropshire – solo. For almost as long as I could remember, Upton Cressett had been the backdrop to my life, but my experience of any building project was limited to a problematic London flat near the Shepherd's Bush roundabout. And with the future of the publishing business I had founded highly uncertain, I felt as if the foundations of my life were falling away beneath me.

What follows is my attempt at establishing some clarity and honesty. It tells the story of how, after my divorces, I attempted to restore my dilapidated house and my quest for a wife. I wanted a chatelaine for the house that had become my home in the early Seventies when my parents swapped our house in Islington for a derelict ruin in Shropshire. Ever since, the house has provided the mortar and walls of my life, even when I wasn't living there. It was always my dream to live in it with my own family, a prospect that seemed increasingly unlikely.

As I began writing, my immediate hope was that my fiftieth would go better than other milestone birthdays. My main concerns were the weather forecast and the fact that a musician friend had agreed to write and perform a 'cowboy ballad' at the church dinner in the style of my namesake, American country legend Johnny Cash. No doubt, the tongue-in-cheek lyrics would cover the hard knocks of my love life as well as my eventual return home to Upton Cressett.

The other thought pressing on my mind was that several dozen of my 'Moneyman' generation of friends – many of whom had careers in banking and finance – were decamping to Upton Cressett for a weekend at which our relative life scorecards would be difficult to ignore. One had called to ask for the GPS coordinates and if I had a 'touchdown zone'.

My thirtieth birthday, in 1996, had been a special low point. I was living in LA and working as US Special Correspondent for the *Daily Telegraph*. I woke up alone to be greeted by the mess of a Napa Valley expat dinner party with the likes of Elizabeth Hurley, Hugh Grant and Auberon Waugh on my little Valley house terrace. If it sounded glamorous, it wasn't. In a letter to my girlfriend Catherine, LA editor of the *Gault Millau* restaurant guide, I described the evening as a 'grim ordeal'. She didn't spend the night and I ate a hung-over breakfast at my local diner. I spoke to nobody all day and spent so much time clearing up that I missed my afternoon flight to England. I arrived back at Upton Cressett two days later.

But even when I was a deracinated expat living in Los Angeles, I felt the hamlet's ancient pull. In a fax from Shropshire to my girlfriend a week after my wretched thirtieth birthday, I wrote, 'Life is a long walk which leads to a dark wood, which leads to a beautiful garden, which leads to a fine brick house, which leads to a panelled bedroom where the evening sun floods in as the woman I love dresses for dinner . . .'

The house, of course, was Upton Cressett. But reaching the oak-panelled bedroom – where in 1580 owner-builder Richard Cressett had carved his initials above the bed – was to prove no easy journey. Many before me had been ruined by the folly of their building or restoration projects. Indeed, mine nearly broke me, not only emotionally but also financially.

People often ask whether Upton Cressett is haunted. I have never seen a ghost, although I do believe that a house's walls and rooms can absorb the spirit of former owners. Nowhere is this idea more evident than in the hold that old English houses have on the national psyche. But our houses are often more than bricks and mortar; they are the very stage sets of our lives. Just as we rebuild and remodel, we change with them. In my case, the house has always been the most durable of my relationships – more reliable than any love affair or marriage.

1

Marriage à la Mort

My story begins not among red Elizabethan bricks but deep beneath the streets of Paris among centuries-old bones. In early June 2009, my second wife, Vanessa, and I were in Paris to celebrate our wedding anniversary. It was meant to be a romantic trip. A nice boutique hotel, a walk in the Luxembourg Gardens, a visit to Balzac's house (where he had once jumped the garden wall to escape his creditors), and dinner at Derrière. Then a taxi ride back to the Faubourg Saint-Honoré and late-night cocktails in the plush, plum-velvet booths of Hôtel Costes.

But the painful fact was that, rather than celebrating our first year of marriage, the trip was more about saving it. In February, less than nine months after 'Love is a Great Thing' was read at our Westminster wedding service, the state of our marriage ('the couple are living apart') had been broadcast across the *Daily Mail* by Richard Kay in one of his ever-revolving gossip-column despatches on our relationship. 'I learn that Vanessa has taken her chihuahua Pitoufa – who featured on the couple's first Christmas card – and flown to her Park Avenue apartment in New York, leaving William to his bachelor flat and their friends wondering where it all went wrong.'

I hadn't helped matters by failing to book the Eurostar and our hotel until the last moment. My inability to make the reservations earlier was symptomatic of the lack of control I had on the direction in which our marriage was sliding. In every department of my frazzled life there was chaos – my writing, my career as a publisher, my social life, my finances, and at home. And I was managing two building sites.

Falling in love with Vanessa had been like discovering an exotic new drug that would cure all my ailments. That she was a beautiful, New York-based philosopher and writer – with a PhD from Columbia University – no doubt added to her allure. With her aqua-green eyes and husky, mid-Atlantic drawl, she was also very much her own woman. She was known in the diary pages as the 'Cracker from Caracas' for her Venezuelan heritage and for having dated Mick Jagger. But she was 'Dr V' to her close friends, while I was 'Bunny'.

Her Cracker nickname was a source of amusement to her. She found it both 'flattering' and partly 'insulting'. When she was previously engaged to a Scottish aristocrat, Willy Stirling, whose great-uncle had founded the SAS, her initial reaction was to rail against her characterisation as a 'cracker'. When her German doctoral dissertation adviser at Columbia read about her affair with Jagger while she was teaching philosophy, he asked her: 'Does zat mean you smoke crack?'

Vanessa had lived in her own apartment on the Upper East Side since she was eighteen. Her Venezuelan father had died tragically when she was just twenty. She was a regular on the international conference circuit, specialising in South American politics and counter-terrorism, invariably arriving in her vintage Hermès poncho and knee-high leather boots. She was also a television political pundit and later a foreign ambassador.

We met in October 2007 and I proposed on New Year's Day 2008, in Mustique, where Vanessa had spent much of her childhood. Her grandfather, Hans Neumann, a Venezuelan industrialist and art collector, had rescued the Caribbean island in 1976 after Colin Tennant, later Lord Glenconner, was unable to finance it any longer (Hans bought Glenconner out). Vanessa regarded Mustique as her spiritual home. Needless to say, the jet-set island was a very different world from my bucket-and-spade holidays in North Wales or Weymouth.

My proposal belonged in a Billy Wilder film. We were in the bar at the Firefly Hotel before having dinner with an old friend, New York-based novelist Jay McInerney, and his wife Anne. As the maître d' tried to usher us to our table, I ran out into a tropical rainstorm to fetch the ring from an old sock hidden inside the glove box of the electric golf buggy we were driving. When I returned to the bar, Vanessa was nowhere to be seen.

'Where's Vanessa?' I said.

'She's gone to the ladies' room,' I was told.

So I rushed back into the storm as the loos were outside. I quickly became drenched as I waited for her to emerge. That Vanessa said yes before she'd looked inside the box I took as a good sign.

When she called her mother in New York with the news that she was engaged, I heard Antonia ask, 'What's his name?'

'William,' Vanessa said. '*Another* William.'

I sensed confusion down the line; I was then handed the phone. 'I'll look forward to seeing you in London at the wedding, or sooner, I hope,' I said.

Cracking Up

From the moment we arrived at the Gare du Nord, I was desperate to make the Paris trip a romantic success. Which is why, looking back now, it seems odd that I thought a good way to celebrate our anniversary would be to visit the city's famous catacombs.

Victor Hugo writes about the macabre labyrinth of an underground open graveyard in *Les Misérables*. It contains the bones of more than six million Parisian citizens whose remains were moved from overcrowded cemeteries to the tunnels of former stone quarries on the orders of Louis XVI. Opened to the public in the late eighteenth century, its seemingly endless piles of human skulls, in particular, neatly arranged in pyramids, have long been a grim tourist attraction.

We entered and walked along a narrow stone passage until we came to a sign that read: 'Arrête! C'est ici l'empire de la Mort.'

'Stop!' translated Vanessa. 'This is the empire of Death.'

After about twenty minutes, I started to feel claustrophobic panic. It wasn't just the surroundings. I had already divorced once and my second marriage was showing every sign of crumbling. The truth is, we had been in trouble after only six months. Vanessa had, indeed, spent much of her time in New York, but I could only blame myself. Paris was my last chance to win her back.

I recalled a line from David Hare's play *Plenty*. It is spoken by an English diplomat, Raymond Brock, when he confronts his volatile wife after a disastrous dinner party at their smart Holland Park house – and she takes a carving knife to the wallpaper. Knowing that their marriage is over, he asks her to admit just one thing to herself: 'In the life you have led, you have utterly failed, failed in the very, very heart of your life.'

The subterranean Paris tunnel was oddly muggy. I had never been down the secret tunnel that locals said existed at Upton Cressett as we didn't know where the entrance was. But I thought an underground tunnel would be dank and poorly lit. This one had electric lighting and smelt musty. As I walked along the tunnel, with a sense of panic closing in on me, my thoughts began to surge, like those in the head of Goya slumped on his desk in *The Sleep of Reason Produces Monsters*.

I experienced a similar invasion of nightmarish images and thoughts, whirling around my mind.

What Richard Kay had not mentioned, or known, was that in addition to my wife bolting to New York there were also serious problems with *Spear's*, the financial magazine and media business I had founded on returning from nearly a decade in LA, and still ran as editor-in-chief. The parent magazine company that had bought the company in 2007 – backed by an American private-equity firm – was now in deep financial trouble, post-crash. Investments had gone wrong. Only a few days before leaving for Paris, I had learned that the parent company was going into administration. *Spear's*, its only viable asset, was heading for the liquidator's auction block. I hadn't told Vanessa yet.

Quite what she thought of taking on Upton Cressett, I never knew, as we had not, after a year, got close to spending a night there. We were still living in the Coach House. For the duration of our marriage, we lived between that cottage and my flat on one of the busiest roads in London's Holland Park. The flat had been another building nightmare to complete before starting married life together. When we moved in, the only bedroom was a windowless shoebox in the basement.

I had plans to build a new bedroom extension in the rear garden. Most of its pre-war acacia trees were dying, but the council was refusing to let me cut them down. All building works were on hold as I battled with the tree-conservation department.

Vanessa, meanwhile, was a published philosopher who taught Wittgenstein on New York campuses. I found dating a beautiful philosopher alluring. Mick Jagger also found it unusual. At the start of her affair with Jagger, she was reading Schopenhauer's *The World as Will and Representation* for fun while on holiday. 'Some light beach reading?' Mick asked as he glanced at the cover.

Maybe that was one reason why I had proposed to her so quickly. She was a glamorous Manhattan version of John Betjeman's black-stockinged 'Myfanwy', the feisty and sexy Oxford student whom he dreams about as an undergraduate. Only Vanessa didn't ride a bicycle with a wicker basket: she drove a Porsche (and later a powerful Mini Cooper). I liked her academic background. 'Dr Cash' had a certain ring to it, at least to my ear. Perhaps a philosopher was what I felt I needed. To provide answers. Even if, most of the time, I didn't know what the questions were.

Such were the thoughts that swirled in my mind as I wandered under the streets of Paris.

Of course, all life is a process of breaking down, but the blows that do the dramatic side of the work – the big sudden blows that come, or seem to come, from outside – the ones you remember and blame things on and, in moments of weakness, tell your friends about, don't show their effect all at once.

So began F. Scott Fitzgerald's account of his own breakdown in *The Crack-Up*. He chronicled, in painfully honest detail, how his marriage and life unravelled, at the height of his fame, in his mid-thirties. But I was now forty-three, with no *Great Gatsby* to show for it, no Babylon to revisit. And I had no Upton Cressett magic wall to jump over to escape my growing stack of bills. Tools were not so much 'down' as nowhere to be seen.

Why did I have two building projects going on at the same time, neither of which I could afford? How long would I still have a job to pay for any renovation? Would I ever get to sleep in that oak-panelled master bedroom with my wife's initials carved above the bed? And would I ever have a family of my own?

Tudor Grotesque

The chief reason for my despair was that my family home in Shropshire, the moated Elizabethan manor and gatehouse of Upton Cressett, had come to resemble an architectural salvage yard. The gardens where I had played tennis and cricket on the Moat Lawn, and my mother had her Tudor rose garden, had long been abandoned.

One thing about building work is that whenever someone mutilates a house you often find that the urge to strip out its interior is a symptom of personal despair or unhappiness. Over the late summer of 2007, on my instructions while I was away on an unlikely two-week holiday – read 'mid-life crisis' – at the Burning Man Festival in the Nevada desert, the house had been ripped apart by my Liverpudlian builder.

While I was in the Black Rock Desert, a vanload of axes, sledge-hammers, iron bars and pneumatic drills had turned my former family home into a wasteland. The builder had long since departed, with his weathered Transit van.

When I took over Upton Cressett in 2007, the house needed to be completely remodernised – new electrics, new lime-plastering, new mullion windows and central heating for the first time in five hundred years. In my parents' day, the main guest bathroom was almost fifty yards from some bedrooms. On freezing winter mornings, I used to hear people running along the upstairs corridor to get to the bathroom. Five minutes later they would run back, after they had discovered that the hot water – there was just enough for two baths a day for the entire household – had run out and they would either have to face a cold shower or use kettles.

I had wanted a fresh start for Upton Cressett. I hadn't just wanted to divorce the past but to obliterate it. Not my childhood and teenage memories of the place, where I had been so happy, but my recent past. I wanted to put my own stamp on the house. I wanted to give it a new identity; my own had been so crushed by my first divorce.

But my builder had gone too far. It was painful to walk around the dusty beamed rooms, their old electric sockets removed, leaving green and yellow wires hanging like the tentacles of some giant tropical weed growing through the walls.

The 1930s porcelain pedestal basin with brass taps that my father used to shave in was upturned and discarded in a corner; the Tudor oak floorboards of his dressing room had been torn out and left like scaffolding planks, their crude sixteenth-century nails scattered in a heap. The beautiful home in which I had been brought up since the age of about five had been gutted. The furniture had been removed, as had almost all of the old wallpapers, chosen by my mother, that had given the house so much of its character, leaving the plastered walls a dirty and scarred off-white. Even the pretty bird-of-paradise chinoiserie paper of the Parrot Bedroom had gone – my friends from school had slept there, or my Uncle Jonathan when he came for one of his archaeological holidays.

The Tudor Grotesque wallpaper adorned with gargoyles had been torn from the walls. Almost every room, from the kitchen to my mother's study, was now unrecognisable. There was no sign of any work resuming. Frayed plastic sheets, taped on to the wooden casements, rustled in the wind where windows had been removed. This demolition was in the late summer of 2007, just before I met – or, rather, became reacquainted with – Vanessa at a friend's party. By 2009, after a year of marriage, the house was in the same derelict condition.

My father had recommended doing up one room at a time – as they had done when he and my mother had renovated the house in the 1970s. 'We had price tags for each room,' he told me. 'Never more than a few hundred pounds a room. You need to be on site.'

Of course, I hadn't listened. Instead, I'd headed off to bury the past in the Nevada desert, only to return to find my childhood home literally demolished. I saw its destruction as a symbol of my own broken life at forty-three.

When my parents moved out of the main house, I inherited a small library of old architecture books in which Upton Cressett featured. These included *The Old Houses of Wenlock* by H. E. Forrest (1914) and *Nooks and Corners of Shropshire* by H. Thornhill Timmins (1899). The other volume that was handed over, like some sacred heirloom, was my father's much-treasured navy album with ox-blood leather corners and spine with 'Upton Cressett Hall, 1971' embossed in gilt on the front. It included his photos of the house restoration.

The first pages show a ruined manor house with broken windows and chimneys and Shropshire pigs happily eating from a trough in what I am guessing is the former pig shed in which I am now writing; and a picture – I'm looking at it now – of me aged five or six, standing in the muddy clay moat in front of the church. I have a pudding-bowl haircut and am smiling in green corduroys and a sweater. I look happy.

Hopeless Romantics

My determination to restore Upton Cressett sprang from the desire to return to or recreate the magic of my childhood and teenage years spent there. Such a quest back to a world of innocence is, of course, a familiar cliché. G. K. Chesterton's first memory was of looking inside his father's Victorian toy theatre, which he described as 'a glimpse of some incredible paradise', and he spent much of his life trying to recapture that lost vision of a childhood Arcadia.

My boyhood adventure had begun on a warm day in June 1970 after my parents read an entry for Upton Cressett in the list of 'Threatened Houses of Architectural Interest', published by the Society for the Protection of Ancient Buildings (SPAB) founded by William Morris. My father had become a member in the late 1960s and had been looking for a 'project' to restore with my mother. What they didn't know at the time was that, if a buyer or leaseholder hadn't been found, the house might have been yet another to fall victim to the wrecker's ball as a way of avoiding a costly Conservation Order. The notice appeared under the county heading 'Shropshire'. The entry read:

Built about 1580 by Richard Cressett, the oldest dated house built entirely of brick in the County. Manor House . . . Interesting features. Unspoilt Shropshire countryside. Requires considerable renovation.

My parents had become afflicted with that most British and expensive of diseases: the 'dream' of finding an old English manor house and restoring it, the more of an overgrown ruin beyond hope, the better. Finding such a crumbling manor, château, castle, Italian villa or French farmhouse to turn into a family home made my parents members of the same club as Peter Mayle, author of *A Year in Provence*. In 1987, Peter and his third wife, Jennie, moved from Devon to a farmhouse in Ménerbes, in central Provence, where they planned to refurbish the property while he wrote a novel. The farmhouse soon took on a life of its own.

My father, Bill, was then a thirty-year-old lawyer in London with political ambitions and a young family. We lived in a terraced house in Islington, north London. 'We drove up over the weekend almost as soon as we saw the ad,' my father recalled, many decades later. 'We had wanted to move to the country but we had no idea where Shropshire was. Most of the properties advertised in the SPAB list were white elephants – old schools, institutions, mental asylums or small cottages. Not suitable for raising a family. This sounded different.'

In the preface to his history of the De Uptons and Cressetts of Upton Cressett, my father describes the sultry day that he and my mother first glimpsed our future family home in June 1970:

The atmosphere was magical, heavy with the humming of bees. The foliage was dense and we walked, with mounting excitement, through high grass surrounding the ancient, derelict buildings with tumbled down chimneys and trees growing through the brickwork, faintly discerning the outline of the moat by the Norman church.

The air of romantic dereliction was permeated by a surge of ancient emotions. It has never lost its medieval character.

Soon after, my parents packed me into their white Citroën Safari estate and we drove up to Shropshire to look at the romantic-sounding Elizabethan manor. This was well before the M40 was built and the journey took us to Oxford and along winding cow-parsley-filled Cotswold roads through Moreton-in-Marsh and Evesham. About eight miles from Bridgnorth, outside the village of Billingsley, we stopped for a picnic. Not long after my mother had laid down a tartan rug and started handing out sausage rolls and sandwiches, we were slowly encircled by cows and young heifers. I was hurriedly passed across barbed wire to 'safety' (we were from Islington).

When we arrived at the Hall, we found a ruin, with pigs strolling around the oak-panelled Jacobean ground-floor rooms. Piles of grain and abandoned farm machinery lay about. There were no locks on any of the doors; once you had battled through the nettles and brambles, you just walked in. My parents had just wanted to take a spontaneous look before requesting the keys – they never expected to spend two hours walking around every room. The church, some hundred yards away, was locked.

Of that first tour of the empty house, I can still remember the fetid animal smell of the place. 'It was a hot day . . . the ground floor stank like a summer farmyard. There was chicken and pig manure everywhere,' my father recalls. The last resident had been a tenant pig farmer called Mr Flood. He had lived in a few rooms without electricity or mains water.

Despite the Shropshire pigs, the cloak of ivy, the broken Jacobean chimneys, the smashed, leaded casement windows, the chunks of ornate plaster work hanging from the ceiling attached to clumps of horsehair, and a tree growing up the oak staircase of the Gatehouse, they immediately fell in love with Upton Cressett.

The result was that I left St Anthony's in Hampstead for Shropshire and was packed off to board at Moor Park School near Ludlow, starting aged seven. One of my earliest Binder Boxes, marked 'School', contains letters sent from Moor Park and a short autobiography I wrote. It begins with an early memory of Upton Cressett:

> *Childhood experiences, I have been told, are the writer's credit balance. Aged four, we moved from London to an Elizabethan house in Shropshire with a Gatehouse, moat and secret passage. My mother gave up breeding children for peacocks. If friends came to stay I would hand them boxing gloves and fight them under a damson tree. Afterwards, I would teach them Mahjong. The house's sequestered location meant there were few newspapers.*

At school, I wrote home every week on Wombles or Tom and Jerry writing paper, offering my verdict of films like *The Land That Time Forgot*, asking for more stamps or to be sent a new jar of peanut butter. Aged ten, I was writing short stories for the school magazine. I even enjoyed exams. In a letter dated June 1982, after I had moved to Downside School in Somerset, during my O-level exams my mother wrote: 'Don't be over-confident. If one question looks easy, always take care and watch your writing. If one exam doesn't go as well as you expect, don't let it get you down. Just persevere. Soon you will be home for the holidays, which will be wonderful. I am enclosing £10.'

Thirty years later, I found one old blue fiver (the kind with the Duke of Wellington on the back) inside the envelope. The note is still surprisingly crisp. That I had entirely forgotten about it was unsettling. Had I read the letter properly, let alone taken my mother's good advice? But for most of the last forty years or so, had I ever taken anybody's advice? Almost certainly not. But, then, if I had taken the advice of friends and family, I would almost certainly never have embarked upon the restoration of Upton Cressett – with no budget, no builder and no experience.

For much of our family's first two years at Upton Cressett, we camped, living in just a few rooms in primitive conditions while work continued. I played with my plastic soldiers in the builder's sandpit. A huge, rickety old seventeenth-century tithe barn – with giant, gnarled oak beams – was my playground.

As a boy, I dressed in plastic armour and re-enacted Roman and medieval battles with my younger brother Sam and our Uncle Jonathan, who was only ten years older than me. He was more like an older brother and introduced me to local Shropshire beer – aged sixteen – down the pub after one of our 'field walks'. He loved the ancient history around Upton Cressett, which he endowed with Romano-British significance. He had curly brown hair, later grew a professorial beard and was innately kind, always carrying boxes of maps and notebooks with neatly written notes. He never travelled without a suitcase of books on classical history.

Little did I know then that his mania for collecting signed first editions of W. H. Auden and Sylvia Plath, *Wisden* and the entire Loeb classical library were symptoms of a hoarding compulsion. He would arrive at Christmas and Easter with cigars, boxes of wine and enough archaeological equipment and 'weather gear' for a six-month stint in the 'trowel pit' at Hadrian's Wall. He taught me how to build a Trojan fort from straw bales. Alas, the Trojan War came to an abrupt halt one day when my brother's tunnelling disturbed a hornets' nest. He was so badly stung that my mother had to drive him to Telford hospital.

Jonathan introduced me to archaeology. He had been taught Latin and classical history at Stonyhurst, in Lancashire, by Michael Tolkien, son of J. R. R. Tolkien, and had a romantic view of Old England as a country that could not escape its almost mythical past. We would walk for miles in search of lost hill forts, mott baileys and medieval villages, or follow the trail of King Arthur, whom my uncle believed might have been a Welsh warrior king. 'You're living in the very seam of English history,' Jonathan would say, as we donned camouflage jackets and binoculars, collected maps and set off around freshly ploughed local fields looking for Roman coins or pottery. 'Upton Cressett is one of the oldest landscapes in old Mercia,' he added. 'It was settled by the Cornovii tribe, well before the Saxons. They were Iron Age Celts who were finally defeated by the Romans around AD 47. Their capital was a large double hill fort on the Wrekin, which inspired Middle-earth in *The Lord of the Rings*. I'll take you there.'

2

The House That Time Forgot

Although it sounds stately, Upton Cressett isn't. It belongs to that long tradition of off-the-beaten-track houses, combining English architectural beauty and homeliness, that were so well described by P. H. Ditchfield in his 1910 account *The Manor Houses of England*, in which Upton Cressett is mentioned. In it, he describes the English manor as a style of dwelling that ranks between the mansion and the farmhouse or cottage.

> *Many of them stand in remote, inaccessible and little-known parts of the country; and their remarkable beauty, their historical associations and architectural merits, may have escaped the attention of those who love to explore the English countryside . . . They do not court attention, these English manor houses, or seek to attract the eye by glaring incongruities or obtrusive detail. They seem in quest of peace, love and obscurity.*

One reason that the Cressett family left the house in the early eighteenth century (although they continued to own the estate) is that,
despite its medieval water garden and deer park, it wasn't grand
enough. Its carved dragon frieze, panelled rooms and hefty medieval
Crown beams – spliced from oak trees tied together as saplings – were
too English, too dark and too far away from the seats of local power in
Ludlow or Shrewsbury.

The house was originally a timbered medieval manor with a Great
Hall and solar wing built in the fifteenth century for Hugh Cressett, a
royal commissioner for the Welsh Marches. Hence it would have been
regarded as a Yorkist safe house in 1483 when the twelve-year-old King
Edward V reportedly stayed with Hugh Cressett, then crossed the
River Severn in Bridgnorth on his fateful journey from Ludlow Castle
to the Tower of London. Hugh and his son, Robert, were successively
Members of Parliament and Sheriffs of Shropshire.

In 1580, the Great Hall was truncated, then encased in fashionable
brick by Richard Cressett, who also added a romantic, turreted
English Renaissance gatehouse (more Elizabethan banqueting lodge).
Twisting and intricate cut-brick chimney stacks towered above the
medieval fireplaces that were the ultimate Tudor status symbols – like
having a Richard Neutra pool-house when I lived in LA. The Cressett
family were powerful Civil War royalists and landowners with close
connections to the Stuart and Hanoverian royal courts. They owned
the house until 1926, by which time it was an ivy-clad ruin.

In 1970, the estate was owned by Colonel Henry Marsh, OBE (of
the Marsh & Baxter sausage family), who lived at nearby Monkhopton
House. But as the inscrutable ecclesiastical architectural historian
Henry Thorold puts it in his classic *Collins Guide to the Ruined
Abbeys of England, Wales and Scotland*: 'There is nothing like neglect
for preserving a place.'

Ever since the Cressetts moved out in 1703, a succession of
tenants, usually farmers, including illegitimate cousins called Corser,

occupied the house, which became a farmstead until the mid-1950s when the lack of water, electricity and its remote location became too challenging even for the 'caretaker' farmer living in two rooms. So, Mr Flood moved out and the pigs and chickens moved in.

Upton Cressett was a highly risky project for my parents to take on. My father had only his solicitor's salary – he was a partner at Dyson Bell, the Westminster-based constitutional and parliamentary law firm – and the sale proceeds of their house in Islington. The idea was to downsize in London and put aside the difference to pay for the restoration. By April 1971, as the works began, I had a new brother called Sam. My mother gave up work to raise her young family and supervise the builders (Treasure's of Ludlow) during the week when my father was working in London.

By 1966, when I was born, she had worked for several years as a 'garden room' secretary in Downing Street where she and others regularly had to fend off drunken, late-night advances from Labour politician George Brown, a notorious philanderer as foreign secretary. 'One would not invite him to cucumber sandwiches with one's maiden aunt,' railed a *Times* leader in 1967 on Brown's suitability for high office. But it was a different political world and my mother – who had signed the Official Secrets Act – just laughed off his behaviour. She would walk from our flat in Lincoln's Inn Fields down the Strand to Downing Street where she often arranged top-secret calls from the prime minister, Harold Wilson, late into the night.

'When I was pregnant, I became a bit scatty,' my mother recalled. 'I remember taking an important late-night call from the White House. I had Lyndon Johnson on the line and said I'd put him through to the prime minister. I got up to find him and completely forgot the American president was on the line! He must have waited for quite a few minutes before hanging up.'

After I was born, my mother worked part time as researcher and secretary to Anthony Sampson when he was writing *Anatomy of Britain*.

She was a Sixties, hands-on loving mother, who used to push me, in the Silver Cross pram, around London parks in her navy-and-cream Hermès scarf. She refused to have a nanny.

Close family and a real family home were always important to her, as she hardly saw her own parents while she was growing up. Her family had a restless streak: a relation had been on Scott's expedition to the Antarctic; her father, James Lee, a keen sailor with a yacht in Weymouth, worked as a senior civil servant in the Commonwealth Office with postings to Kenya and Malaysia. For my mother this meant staying with friends in the school holidays and often not seeing her parents for six months or longer. Upton Cressett was the 'much-loved family home' she had never really had before.

'Many of our friends thought we were mad,' recalled my father, 'which was why neither of us told our parents about Upton Cressett for two years after we had moved in. We just didn't dare. They would have thought we were crazy and irresponsible.'

That spontaneous Sunday-afternoon drive to Shropshire turned out to be lucky timing. By 1970, James Marsh, son of Colonel Marsh, didn't have the appetite for a costly two-year restoration so the colonel's priority was to find a leaseholder – fast. Thanks to the SPAB having alerted the local council to the Hall's 'frightful' condition, he knew he was in grave danger of being served with a Conservation Order, requiring him to make expensive repairs.

The property had been advertised for two weeks as far back as July 1969 by the colonel's land agent Nicholas Collis. He had written to Mrs Dance, head of the SPAB, on 13 August 1969: 'The present position is that I advertised the Hall and Gatehouse in national and local papers about two weeks ago. The response was terrific, some ninety applicants. Our intention is to offer a long lease of twenty years to someone who has the time and money to return both of the buildings to their former glory. I have six applicants who are of that calibre and it remains to choose the right one and have the lease signed. We will watch very carefully that nothing is done to destroy the place and, although it may take a few years to restore, it will be worthwhile.'

Why none of the original six applicants took on Upton Cressett is unclear. They probably thought it was a crazy, money-pit project. By 8 July 1970, Mrs Dance was writing to Colonel Marsh that they were down to 'two people who are exceedingly keen'. One of the two was my father.

Eagle's Manor

My father could recall very little of his own (real) father growing up as my grandfather Paul Cash had been killed in action during the Normandy landings of 1944. He won the MC just days before he died on July 13 while defending the fifteenth-century chateau of Fontaine –Etoupefour, near Caen, whose turreted moated gatehouse bears an uncanny resemblance to that of Upton Cressett.

As Jack Hayward, a sergeant in my grandfather's regiment (Wessex Wyverns and Royal Artillery), described the bloody battle for Hill 112, a critically important vantage point between the valleys of the River Odon and Orme: 'The guns became so hot that the paint started to peel off. It was at this time that we were told that our Troop Commander, Captain Cash, had been killed. We had lost a great leader, a wonderful officer and a real gentleman.'

My grandfather was only twenty-six. A fellow officer wrote to my grandmother from convalescent hospital: 'During an attack, we got into a very sticky place. Paul was in a tank but had to abandon it when it got too hot. During that battle Paul was magnificent although I know he realised, as I did, that it would be a miracle if we survived.'

I am sure the emotional scar of losing his war hero father when he was just four defined much of my father's life. As a young teenager, while on a summer holiday in Normandy, I remember we tried to find my grandfather's grave but had difficulty locating the exact cemetery (my father has since been back several times). Part of the reason was that for the rest of her long life, despite happily remarrying, my grandmother Moira found visiting her husband's grave simply too painful.

My father can still vividly recall the awful news arriving. 'I opened the door. Then a huge man, some sort of policeman, handed my mother the letter. She collapsed. I then remember going up to her bedroom where she was in a terrible state and saying, "Don't worry Mummy, I'll look after you."'

On that August day in the late 1970s when we failed to find the exact location of my grandfather's grave, I recall taking a swig of red wine and biting hard into a baguette to stop myself from crying when I saw the rows and rows of those killed – and their ages.

My father possessed a treasured framed photo of his father's sports car with my young grandparents standing beside it holding him as a baby. This was placed on a table in the drawing room at Upton Cressett, alongside his father's Military Cross. My father used to enjoy pointing to the 'Just Married'-style sign hanging above the numberplate, which read: 'To Hell With Hitler.'

In a darkly comic twist, the only person who expressed any interest in occupying the hamlet of Upton Cressett during the Second World War seems to have been Adolf Hitler, or his Nazi high command. According to German military papers put up for auction in 2005, maps show that Hitler's generals were eyeing up Bridgnorth, on the River Severn, for their headquarters after the invasion. And according to historian Andrew Roberts, Upton Cressett Hall, hidden on top of a treacherously steep hill, might have become Hitler's 'Eagle's Nest' in England. A look at the German maps shows that Upton Cressett had probably been circled because of its remote location at the end of a three-mile cul-de-sac lane with no neighbours.

But Upton Cressett has always been a survivor. After the war, it was lucky not to have been one of the 'Lost Houses' that were named in

1973 on the roll-call of demolished houses that featured in the Victoria and Albert Museum's show, *Destruction of the English Country House*. In *No Voice from the Hall*, architectural historian John Harris describes how the predicament facing English historic houses post-1945 had no parallel in Europe. In 1955 alone, one country house was being demolished every two days, with 1,116 houses being lost in the 100 years to 1973.

Upton Cressett survived the twentieth-century dissolution of the country house because it was largely forgotten. After the last Cressett descendants – the Thursby-Pelhams – sold the estate, the Cressett family crypt, lined with carved marble effigies, was blocked up and the church fell into neglect and disrepair. When we arrived in 1970, my father was offered St Michael's Church for just £1,000. By then, it was in a chronic state of disrepair.

In the summer of 1938, writing their entry for *Shropshire: A Shell Guide*, John Betjeman and artist John Piper had to fight their way through thick nettles, fallen branches and four-foot-high brambles to reach the little church, with its 'rich Norman chancel arch and a little late Flemish glass'. Betjeman described the derelict manor house, set in the 'loneliest of valleys', as among his favourite places in Shropshire. Although he was writing for a motoring guide, he noted that Upton Cressett was 'best approached on foot, horse or bicycle' so that its beauty, peace and history could be 'appreciated'.

In 1958, the rare Flemish glass, along with the Norman font and Cressett family brass, was removed by the Hereford diocese before they closed the church for 'safety' reasons. The real damage to both house and church had been done by salvage thieves, farm tenants and neglectful owners of the twentieth century. There is a photograph, taken in August 1909 by the Scottish philosopher and mathematician John Edward Steggall, of the derelict Gatehouse almost entirely covered with ivy. While neighbouring Aldenham Park – the former home of the nineteenth-century Liberal statesman and historian Lord Acton – was used as a girls' school during the war, and Morville Hall was also requisitioned, Upton Cressett was just too isolated.

That my parents were Londoners looking to restore a derelict old manor in a part of England they had hardly heard of fits the template for the typical *Country Life* reader.

They were members of the 'restore-a-wreck' brigade. When friends came to stay for the weekend in the 1970s, they would know that they weren't being invited for tennis and swimming. Rather, they would find themselves being handed paintbrushes and SPAB instructions on how to mix lime mortar. I remember my brother's godfather, the French Revolution historian Dr Colin Lucas, my father's former Oxford flatmate, building the brick-edged pathway in front of the Gatehouse.

The new breed of country-house owner in the 1960s and '70s often had little in common with the landed aristocrats who gathered at the V&A for the owners' preview night of the *Destruction* exhibition in October 1973. Worried about negative publicity, curator Roy Strong insisted no journalists were to be invited to the privately funded opening-night dinner – and issued a press embargo. 'I feared the newspapers caricaturing rich country-house owners quaffing champagne while the Museum pleaded their cause would be counter-productive,' he later wrote.

The V&A exhibition argued that country houses are the envy of the world and one of the main reasons that people came to Britain; the imminent threat of a wealth and inheritance tax could potentially kill off the English country house as an art form and national treasure. An early draft of the exhibition brochure in the V&A archives states: 'Taxation has broken up the estates which supported them. It has forced the disposal of the contents they were built to house. It has made the gardens around them unmanageable. Above all, they have gone because the nation as a whole was asleep to their beauty. They have gone because politicians have not been moved to do anything positive to preserve them.'

Upton Cressett was a case in point. In the 1960s, house-breakers had stripped the exquisite, carved, sea-dragon frieze panelling on the first floor that the National Monuments Commission had photographed for their records. By the time my parents arrived in 1970, it had gone, along with most of the beautiful studded Elizabethan oak doors. My father found one surviving panel of the sea-dragon frieze in the attic, along with a priceless (to us) original Elizabethan window casement. Its green-leaded glass was broken but it could be copied.

The V&A show promoted the idea that if more noble and symbolic temples of visual beauty were to be lost, our national, cultural and aesthetic identity would suffer a severe blow. The public reaction to *Destruction* showed that the English house played an important role in our sense of place, and who we are.

But there was a flip side to the toll of destruction that was not much noted. By the late 1960s, when my parents began country-house hunting, many derelict properties were available to buy, usually inexpensively; and builders were cheap. This led to a new golden age for the 'rescued' historic house and an unexpected revival of the 'cult of the country house', as Evelyn Waugh described it in his revised 1959 foreword to *Brideshead Revisited*.

Many new owners were not especially well off. They were just romantics who often bought their run-down wrecks on a whim or wanted to change their lives, often escaping from London with the dream of swapping their urban backyard for a real English garden.

My mother's bedside table was heaped with books like *The Pleasure Garden* (1977) by Anne Scott-James and Osbert Lancaster. The English roses she grew in her Elizabethan garden had names like 'Munstead Wood', 'Gertrude Jekyll' and 'Boscobel', the latter no doubt chosen because of the association with the nearby 'Royal

Oak' at Boscobel House, the seventeenth-century hunting lodge near White Ladies Priory where the young Charles II hid while fleeing from Cromwell's soldiers after the Battle of Worcester in 1651. Boscobel had a box hedge knot garden with parterre beds filled with old species of lavender and honeysuckle that my mother admired and tried to replicate.

Two of my childhood friends lost their Shropshire homes while I was growing up – events that seemed (to me at least) some traumatic violation of the natural order. Seeing the contents of Wenlock Priory (my parents bought an Oriental dinner gong) being laid out on the lawn close to where I used to play cricket with my friend Mark was perhaps the first time I realised how much of my identity and childhood happiness were rooted in my family home. The magnificent Cluniac priory, where Henry James used to stay, was sold for just a few hundred thousand pounds in the early 1980s after the four brothers who owned it couldn't agree on a succession plan. It was bought by the late artist Louis De Wet and his actress wife Gabrielle Drake, who devoted themselves to restoring the house to its medieval self.

Whereas shared inheritance laws across Europe have meant that the French and others have adopted a sanguine attitude towards the selling-off of old family houses, in Britain we tend to be more sentimental. We cling to them until the bailiffs and the estate agent's photographer – or Christie's porters – are pounding at the door.

In September 1992, *le tout* Shropshire had gathered morbidly to watch the contents of Pitchford Hall near Shrewsbury – one of the country's finest black-and-white timber houses – being sold, along with the house. The house belonged to former stockbroker and Guards officer Oliver Colthurst and his wife Caroline, having been handed down her family for nearly five hundred years. I had grown up in Shropshire with their two daughters, the elder of whom was called Rowena. 'People were sitting in a tent bidding for paintings by

Reynolds, or the lumpy bed that Queen Victoria had slept in,' says her husband James Nason. 'And then a porter would just carry them to the front door of the house to be put into vans and cars and driven away. It was surreal.'

James's parents-in-law had been forced to sell the historic forty-two-room house following catastrophic Lloyd's of London losses.

'My parents went to Mexico,' recalled Rowena. 'It felt like a bereavement. But when we lost the house, James and I made a vow that we would try to buy it back. We felt a wrong had been done and we wanted to set that right.'

The house, plus seventy-six acres (the family kept a thousand acres), had been bought by a Kuwaiti princess who had plans to turn the sprawling manor – with a badly leaking roof – into a stud farm. But she never spent a night at the house. Some twenty-five years later, Rowena and James were able to buy Pitchford back. When I visited, there was still a yellowed copy of the *Daily Telegraph* in the kitchen from the week the family moved out in 1992. When the house was up for sale, the National Trust and English Heritage had both turned it down. John Major's heritage minister David Mellor thought the iconic black-and-white timber house wasn't important enough to be rescued.

Taking on Upton Cressett in 1970 was a gamble as my father was able to negotiate only a 79-year lease with Colonel Marsh. Cecil Beaton's bitter-sweet account of his years as the tenant of Ashcombe House in Wiltshire (from 1930 to 1945) is full of grief for the loss of a house that he transformed from an overgrown derelict wreck into a rural salon for the bohemian demi-monde. His memoir, *Ashcombe: The Story of a Fifteen-Year Lease*, is a literary act of re-possession for the 'small universe' that he loved, but his eviction left a shadow hanging over him that he was never able to shake off. Our home was only saved from possible future family expulsion when my father bought the freehold following Colonel Marsh's death.

Car Park Lefty

In the late 1970s and early '80s, I spent a lot of time sitting in car parks around the country while my father was interviewed by local Conservative Associations in the hope of getting a Commons seat. He often made it down to the final shortlist. The reasons he was never selected were always abstruse. Once I remember my mother saying it was because he had worn a suit 'with turn-ups'; another time it was 'because he was a Catholic.' As the 1983 election approached, his deepening frustration at not finding a seat was enough to put me off having any personal interest in politics.

While I sat in our Ford Granada in Conservative Association car parks in Folkestone, Poole or Beaconsfield, babysitting my brother Sam and younger sister Laetitia (my mother would be inside with my father), I was usually reading a Graham Greene or George Orwell novel. Although I didn't let on at the time, I identified more with the politics of my left-leaning, liberal or dissenting literary heroes – William Hazlitt, John Ruskin, W. H. Auden, J. B. Priestley, John Betjeman and Christopher Hitchens (whom I later got to know after we enjoyed a three-bottle dinner in Washington).

Above all, I enjoyed the caustic literary style of Clough Williams-Ellis, the plus-fours-wearing and Labour-voting founder of Portmeirion, the 'Italian seaside village' in North Wales. He was the iconoclastic author of *England and the Octopus*, a 1928 diatribe about the destruction of the English countryside, thanks to poor planning laws and ribbon development. It helped lead to the founding of the Council for the Protection of Rural England (of which I am a long-standing member).

My anti-Establishment sentiment came, I am sure, from my Quaker roots, with seven Liberal MPs in my political family. My father was proud to be a cousin of John Bright, the radical Liberal statesman, repealer of the Corn Laws and mentor of Abraham Lincoln (who had a photo of Bright in his pocket when he was assassinated). After my father finally won a seat in 1984, selected for the Stafford by-election following the death of Sir Hugh Fraser, he would always say, 'Meet me by John Bright', referring to his ancestor's marble statue, whenever I went to see him in the Commons.

So, we were self-made entrepreneurial Quakers who moved from Scotland to the Midlands where our family became financiers, railway-builders and prosperous nineteenth- and twentieth-century silk ribbon weavers ('Cash's of Coventry'). We had a royal warrant and factories in America and Australia. We made name tapes for generations of school children as well as labels for Levi's, Harris Tweed and Jermyn Street shirtmakers.

The head of our branch of the family before my father was Sir William Cash, former chairman of Abbey National and chairman of the Girls' Public School Day Trust, who died in 1964 after attempting to stand several times as a Labour MP. *The Times* obituary referred to him as a 'tall man of great presence' who bore a 'striking resemblance' to the late Earl Kitchener. Sir William was described as a 'financial genius' (a DNA quality that I never shared), with his entire life and work dominated by 'his deeply religious outlook'.

Alas, my father never received any significant Cash inheritance as Sir William left most of what remained of the family fortune to Balliol College, Oxford. Cash's of Coventry, once one of the most important textile manufacturers in the country, was sold in the recession of 1976; its traditional Jacquard looms were unable to keep up with Far Eastern competition.

As I grew up at Upton Cressett, my father had to work hard as a constitutional lawyer as well as an underpaid MP (salary of £15,090) to fund the school fees. He subsidised one term's with the sale of his Holland & Holland shotgun after he decided he 'absolutely hated' shooting. He was no Tory squire.

The house was decorated with portraits of worthy Cash relations and I always felt connected to my liberal heritage – up to a point. My family's values (as leading nineteenth-century Quaker insurers and accountants) were to be prudent and community-minded. Worse, they were usually non-drinkers and non-smokers. My London–Brighton railway-building ancestor William Cash was even chairman of the National Temperance League (alas, he was to die of cholera after ordering a glass of water at a board meeting when his fellow directors ordered beer). He was reported to have converted the rakish and hard-drinking Victorian caricaturist George Cruickshank – who illustrated books for Dickens and had eleven illegitimate children with one mistress – into a fanatical teetotaller. Later, I struggled to live up to such sober standards.

In the dining room at Upton Cressett hangs a rather forbidding oil portrait of another member of our family, Samuel Lucas, whose MP son Frederick (who converted to Catholicism in 1839) in 1848 founded *The Tablet* magazine, the self-described 'progressive' Catholic weekly. His other son, Samuel, was a fervent US abolitionist and the 'managing proprietor' of the *Morning Star*, founded by his Quaker brother-in-law John Bright and Richard Cobden in 1859. This was the only national newspaper in Britain to support the Unionist cause in the American Civil War. I was brought up to identify with outsiders and underdogs.

Politically, I had no loyalties. I stood with Greene's observation that 'a writer must be able to cross over, to change sides at the drop of a hat. He stands for the victims and the victims change.'

Family Theatre

The 1970s was a good time to be brought up in a restore-a-wreck family. The heritage boom was just beginning. The Historic Houses Association was founded in 1973, my father an early chairman of the Heart of England region. The V&A *Destruction* show heightened public awareness of the pleasures to be derived from visiting the many country houses that were opening their doors for the first time.

It wasn't long before a trip to an English country house had become the new leisure activity. As a boy and a teenager, I was dragged around the sweeping avenues, parks and gardens of our great country houses, and came gradually to see that this 'day out' was replacing the Victorian experience of going to the seaside.

What people now wanted, largely thanks to the car, was a twentieth-century equivalent – a resort-like estate with ice-cream, tea rooms, avenues and car parks, a famous garden, like Sissinghurst's, or a safari park. Instead of walking along the beach at Brighton or Broadstairs, today's tourists wander with their dogs and children up the sweeping drives of stately homes, like Blenheim and Castle Howard. The avenues and parks are today's esplanades, beaches and piers.

Growing up at Upton Cressett, I felt we were like a small seaside theatre company that could go under at any time after a bad season. I was stagehand, luggage boy, chair carrier, guide and postcard seller. But I loved it, and leading tours not only gave me confidence and a bit of pocket money but also taught me that the story of Britain is also the story of the houses, abbeys and churches that were built, demolished and rebuilt by those for whom their houses and architectural ambitions (often ending in financial ruin) were often their most lasting legacy.

Visiting houses during the summer holidays, with *Hudson's Historic Houses & Gardens* as our family Bible, taught me how our understanding of so many historical men and women – statesmen, seafaring buccaneers, soldiers, war heroes, artists, writers, industrialists, wives, mistresses and heiresses – is enlarged by seeing the houses and follies they built, or changed in their image. I learned about Sir Francis Drake bringing tobacco to England from America in 1586, for example, through visiting Buckland Abbey in Devon. I can still recall the garden spot where a bucket of water was thrown on Drake when he lit up his tobacco pipe. The servant had thought his master was on fire.

I absorbed the past by visiting the domestic stage sets where so much history was shaped. The same applied when we went abroad on holiday, whether it was camping in Normandy, visiting the tomb of Agamemnon at Mycenae in Greece, or tramping around Tintagel Castle in Cornwall with Jonathan on one of our 'In Search of King Arthur' road trips.

As a boy, I became an avid autograph hunter. In the first freezing week of January 1979, the BBC came to film the last episode of the Dickens drama *The Old Curiosity Shop*. I helped serve plastic cups of tea and sausage rolls from an old catering truck and collected cast autographs, which included those of the veteran character actors Sebastian Shaw and Brian Oulton, to whom I gave a tour of the Norman church. ('Thank you for showing me your wonderful chapel,' Oulton wrote.) Shaw was to achieve cult fame as Darth Vader in *The Return of the Jedi*.

Now – along with the 1976 Leeds United football team – most of the names in my autograph book are already largely forgotten. Signatures are transitory, but bricks and mortar are more durable. I learned that almost anything wrecked can be made beautiful again as long as the essential fabric – the original mortar, wattle and bricks of a house – is still there.

I also learned that in the country-house rescue business value had little to do with price. Much of my teenage life was coloured by stories of improbable bargains picked up in antiques shops or salerooms. The panelling in the entrance hall at Upton Cressett came from an antiques shop in Camden Passage near where we lived in Islington. It was lime-green and my mother spent weeks stripping it off with a wire brush, washing her hands in turpentine. The carved oak overmantel above the fireplace was rescued from a Shropshire butcher's shop. Part of it was half of a Jacobean headboard.

It was an early education in optimism and the power of buildings to heal. It wasn't just a return to my childhood that I was seeking after my failed marriages; it was a return to a world of emotional stability and aesthetic transformation in which ruin, chaos and disorder are defeated by imagination, love and beauty.

Deep down I always thought of Upton Cressett as my haven, a mini-world in which broken twisted chimneys, ten-foot-high brambles, corrugated roofing, abandoned farm machinery, neglected wells and outdoor brick loos were transmuted by my parents' efforts into a house of Elizabethan glory. The adventure was a form of time travel as well as architectural rebirth.

3

Fawlty Turrets

To help keep the show on the road, and pay the school fees, my parents were members of a club-like organisation called the Heritage Circle. It targeted rich Americans and was run by Elizabeth and John Denning of Burghope Manor in Bradford-upon-Avon in Wiltshire. The idea was to tap into the early 1980s *Brideshead* dream. I still have a copy of the 1980s brochure, which describes the Circle as a club-like collection of historic country houses that offered foreign travellers a 'unique opportunity to stay in some of the most lovingly preserved castles, manor houses, halls and other period dwellings'.

The critical difference from holiday cottages, such as those offered by the Landmark Trust, is that at the Heritage Circle properties you did not have to self-cater. The club's motto was 'Heritage and Hospitality'. Guests were invariably on what was called the 'de luxe country house grand tour'. The whole point was for your owner-host to mix your gin and tonic before a black-tie dinner with the family. I ended up giving house tours while my mother did the cooking.

As a young teenager, I would wear a blue velvet jacket from C&A, with a clip-on bow-tie, and pass round prawn crackers and crisps. It was my first introduction to country-house stage-set acting.

'You are warmly invited into our homes where we will offer you courteous and friendly personal service in the great tradition of British country house hospitality,' stated the brochure. With my father working in London, it was often just me – a bookish teenager with glasses – and my glamorous mother or, during term time, my mother on her own, helped by Syd Smith, our stooping gardener turned occasional butler. Syd was a kind, country soul and belonged in another century, with prickly white side whiskers. I never saw him drive. He was much more comfortable double-digging the rose garden than carrying my mother's duck à l'orange from the kitchen to the dining room. His wife, always called Mrs Smith, would polish the oak newel stairs with beeswax until they gleamed. Guests – especially in high heels – regularly ended up sliding down them on their rear.

The eighteen Heritage Circle members included various Scottish castles and Renishaw Hall in Derbyshire (the ancestral seat of the Sitwell family). Several properties offered shooting and hunting ('in the appropriate season'). We certainly didn't have any shoots. The only birds we reared were my mother's Indian Blue peacocks bred from her champion, Rosalind.

Things had a way of going wrong. One American woman arrived with a green African parrot in a cage. After I had deposited the bird in the Gatehouse, I was handed a bag of seed and asked to feed it during her stay. When I went up to do so, I found the parrot flying around the ancient rafters squawking.

I used to type up the menus in French, using our old Adler ribbon typewriter. My mother had learned French cooking while studying at the Sorbonne in Paris. 'You really have such a great chef,' American guests would say. 'Can you give him our compliments? Can we leave him a tip? We can't get French chefs in Dallas. They don't like the heat.'

They had no idea my mother was cooking in the kitchen, then running out in her cocktail dress and heels to host the dinner. I remember how civilised and gracious most American guests were. They wrote to thank us from their next stop on the tour, so letters would arrive on thickly embossed paper from Gleneagles or via airmail from the Ritz in Paris. They were worldly, rich and fascinating, and usually polite to the point of indifferent if the hot water only dribbled, there was a power cut (quite regular) or they were dive-bombed in bed by medieval bats.

The next promise was also a little wide of the mark: 'We endeavour to blend the atmosphere of an historic private home with the high standards expected of a good hotel.' The truth was that most Heritage Circle bathrooms harked back to the post-war 1950s era (when you turned on a tap, out came rust-coloured water) and were a world away from the standards of a luxury hotel, or at least the type that those much-travelled guests were used to. But, while plumbing standards were challenging in most Heritage Circle properties, few visitors complained. They were coming to country houses to experience something different, authentic and unique – holidays in English history. One lovely Californian family, called Norton, first came in the mid-1980s when the top-floor tower bedroom in the Gatehouse had just one light switch, as their daughter Meghan remembers. 'It was twenty yards away by the door so you had to navigate in the dark to find the bed.'

After her mother Gayle had revealed that her fifteen-year-old daughter had inherited a water divining talent from her grandfather (she had half-jokingly described herself as a 'Water Witch'), Meghan found herself volunteering to help find Upton Cressett's famed secret tunnel, built for smuggling out either priests or the house's royalist owners. After requesting an old pair of pliers, Meghan duly went out in the driving rain the following day with my father following behind with a rusty pair of divining rods. They soon started whirring around like helicopter blades.

'As I walked past the Gatehouse, I could feel the energy,' Meghan recalled. 'My hands started shaking. The tunnel led from the Gatehouse to right under the main house and then dog-legged by the moat to the church and ended behind the altar.'

Alas, my parents never did anything about excavating the tunnel, which we had been told by an elderly farmer was brick lined. It was said to emerge in a field some quarter of a mile from the church so that escapees could vanish into the woods.

'Health and Safety' breaches were commonplace. Once, when we had some rich Texans staying, a mouse appeared in the drawing room just as we had drinks before dinner. As it scuttled into the middle of a Persian rug, my mother's face dropped. She looked at me. But it was too late. The Americans had seen it.

'Oh, my, isn't that a little mouse?' the woman said. 'He's so cute. I've never seen a mouse like that before. Do they come out often?'

I remember one Californian woman, back in the 1980s, being entirely nonchalant when she mentioned to my mother that she had enjoyed a wonderful night's sleep in the Gatehouse. She had woken, though, when she felt something warm dripping on her face.

'I'm so sorry,' my mother said. 'Elizabethan tiles do have a way of letting the rain in occasionally.'

'Oh, it wasn't rain,' the woman said. 'It was a squirrel above me in the rafters going to the toilet – or was it a bat?'

My mother and I looked at each other. We were speechless.

'The bat didn't really trouble me,' the American woman went on. 'I guess it's all part of the charm of a lovely old house.'

The roof has long since been repaired and a four-poster bed installed. So such an incident could never happen today . . . I'm almost certain of that. Almost.

On another occasion we had a wealthy Anglophile Australian polo-playing family staying. Leslie Hill was a friend of Prince Philip and his son Sinclair taught polo to Prince Charles. Prince Harry was later to work as a jackaroo for the Hill family at one of their huge cattle ranches. I had been told to clear the plates after dinner. I was just about to do this when I saw that Mr Hill senior was starting to pile the plates down the table. When I tried to intervene, he laughed, then told us that the same thing had happened when Prince Philip had stayed with the Hill family at their ranch in New South Wales.

'I said to the staff, "With British royalty, you do *not* stack the plates after dinner. You carry them out." But then, when dinner finished, to my horror, I saw Prince Philip stacking up all the plates on the table around him! He stood up and carried the pile to the side table. "Oh, don't worry, Leslie," he said. "We do this the whole time at home."'

The house has had many facelifts, modernisations and incarnations. In its entry in *The Best Thousand Houses of England*, Simon Jenkins describes his frustration at trying to understand the architecture of the house, saying, 'It is not easy to read.' He was right. But I liked that aspect. It was a house of secrets and surprises.

My father had once invited Britain's foremost priest-hole expert, Michael Hodgetts, a world authority on English recusant history, to visit Upton Cressett. One of the favoured forms of priest hides, designed by the Jesuit carpenter and saint Nicholas Owen, was to incorporate it inside the garderobe (Elizabethan lavatory) shaft that dropped down to the moat. We discovered exactly such a shaft leading off the fireplace in the master bedroom.

As a boy of twelve or thirteen, I spent many days with a trowel and bucket being lowered into the hole as we excavated it in the hope of finding a secret chamber leading off it. All we discovered was an

Elizabethan pewter bowl and a spoon, which may have been used for feeding a priest hidden in the shaft. As my Uncle Jonathan said, 'You've spent the last two days digging through Elizabethan shit!'

He was convinced there was a major Roman military settlement and maybe a general's villa just a few fields away from the house that needed to be professionally excavated and designated a Scheduled Ancient Monument. Nobody knew more than he did about the historic topography of Upton Cressett. The main area of our attention was the fields at Parlour Coppice, behind our house, where the farmland had lain undisturbed for almost a thousand years until the farmer ploughed it after the war.

In the mid-1980s, my uncle made what should have been a life-changing career breakthrough. I remember his fevered excitement when he arrived at the house, his dark hair wet and with clods of mud on his boots. He had just met with farmer Derek Pugh to ask him for permission to look at the 'plough soil'. The Pughs had bought land around Upton Cressett during the war very cheaply ('a few shillings an acre', my father said). When my uncle entered the Pughs' old farmhouse, Mr Pugh led him into the kitchen, told him to sit down and that Mrs Pugh would give him a cup of tea.

'Wait here,' he was told. 'I've got a few things to show you.'

A few minutes later he was taken into a back room where a large collection of Romano-British pottery, axe and arrow heads, coins, brooches and coloured flint heads lay on a table. This previously unseen hoard of artefacts – now known as the 'Pugh Hoard' – had been collected from the plough soil since the war. The broken pottery pieces were kept in racks and laid out like a school exhibition. It was quite a find. Over 1,500 Roman sherds were piled up, including examples of local Malvern and Severn Valley pottery, Roman beakers, flagons, mortaria and quern stones.

'Can I take some photographs?' asked Jonathan, taking off the Praktica camera that was slung around his neck.

'I don't mind,' said Pugh. 'You can take some pieces away to have them date-tested if you want. Must be Roman or Bronze Age.'

Life-changing moments can be difficult to recognise when they happen. The discovery of the Pugh Hoard from Parlour Coppice was just such a moment for my uncle – or at least it should have been.

'Look at these,' Jonathan said, as he hurried into our kitchen, taking off his camera and waterproof. He pulled out a few large fragments of pottery and placed them on the kitchen table with as much pride as if they were gold coins recovered from the *Mary Rose*. 'This looks like Samian ware, which traded across the continent,' he announced. 'It makes it all the more likely that my hunch that this was an important Roman site is correct. Perhaps even a lost Roman hill fort.'

Jonathan helped me understand that the landscape around Upton Cressett was magical, mysterious and symbolic. I had thought of Upton Cressett as early medieval, or Saxon, with the site of the original old hall and church dating back to when it was known as Ulton in the Domesday Book. But, in fact, it was an ancient hamlet that dated back well beyond the medieval period to the Romano-British age.

Our favourite archaeological tramp was up the Wrekin to see the ancient double hill fort remains. As you stand on the summit, with the wind blowing in your hair, the vista towards the Malvern Hills is celestial. The sweeping views across Shropshire and Wenlock Edge from there have inspired generations of artists, writers and composers, including A. E. Housman, Edward Elgar, Ralph Vaughan Williams and J. R. R. Tolkien. Jonathan explained that Tolkien used to walk up the Wrekin and used the famous defensive hill as a model for the Shire in *The Hobbit*. At the top, we would see kestrels swooping and tumbling in the sky in front of us. We could have been perched in the crow's nest of the *Golden Hinde* looking out across a sea of hills and valleys.

As the bitter wind blew into our faces, Jonathan and I imagined that we were standing where King Caractacus of the Ancient Britons might have fought the 'Last Battle' with the Romans. We felt as if were standing in the very heart of England, and the very soul of Housman country, with the 'blue remembered hills' of Shropshire rolling beneath us.

Ted Hughes described Housman's elegiac poetry as 'the most perfect expression of something deeply English and a whole mood of history'. It was a landscape I came to love and I understood from an early age why it was worth fighting for.

4

Wapping Graduate

In a Binder Box marked 'Cambridge' there is a cream envelope, post-marked September 1987. In the summer holiday before I started at Magdalene College, I found myself sitting two tables away from Graham Greene in Chez Feliz, a restaurant just inside the walls of the old Antibes port. The following day, I returned with a copy of a short story I had written in an envelope marked 'c/o Monsieur Greene'.

Quite why I was carrying short stories around with me on holiday I cannot recall. But two weeks later, back at Upton Cressett, I received a typed letter from Greene, signed with his spidery writing, saying that he liked the story 'very much' and advising me on how to get it published. I was eighteen and blindly imagined that literary success came easily.

Within a month or so, I managed to get myself accredited as the literary editor of *Varsity* for the Booker Prize award ceremony in London. I'll never forget it; I ended up carrying the horizontal (and quite heavy) figure of Peter Ackroyd out of the dinner with his agent Giles Gordon. I took his head, Gordon took the legs and Melvyn Bragg, I think, took up the portly midriff as we somehow managed to get him into a taxi, then headed off towards the Groucho Club. Ackroyd was comatose through drink, his eyes closed. He had been shortlisted for his novel *Chatterton* and so nervous that he had scooped up his table's entire drinks supply. The incident was later recalled in the *Guardian* by Christopher Sinclair-Stevenson, his friend and publisher. 'The waiter asked if anyone wanted a glass of brandy or port or whatever. And most people were saying no. And Peter said, "You're all to have one because then you can shovel them across to me." And he swallowed one after another.'

I thought this *nostalgie de la boue* literary world of boozy dinners was much more appealing than getting up at 6 a.m. to work as a summer intern for an American bank. I bunked off my lectures in November 1989 to report on the fall of the Berlin Wall, taking the ferry from Felixstowe and driving to East Berlin in my small Peugeot with two fellow English undergraduates. On my second night, I had lost my friends, and an East German student brunette led me up a ladder to the roof of a building to drink beer and watch some fireworks. We were alone. As she asked me to light her Marlboro cigarette, she leaned forward to kiss me. It was like VE Day in 1945. But I fumbled with my lighter. I still hadn't a clue about girls.

Then I arrived in snowy Prague – by plane – two days before the Velvet Revolution and ended up with my first foreign cover story for a national paper (the long-defunct *Sunday Correspondent*). When I should have been working for my finals, I was flying head-first down an ice tobogganing run at 80 m.p.h. on a skeleton sled in Switzerland, having trained on trays down the staircase of a Cambridge club, with Harry Dalmeny, later chairman of Sotheby's, being the most fearless team rider.

I was taught English by the brilliant Trinity don Eric Griffiths. He told us that the 'printed voice' of authors and poets – from Victorians like Tennyson to modernists like Geoffrey Hill – was a living form of communion with the past. Letters or poems to those we have loved, or still love, can live on, long after the relationship is dead. I am sure this contributed to my chronic inability to let go of my past, and my habit of photocopying and collecting my letters.

I was part of the Moneyman generation – or the *Bonfire* generation, to be more specific. Everyone, it seemed, wanted to become a banker. I was in my first year at university when I got my hands on a copy of *The Bonfire of the Vanities* in 1987. I read Tom Wolfe's Dickensian tale of the money-fever-obsessed world of 1980s New York through the night, fuelled by takeaway pizza and dreams of one day working in America.

My late-1980s contemporaries were the new financial warriors of Wall Street and London, including the investment banking houses of Goldman Sachs, JP Morgan and Salomon Brothers, as well as German and Japanese banks. Strangely, Gordon Gekko, the greed-is-good corporate raider anti-hero of Oliver Stone's *Wall Street* – which came out in December 1987 – was almost regarded as an aspirational role model by many, although few were so dumb as to say so in their 'milk-round' job interviews. It was all anathema to me, working as a slush pile reader and lowly salesman for a Soho Square-based publisher in the university holidays.

In 1986, the Big Bang had revolutionised not just the City but the financial and work universe. An article that year in the *Spectator* by Nicholas Coleridge caught the *zeitgeist* by describing how 'Money is the new club.' It was difficult to estimate the number of young investment bankers, stockbrokers and commodity brokers earning £100,000 a year, he wrote. 'Most are between 26 and 34 and two years ago they were being paid £25,000 . . . the majority of highly paid City boys are not *nouveaux riches* at all; they are traditional upper-middle-class pinstripes who are banking the cheques as fast as they can while the going is good.'

In the late 1980s and early to mid-1990s, you could buy a two-bed flat in South Kensington with a year's salary and bonus – in your twenties. The average London house price in 1986 was £56,000. The idea that success was something to look forward to – let alone be earned – became quaint or petit bourgeois. The Moneyman credo was that success and self-worth were defined largely in dollar terms, and you could have it all, now.

In my second year at university, Michael Lewis's book *Liar's Poker* came out. Whenever he spoke to bankers, he sensed they felt 'cheated' if somebody was paid more than them. His book was like a graduate career training manual to my friends. On his first day at Salomon Brothers, turning up to work just before 7 a.m., Lewis described how he saw an army of 'worried men in suits' marching along Lexington Avenue. 'Oddly enough, I didn't imagine I was going to work, more as if I was going to collect lottery winnings.'

But I never wanted to be a banker, or a Master of the Universe in red braces. I was looking to accumulate another form of capital I thought more valuable – experience.

I took a graduate trainee's job at *The Times* on £14,000. After a year, thanks to foreign editor Martin Ivens, I got to fulfil my ambition of working in America. I had introduced the idea of being posted to Los Angeles at the *Spectator* summer party in July 1991, after which I'd written him a rather bumptious letter about the merits of *The Times* covering both 'high' and 'low' culture, and how I was unsuited to Wapping desk life. This somehow won him and op-ed editor Graham Paterson over to the idea of sending me out to California.

The appointment truly was a dream. I was soon having dinner at the Washington home of Michael Lewis and I began a correspondence with Tom Wolfe. As part of my finals I had written a 15,000-word thesis on Wolfe's satire, full of obtuse references to Swift and Juvenal, and had brazenly sent him a copy (c/o Farrar, Strauss & Giroux) with a covering letter on *Times* stationery. Wolfe politely wrote back in his florid eighteenth-century octopus script thanking me for the monograph on his work which he enjoyed: 'I might add that since you mention me in the same breath with Evelyn Waugh, Thackeray and Wyndham Lewis – you'll notice I say the same breath and not the same league – I now feel positively historic. But alas, I have been forced to put my feet in the stocks to compel myself to complete a book against a ferocious deadline.' But, he asked, once he had finished his follow-up novel to *Bonfire*, would I like to meet up at his East 79th Street apartment in New York?

This typed letter – dated 31 January 1991 and addressed to 'Mr Cash' with its triple-spacing and Thackeray-esque signature – meant so much more to me than any Wall Street bonus.

It was also in America where I discovered another form of adulation. For it was in LA that my Binder Box love letters, and my heart's voyage, began.

II

5

Good Intentions

When I headed for America in 1991, I was following in a family tradition of New World adventure and reinvention. Bizarrely, I am related to the American country singer Johnny Cash, whose Anglo-Scottish ancestor settled in America in 1667 after being the captain of a pilgrim boat in the late seventeenth century. As the *Guardian* wrote in a review of a BBC radio documentary on the Scottish roots of the American country legend: 'The American connection was established when mariner William Cash sailed from Scotland to Salem, Massachusetts.'

His pilgrim brigantine ship was called the *Good Intent* and its enterprising owner was from my family. This improbable genealogical story dates back to the 1970s, when Johnny Cash was flying on an American Airlines flight and found himself – dressed in trademark black suit – seated next to Major Michael Crichton-Stuart, hereditary keeper of Falkland Palace in the Kingdom of Fife in east Scotland. When the singer remarked that he had heard that that the American branch of the Cash family were originally from Scotland, Crichton-Stuart told the Man in Black that there were villages, farms and streets in Fife that still bore the Cash name (such as Easter Cash and Wester Cash) as well as Loch Cash near Fife.

Johnny Cash's official autobiography opens:

> *My line comes down from Queen Ada, the sister of Malcolm IV, descended from King Duff, the first king of Scotland. Malcolm's castle is long gone but you can still see some of its stones in the walls of the church tower in the little village of Strathmiglo. The motto on my people's coat of arms was 'Better Times Will Come.' Their name was Caesche; with emigration in the sixteenth and seventeenth centuries, it came to be spelled the way it was pronounced, C-A-S-H . . .*

Although my father had long been aware of our shared American ancestry with New World pilgrim ship captain William Cash – due to a detailed exchange of letters in 1974 with a San Diego-based family historian – we had no idea that we also shared a direct family 'bloodline' with Johnny Cash. This only emerged when Johnny's country singer daughter Rosanne contacted my father at the House of Commons when she was on tour in England to promote an album that explored her Cash family roots. On a previous album, *Black Cadillac*, she had written a song called 'The Good Intent' about our ancestor William Cash, and his New World pilgrim ship.

Born in Strathmiglo, Fife, William was a 'Master Mariner' in the American colonies trade who – from his twenties – transported pilgrims (paying their own way) to New England. On his final voyage in 1667, he brought his nephew, also confusingly called William (traditionally the name of the eldest son), and ended up settling in Essex County, Massachusetts with his wife and family. His perilous but profitable maritime operation (navigating by the stars or with the most basic of instruments) allowed his descendants to own a large tobacco plantation in Westmoreland County, Virginia.

When William Cash (the nephew) died in 1708, his will not only set out the division of his Virginian lands to his sons and Quaker wife Elizabeth but also made clear his strong religious temperament. 'In the name of God Amen!' William begins his will, 'I give my soul to God which gave it'.

The Cashes then moved on to Georgia, where the plantation of Johnny Cash's great-grandfather was burned by General Sherman after he fought for the Confederacy in the Civil War. His son, Johnny's grandfather, was another William who was a 'circuit rider', a farmer and travelling minister. He 'rode a horse and carried a gun' and never charged a dime for his preaching. Preaching and God were in Johnny's religious dissenting family blood.

Johnny Cash was brought up in Arkansas, where his father, following the Depression, scratched a living doing whatever work he could find, from working in a saw mill to picking cotton. Better times only finally came with Johnny's first hit, 'Walk the Line', in 1956 on the Sun label. His Celtic spirit and religious moodiness – in addition to his deep baritone-bass voice – helped him to sell over 90 million records, making him one of the best-selling artists of all time. Cash saw his 'hard knocks' life – derailed by addiction, alcohol, drugs and divorce – as a road trip into the soul. But his scorching and unforgiving emotional honesty helped him to become an American icon.

I was just twenty-five when I arrived at LAX airport as West Coast correspondent of *The Times*. What most surprises me now about *Educating William*, my book about my early years in LA, is its almost complete lack of any girlfriends, or any 'romantic interest'. That was because there wasn't much to report. The only exception was that I spent the first month or so living in a rickety house on stilts in the Studio City Hills with an attractive LA film producer, a few years older than me, whom I had met at Madonna's 'Truth or Dare' party at the Cannes Film Festival. Her name was Holly McConkey and she ran a company called Wild Dog Films.

I was staying some miles from Cannes at the Grand-Hôtel du Cap Ferrat, which the travel editor had let me review. I somehow persuaded Holly to travel back to England and invited her to Upton Cressett. Having crashed my own car in Cannes, I hired one. We spent a few days staying in little hotels as we drove through the Loire Valley to Calais. She then invited me to live with her when I arrived in LA as a young, ambitious and romantically inexperienced foreign correspondent. She was a lovely girl – fun, kind and bright, although not quite (yet) the A-list Hollywood producer I had envisaged.

The relationship lasted a month before we changed the sleeping arrangements. I was to move out of her bedroom and pay her $30 a night to sleep on her sofa until I found my own apartment. I was a bookish Englishman, selfish, over-excited to be in LA, and more interested in my deadlines than the pursuit of romance. In my book, I wrote an account of my first few weeks in LA, with Holly's name changed. After the book was published, I tried to get back in touch but couldn't reach her. There was no record of her in any LA area phone directory.

Then, after covering the O. J. Simpson trial, I found myself interviewing one of LA's top private investigators involved in the Simpson murder case. He specialised in working with the LAPD to track down missing persons so I asked him to run a name-check on Holly. On his screen, her name and date of birth flashed up, along with the information that she had died, cause unknown. I was beginning to understand why LA was regarded as the most unromantic city on earth.

For many years, I didn't even have a photograph of her. But while rummaging through some old cardboard boxes in a storage barn in the weeks before my fiftieth, looking for something entirely different,

I found an envelope dating back to 1991 containing several letters on lined exercise paper. Reading them all those years later made me wince. In one, Holly had written: 'You are very different from most men I meet. You seem to take matters into your own hands successfully, at times, though it seems like a fantasy. You are a very sweet person and very loving. I only wish you would talk to me more. You're just not used to being intimate with a woman.'

Holly was right. I was an immature hack in a hurry and had never been in love before. I could bond emotionally with a house but had yet to have similar feelings for a woman.

Clearing out the storage barn where my LA papers had been stored, I came across an unsettling letter from my mother in a cardboard box whose bottom was rotted with mould. It was dated 10 September 1992, after my parents had come out to see me in Los Angeles for the first time.

On their arrival, they were surprised to find me still living in a hotel and driving a rental car although I had been there for nearly a year. They stepped in to help, found my lovely rustic house in the Hollywood Hills (next door to David Hockney) and gave me a party for my birthday. But the letter is painful to read now.

I have to say Daddy and I were extremely upset by the unwelcome you gave us. Considering we had provided the home for you and invested a great deal of time and money in it – it is very irksome to hear you complaining the entire time we were there which was only two and a half weeks anyhow. For the first two days, you moaned about your back while we got your office organised, sprang me with a party for 40, got drunk and were bad-tempered for 10 days. For most of the time, you were very uncompanionable. Your lack of effort to be tidy and organised will stop you achieving success. And your inability to manage your financial affairs is intolerable.

You are extremely fortunate that you are one of the very few
people with a job and opportunity to earn a lot of money through
writing and very lucky to be in America at this time. I should make
the most of it.

Life here is very, very critical.

Love, Mummy xxxx

I remember feeling devastated on reading it and vowed to change.
It also reminded me of the power of words to hurt and also heal. Words
mattered. My mother also recognised that living in a hotel was not
good for my health. I needed a home.

My mother had found my house through an ad in the rental section
of the *Los Angeles Times* and had paid the deposit. She had also used
her considerable charm on the owner, a notoriously tough, ball-
breaking LA entertainment attorney called Martin ('Mutt') Cohen,
who lived next door, surrounded by his own LA vineyard and orange
grove, which we shared. I could have been in Tuscany.

My first housemate was a budding English screenwriter called
Simon Kelton, whom I had first met when he was the opposing captain
of the Oxford Cresta Run team. Neither of us knew what to make of our
colourful Jewish landlord, who often behaved like a Brooklyn gangster.
He had almost expressionless dark-brown eyes and an awful temper,
combined with an unpredictable streak of warmth and generosity.
Along with his brother Herb, Martin was known as a ruthless music
rights lawyer who made a fortune (50 per cent) from the talents of such
singers as Tom Waits, Frank Zappa and Linda Ronstadt.

By the time I knew him, he was on his fourth wife, a lovely Irish
woman called Trish who was many years younger than him. She may
have been the aunt of *Downton Abbey* star Michelle Dockery, but the
Cohen household was not known for its *noblesse oblige*. Martin was
always shouting at people (Simon and me included if we were late
with the rent) and he 'died of anger', according to an ex-wife. He was,

however, a legendary LA host, throwing regular Sunday-afternoon parties ('No Children or Vegetarians') in the cellar and garden of his house, where he would offer guests a 'sampler' of his own wine (undrinkable). He then began opening his cellar of French *grand crus* and Napa Valley 'super-premium' wines. He also had an underground cigar bunker.

He had been born in a tough part of Brooklyn, the son of a Russian Jew whose family had fled Germany for America. His aggressive approach to life was an education. As I stood beside Trish as we trampled his grapes barefoot, he said, 'If a drop of your fancy nail varnish gets into my wine, I'll fuckin' kill you.' When I once brought my former old Etonian actor friend Clement von Franckenstein to one of his parties, he looked at Clem and said, 'Who the fuck are you? Get the fuck out!'

Clem was known as 'The Baron', being the only son of the former Austrian ambassador to London, Sir George von und zu Franckenstein, who was tragically killed – along with Clem's English mother – in a Frankfurt plane crash in 1953 when Clem was just a young boy starting at prep school. He became a dear friend and I lived on a mattress on the floor – shared with his cat – at his Carthay Circle house for several months when I was homeless for a while in LA. With his monogrammed slippers, Basil Rathbone voice and 1970s suits, he was an expat legend and one of the last of the breed of gentleman-playboy Brits that came to California in the 1960s and 1970s, chasing the Hollywood dream . . . and more.

After I was 'detained' in a Disneyland cell after *The Times* asked me to report on the sixtieth birthday party of Liz Taylor, Clem picked me up in his white BMW. As we drove past a 'Ye Old England' Tudor pub in Anaheim, he said: 'That's where I began my Hollywood career in 1972, dressed up as Henry VIII. I sang bawdy English ballads as I had trained as a classical tenor. In the 1970s life was easy, everyone was laid back, everyone had a good time.'

He was referring to his Scandinavian attitude to sex. Living with Clem was probably the low point of my romantic single adventurism in LA. Clem was in his late forties when I met him and had never married (and never did). He was proud of being named as one of 'America's Top 50 Bachelors' in *People* magazine and regarded himself as an LA *boulevardier*. I'd often be awaken in the night by the sound of stiletto heels on the parquet floor and the sight of a curvaceous black woman smelling of a musky perfume clomping over my head and mattress, only for another such woman to appear several hours later. In addition to his opera training he was proud of his literary work, which included a piece – 'The Art of The Orgy' – for the *New York Press*.

In addition to being a cabaret singer, he appeared in around eighty films (playing alongside many stars including Jean-Claude van Damme, Melanie Griffith and Mel Brooks in *Robin Hood: Men In Tights*). He often played a debonair figure who looked good in a dinner jacket, or on the arm of a leading lady, sometimes wearing only a leather thong.

One bright Kodak-blue weekend morning, he appeared from his bedroom dressed in one such thong and said: 'William, it's a beautiful day and we are going sunbathing.'

'The beach?' I said.

'No. We're off to Elysium Fields for Sunday lunch. Have you ever sunbathed nude?'

An hour later, we turned off the Pacific Coast highway in Malibu and wound up the craggy road leading to Topanga Canyon.

'This area used to be a free-love colony in the seventies,' Clem said as we pulled up in front of a wooden house set back up a discreet driveway. A white nylon banner proclaimed: 'Elysium Fields – Isn't it time for another adventure?'

Sitting behind the desk was a respectable-looking British woman of around forty. She and Clem knew each other. After we paid $14 each for a 'One Day Vacation Special' pass, Clem whispered into my ear: 'She's the wife of a well-known member of BAFTA.'

As she handed me my locker key, she said: 'By the way, we don't use the word "nudist". Elysium is "clothing optional".'

It wasn't long before Clem had stripped off and was splayed out in a deck chair reading a movie script, smothered in Venezuelan carrot oil and smoking a cigarette. 'Get your kit off William,' he drawled. 'You're making a lot of people very uncomfortable in that English linen jacket.'

I obliged and as Clem nodded off after our sandwich lunch and bottle of cheap Spanish wine bought at a local gas station, I explored the seven-acre park in *puris naturalibus*. After I walked through a secluded wood, I came to a huge bubbling Jacuzzi. A sign stated: 'Leave your hang-ups here.' The swirling hydro-pool was scattered with dead leaves and steaming like a sulphur spring. A bald muscle man in Kojak-style sunglasses – a film cameraman – strummed on a guitar singing Bob Dylan. A fiftysomething woman, her body like a pregnant jellyfish, was floating on her back, her trunk-like legs spread at 45 degrees.

'Come on in,' she gurgled. 'It's like a bath.'

I was rescued by the timely arrival of Clem, who wasted no time in discarding his sandals and plunging into the soupy water with a booming shout of 'Let's party!'

As we drove back in the early evening to Carthay Circle, I reflected that I wasn't going to find a wife to return to England with from hanging out at Elysium Fields.

Clem seemed despondent. 'The place has changed. Didn't know too many people. The Seventies swinging lot weren't there. Nudism and swinging tend to go together – I went off to the Meditation Room, which used to be a very cosy place where people went to have sex. Now it is somebody's bloody bedroom.'

This was all a world away from my parents' Sunday-lunch parties in Shropshire where I used to mix the Pimm's. The 'very, very critical' reference in my mother's 1992 letter referred to the Maastricht Rebellion that my father, an outspoken Eurosceptic Tory MP, was leading at the time from a house in Great College Street loaned by Lord McAlpine. The rebels were a determined clan of like-minded MPs (whom Prime Minister John Major called 'bastards'), who aimed to stop the Maastricht Treaty – which gave EU law supremacy over UK law – becoming enshrined in UK law. I was apolitical (a 'classical liberal', if asked), but I knew my father was obsessed with fighting to save the 'freedom and democracy' that his father had died fighting for.

While I was moaning about my back in sunny LA, my father was involved in backbench warfare with treachery and loyalties tested in scenes worthy of *Julius Caesar*. It was around this time that the playwright John Osborne – who lived not far away in Clun – started to come for Sunday lunch; he had begun writing about his political views in the *Spectator* and my father enjoyed his company. When I was back over Christmas, Osborne arrived in a hand-knitted sweater boasting a British Bulldog and Union Jack.

But as Osborne and my father sank another bottle of claret over Sunday lunch, talking politics, I felt a curious sense of detachment. I wanted to ask John about his relationships with Kenneth Tynan and 'Terry' Rattigan, and how on earth he'd ended up marrying *five* times.

6

Binder Box Beginnings

The first love-letter Binder Box from the LA years is labelled 'P' for Philippa, the tennis-mad daughter of my screenwriter friend Allan Scott (his many credits include the hit musical *Priscilla, Queen of the Desert* and several of Nic Roeg's films, including *Don't Look Now*). Philippa was a beautiful original whose dark Celtic eyebrows hid a more complicated side, which I found attractive. She had intense green-hazel eyes, thick dark hair (like Mary Queen of Scots) and a voice whose cadence speeded up to make a point.

I adored her. She was the first girl I ever thought about marrying. But she crushed my romantic hopes when we went to Australia on a book tour. On the way back to LA, we sat in different sections of the plane.

The relationship spluttered on for another six months. In one of my very first Binder Box love letters, written at Upton Cressett on Christmas Eve 1994, I told her that I had been thinking of her 'in the darkest hours of the night as I lay freezing in my room here'. I said what a relief it was to be back in London after months in rootless LA. I had been 'behaving badly,' I added, 'roaring around London on the back of a BMW motorbike without a crash helmet', and had spent the weekend before Christmas at Sudeley Castle, the Gloucestershire home of my friend Henry Dent-Brocklehurst, whom I'd met in LA.

Most expats returned home at Christmas, almost as if mid-December marked the end of the LA school term. Few had proper jobs. Regular house guests at Sudeley, especially around Christmas, would include the likes of actress Elizabeth Hurley, Hugh Grant, American banking heir Matthew Mellon, Trinny Woodall, her musician husband Johnny Elichaoff, the writer AA (Adrian) Gill and his girlfriend Nicola Formby. Jeremy Clarkson would sometimes be a guest. He once got a brand new Range Rover stuck in a muddy field and had to be humiliatingly towed out, much to passenger Adrian's amusement. Of this group, Matthew, Adrian and Johnny were all to die tragically young.

I naïvely believed that Upton Cressett could work some sort of romantic magic on my relationships. 'Please, please come up for the weekend,' I had faxed Philippa (abroad) as I cracked Brazil nuts by the fire in the drawing room and listened to carols on the radio. I thought that everything would be resolved once she came to stay. I invited her to a belle-époque-themed fancy-dress party where 'everyone will be behaving rather badly'. In early January 1995, she found herself attending playwright John Osborne's funeral in Clun after he died before Christmas. There is a letter describing the small service on that icy day with actor Edward Fox and other theatrical luminaries carrying the coffin through Clun church. Cars had to be dug out of the snow to get to the champagne wake.

The end of our relationship came a few days after the fancy-dress party, where things had, indeed, gone very badly. If I'd hoped Upton Cressett might perform some alchemy, I was wrong. After the disastrous party, we sat in silence during a half-hour drive from Upton Cressett to Wolverhampton station. I was soon back in LA.

Whisky Suite

It had been over that Christmas that I had heard the details of Margaret Thatcher's stay at Upton Cressett in October 1994. My mother recalled the visit with the anecdotal perspective that perhaps only an MP's wife, who had to do everything to prepare for it, could give to the visit of Britain's first female prime minister. She was now Lady Thatcher, and had arrived half an hour early.

'I had my hair in curlers and was standing in a towel in my little bathroom down the corridor [some fifty yards from her bedroom] when I heard dogs barking, peacocks screeching and saw two black cars pull up,' my mother recalled. 'Of course, I had been getting the Gatehouse ready and we had spent about an hour trying to squeeze a sofa up the oak spiral stairs. I remember running down the corridor in a small towel, praying that Margaret hadn't looked up to the window at the time, and grabbed the very first pair of shoes I could see. High heeled suede and sequin beige evening shoes from Paris. I put on a top and headed downstairs to meet Margaret – Bill was nowhere to be seen. Probably mowing the lawn.'

My mother just about managed to get the curlers out and be standing by the front door when Margaret and Sir Denis arrived, escorted by security guards who had begun to fade into the topiary hedge background of the Gatehouse lawn.

Margaret was wearing a tweed suit with black shoes and trademark handbag. Very much dressed for the president's lunch table at the County Show.

'Hello, Margaret,' my mother said.

'Hello, Biddy,' she replied, looking at my mother's feet. 'What strange shoes you're wearing.'

A pause.

'What a nice garden you have – very green and plain. Lots of lawn. How appropriate for a local Member of Parliament.'

My mother gulped and said nothing. Compared to Jimmy Goldsmith's Château Le Montjeu, where they had been together just a few weeks before, Upton Cressett's garden borders were, indeed, a little humble. Margaret was more bothered, though, by the worrying standards of cleanliness that she had found so lacking on that recent visit to Sir Jimmy's grand castle in Burgundy.

Jimmy had restored the guarded château and its gardens extensively. He had bought it in the 1980s following previous grand owners, who included the Duke of Valois and various Talleyrands. The formal gardens by André Le Nôtre – who had designed and laid out the parterres of Versailles for Louis XIV – had especially impressed Margaret. No wonder she wasn't exactly gushing about the topiary at Upton Cressett. The yew had been planted in the 1970s. I used to jump over the little trees with friends, pretending they were Grand National fences.

Once, at the Goldsmith château, Margaret had run her finger along the edge of a table in one of the formal reception rooms, like a housekeeper. When she saw the small amount of dust that had accumulated, she turned to my mother and said, 'Not very clean – I would like to get a duster in here myself.' Her visit to Upton Cressett was only two months later. The dust comment had sent my mother into a frenzy of cleaning.

True to form, my mother recalled that when she led the Iron Lady into her Gatehouse bedroom on the first floor she began opening the drawers and inspecting them for dirt. She repeated this ritual in the main house. During her stay, she addressed my father's Stafford constituency association annual dinner. After they got back to the house at around 11.30 p.m., she walked into the drawing room, kicked off her shoes, and said, 'Do you know, Biddy, this is always my favourite time of the evening. Time for a whisky. And Denis will be joining us.'

They talked about the future of Europe until 3 a.m., when Margaret and Denis staggered up the Gatehouse's spiral stairs. A bottle of Famous Grouse whisky my mother had placed in the sitting room of the Prince Rupert Bedroom had been demolished by the morning. It was later dubbed the Whisky Suite.

Was I sorry to have missed her visit? Or that of a young journalist called Boris Johnson the following year? The truth was that in LA, I was getting to meet and know American political and literary figures from right and left, including Arianna Huffington, Gore Vidal – who lived just down the canyon from me – and my good pal TV writer Rob Long, a lone Hollywood Republican who was the co-writer of *Cheers*. I was being commissioned by the *New Yorker* and the left-leaning *New Republic* as well as being appointed American correspondent-at-large for the *Daily Mail*. I was a roving political agnostic.

Vile Young Things

Elizabeth Hurley, Henry Dent-Brocklehurst, Charles Finch (son of actor Peter Finch), Old Harrovian producer George Waud, Julia Verdin and various other expats were all part of a largely British set dubbed the Viles (after *Vile Bodies*) by the media, helped in that Evelyn Waugh's granddaughter, Daisy, was in LA trying to make it as a screenwriter. Hence, she and her father Auberon, known as Bron, were at my thirtieth-birthday dinner at my suburban Valley house.

Decadent fun and naughty house games were very much the order of those louche days, including the notorious Spanking Game. It was based on the French parlour game *La Main Chaude* and involved house guests taking it in turns to guess who was spanking their behind after being blindfolded and bent over an ottoman in the Sudeley Castle drawing room. I was soon moving in a social world far removed from my boyhood existence in Shropshire.

When I first met Elizabeth Hurley in 1992 she was trying to get her Hollywood break as an actress after starring in *Christabel*, a 1988 BBC drama written by Dennis Potter based on the memoirs of Christabel Bielenberg, an English woman married to a German lawyer during the Second World War.

This was well before she wore That Dress – held together with oversized Versace safety pins – to the London première of *Four Weddings and a Funeral* in 1994. Hugh Grant was rarely around and, after Simon moved out, we ended up sharing my house on Woodrow Wilson Drive, high in the Hollywood Hills. In addition to David Hockney, we were also close to near neighbours like Billy Connolly, Berry Berenson (ex-wife of Anthony Perkins), Henry Dent-Brocklehurst and house-mate Matthew Mellon. Elizabeth was also the reigning queen of LA's growing rank of Mid-Atlantic Bright Young Things, a demi-monde of tanned Lilo-lizards, hons, vons, fugitive AA aristos, WASP banking heirs, Euro playboy counts, Young Rotters and hope-to-get-rich Oxbridge and film-school graduates, whose festive lifestyle under the bleached-blue California sky had us marked as, socially speaking, Hollywood's criminal underclass.

While Elizabeth was a sort of Diana Cooper figure for the expat Brits, serving her home-made shepherd's pie to us at supper parties, the playboy Euro-party prince of LA was the impossibly handsome Count Erik Wachtmeister (known as 'Vuckmeister'), who became a good friend. Erik was the son of the Swedish ambassador to Washington and went on to found A Small World, the social media website. This was a jet-set 'private' version of Facebook for 'beautiful people' in which Harvey Weinstein invested heavily (perhaps he thought owning it might make it a good personal dating platform).

Before Elizabeth moved in with me, she lived as a room-mate at Erik's Bel Air mansion, which he rented with financier and backgammon player Sebastian Taylor. This was 'Eurotrash' society HQ, and I can recall parties with Californian super-models roller-skating through the house in tiny shorts.

California in the Nineties bore a close resemblance to Kenya in the 1930s and '40s. Their decadent way of life was epitomised by the notorious Happy Valley set, whose Gucci-loafer-wearing spiritual heirs descended on Hong Kong and New York from the 1960s onwards, where at least most had jobs. James Fox put his finger on the type in his book *White Mischief.* 'Many had money,' he wrote. 'Many were remittance men who had been paid off by their families and sent away in disgrace. Once their spirits and sense of status had been restored in this feudal paradise, the temptation to behave badly was irresistible.'

I wasn't alone in feeling the pull of England in LA, where there was no shortage of British 'pubs' and cricket was still played on Saturdays under the Hollywood sign in a dog-lavatory park with the likes of Mick Jagger and Julian Sands, just as it had been in the 1940s. There was, however, one crucial difference between the world of the Viles and the Happy Valley set, in which wife-swapping and cocaine were rife and titles counted for everything. During the Nineties, my mid-Atlantic British friends were going to almost absurd lengths to be 'classless'. Henry, for example, called himself plain 'Henry Brock', drove a black Range Rover with tinted windows and dressed in Armani, like a character in *Miami Vice.* Clem Franckenstein went so far as to change his name to 'Clement St. George' when it came to castings.

The decadent and self-destructive *Vile Mischief* world I became submerged in was also very different from the tiny expat Hollywood world of the 1920s and '30s when monocle-wearing Brits, like Basil Rathbone and David Niven, played cricket in cream linen flannels under the palm trees. As Sir Ambrose Abercrombie, president of the Hollywood Cricket Club in Evelyn Waugh's black satire *The Loved One,* says, 'We Limeys have a peculiar position to keep up, you know. They might laugh at us – the way we talk and the way we dress; our monocles – they might think us cliquey and stand offish but, by God, they respect us.'

No longer. When I arrived in 1991, there were at least half a million Brits living in LA. Many had about as much legal status as the Mexican maids who ironed their duty-free shirts. The barrier between the Hollywood community and the Brits – until the 1960s – used to be no more than a garden fence. By the Nineties, a social Berlin Wall existed that effectively divided the world of the studio executive and agent-world suits – the 'industry' – and the party world of the Viles.

To their deep resentment, the Viles were mostly looked down on from the power suites of the studio lots and Wilshire Boulevard as LA's equivalent of the Eastern bloc. Some of us may have been brought up in castles or manors but we were regarded more or less as homeless refugees. To compensate for their lack of status, many decorated their houses with family crests and prints of their castles or estate maps of their country homes. When I first met Henry during the early 1990s, he was living with banking heir Matthew Mellon in a mock-Tudor manor in the Hollywood Hills. Henry had a huge framed poster of Sudeley Castle (as sold in his gift shop) in his LA house. I absurdly had copies of *Country Life* on the coffee-table of my LA sitting room, along with a framed print of Upton Cressett on the wall.

Although American, Matthew preferred to hang out with the party-loving Europeans and Viles. He used to joke that he had been to so many rehab clinics he could write a Zagat world guide to the best. In LA, few knew who he was, which he liked (he inherited $25 million on his twenty-first birthday), so he could be relatively anonymous. Yet his mock-Tudor pool-house was filled with a library of books on his famous (self-made) nineteenth-century banker ancestor Thomas Mellon, financier to the likes of Andrew Carnegie and Henry Clay Frick. When I asked him where he had been brought up, he replied, 'On a yacht.'

Matthew and Henry's Hollywood Hills house was known as 'Model Central'. It had castellated walls and a swimming-pool moat. Matthew would spend much of the day floating around the pool in an inflatable plastic crocodile armchair, his mobile phone clamped to his ear, arranging 'modella' pool parties, doing yoga classes in sunglasses, or a wide array of 'deals'. Women adored him, and not only because of his good looks and the gilded life that belonged in a Jay McInerney novel. He was also kind and irrepressibly funny.

A typical example of the *Vile Mischief* expat lifestyle was exemplified by the weekly LA city garbage-collection routine of my Oxford-educated friend Rupert Wainwright. After beginning his film career with a part in *Another Country* alongside Rupert Everett, Wainwright had reinvented himself as a mid-Atlantic director working with stars like Michael Jackson. On his street at the bottom of Franklin Drive, the recycling bins would be neatly put out by residents for early collection on Monday morning. Most would leave a single green bin filled with empty soya milk and juice bottles. Rupert would have several bins stacked up to six feet high, with empty champagne magnums, vodka and whisky bottles and a towering stack of Pimm's.

'I do get complaints,' Rupert told me. 'Sometimes we're still up at seven a.m. when we hear the garbage truck pull up, so we just toss in the last bottles ourselves.'

Walk the Ledge

The goings-on of this louche world were usually what I described in lurid detail in my Binder Box letters to friends such as Elizabeth Hurley and various girlfriends. Elizabeth was too good a friend for being that – and anyhow I placed her far too high on my usual pedestal for anything more than being her confidant. We wrote regularly and she became a big-sister figure, not only to me but also to our group of often socially misplaced expat friends. Whenever a relationship broke down, she was invariably there for me, or the first to know about a new love. This is a fax I sent her in 1995.

7357 Woodrow Wilson Drive, Los Angeles

Dear Elizabeth,

Happy birthday, sweet creature! I would make up some crazed birthday poem but I don't have time. I have been introduced to a fine Russian-Turkish sweat/steam joint in a sleazy part of West Pico where fat moguls sit around in togas. Henry [Dent-Brocklehurst] can hardly walk after having his back broken by a 25-stone Russian beefcake masseur who Henry claims put his finger up his bottom. I ran over John Travolta in the car park.

W xxx

PS I have a new sex slave.

This was before the days of email or texts. Elizabeth was an old-fashioned sort of letter-writer and I would regularly wake up in the morning in our house to find a handwritten fax in my office that had been sent in the middle of the night on fancy headed hotel paper from Cape Town or Paris. The one below referred to a new decorating scheme I was planning for the house. More than a decade before I began thinking about painted ceilings and hand-blocked wallpapers for Upton Cressett, I was busy with paint colour charts in LA. The urge to redecorate my hillside house was also about wanting to change my razor's-edge life. Meanwhile, I was also the house chauffeur and was later to become a studio-lot waiter of sorts.

Campton Place Hotel, San Francisco

Dear Sweet Cashpoint,

Thank you for your fax – I shall arrive in LA on Monday. Might Cash-Limo Service be in action? I'm very excited to see the yellow/ blue colour scheme and DREAD my cobwebs. I miss you.

With love from Favourite Room Mate xxx

Limo driver? Well, yes. The history of my various cars in LA tells a story of career slide. Twice in my life I have bought second-hand cars from Elizabeth at a knock-down price.

Elizabeth was living with me in 1995 when Hugh Grant had his notorious back-seat encounter on Sunset Boulevard with Divine Brown. I described to her by fax how our LA house had been under siege from a zoo of global paparazzi as they thought she was in the house. Elizabeth was actually in England and had retreated behind the protective castle walls of Sudeley with the baying British press camped outside. I described how a segment on NBC news, interviewing Henry outside his home, had 'resorted to subtitles' for the benefit of American audiences incapable of understanding his English 'drawl'.

What I didn't mention (as I didn't know at the time) was that Martin Cohen, our Woodrow Wilson Drive landlord, was also Divine Brown's lawyer. I never liked to ask how she paid him. I then filled Elizabeth in with the latest news of our Woodrow Wilson Drive neighbour. I had been around to dinner at Hockney's 'beach shack' in Malibu when an art-world figure called Joe Simon appeared with a 'monstrous sized butterscotch Great Dane' that he had adopted. I wrote: 'The Great Dane sees what looks like a good dinner and starts eating Boogie [one of Hockney's dachshunds] for his first course. Hockney screams and tries to fight the Baskerville-sized beast off his precious little creature. Blood everywhere. Dog alive but in acute shock. Hockney – by now almost delirious – covered in blood, decked out on the floor.'

But such hilarity hid much unhappiness and loneliness. I remember once doing an interview with actor Dudley Moore (star of films like *Arthur* and *10*) at his restaurant close to Venice Beach. We were almost the only people eating there and the air-conditioned atmosphere was sepulchral. At the end of our lunch, which had been difficult due to his memory lapses, I went to the lavatory, leaving the tape recorder still on at the table. When I later transcribed the tape, I discovered that

Dudley had leant towards the microphone and said, 'William, I think you need help. I know a good therapist if you want to call me.'

I was desperate to leave LA and return home to write at Upton Cressett. Much of my frustration was with myself and my lack of progress with my LA novel, which was to be called *The City of Punishment*. Just as I was starting it, I was poached by Veronica Wadley from the *Daily Mail* to become the *Daily Telegraph*'s US Special Correspondent, including writing about the O.J. Simpson trial from LA. She was to be my editor for many years, continuing when she was editor of the *Evening Standard* in London. Veronica was to become a good friend and later senior adviser to Boris Johnson and Chair of Arts Council London.

As a *Telegraph* writer, I also began to know Conrad Black (owner of the *Telegraph* and *Spectator*), who invited me (and my parents) to his annual December and summer soirees at his vast Kensington house (several houses knocked into one). It was at one such party (there was an indoor swimming pool) that I first met Boris before he became editor of the *Spectator*. Boris was always one of the most scruffily dressed of guests, with his shirt invariably hanging out, his flaxen mop of hair unbrushed and glass in hand – but also undeniably amusing company as he was surrounded by a mini-court of politicians and attractive hackettes such as Petronella Wyatt. I never found Boris very easy to talk with, however: he seemed to prefer female company to men.

It was around this time – in the mid-1990s – that I had first met Catherine Jordan, LA editor of the *Gault-Millau* guide, who was to become a serious girlfriend when I was in my thirties. Her mother was English so she didn't count as fully Californian. She was a striking brunette with a similar mole and looks to Christy Turlington and was great friends with another of my closest LA pals, Christina Knudsen, Roger Moore's beautiful, blonde, half-Danish and half-Swedish step-daughter. Christina loved to ride in the mountains. She was free-spirited, beautiful and often one of the last to leave any pool party, like those of Bond producer Tony Broccoli.

My creative entropy during this period in LA unquestionably caused me to become unbalanced, frustrated and consumed with self-loathing. My journalism was in demand (and well paid) but my novel was going nowhere as I kept having to meet deadlines to pay the Woodrow Wilson rent.

Things came to a head around my thirtieth birthday. In one angst-ridden and self-indulgent letter, I deplored my lifestyle and failure to make progress with my novel. The letter was written from a desert hotel in Morocco, where I was staying in the spare bedroom of Elizabeth Hurley's suite when she was filming *Samson and Delilah*. My classic-car-racing friend, Charles Dean, and I had gone out on a *Tin Tin*-like adventure to play costumed extras in the location set where *Lawrence of Arabia* was filmed. We ended up drinking late at the hotel bar most nights with Nic Roeg and the encyclopaedically informed Michael Gambon, whose favourite subject was his collection of over 800 antique weapons. I wrote to Catherine: 'Just having a good time is a road to ruin, self-destruction and misery. Meanwhile, our lives, our happiness, our children, this whole "human-being business" is passing us by . . .'

Looking back and reading my actual words – to ex-lovers, ex-wives and friends – of more than two decades ago reminds me of the magic of the handwritten word as opposed to electronic words – communion for the heart. The LA Binder Boxes belong to a different pre-digital age when people could only fax, telephone or write.

The advantage of using letters and faxes (of which, unlike a posted letter, one gets to keep the original pages) to frame the voice of a biography of a heart is that private letters allow the narrative to be heard through the author's own words. The emotional recall of old handwriting on onion-skin or heavy-laid paper or an Italian postmarked card is not the same as with a text or email. Who would have thought that a love fax sent to Catherine at 9.45 p.m. on 20 September 1996 from a hotel on Ischia would keep so well?

I always loved the romance of a letter or fax. Before social media, courtship required more effort. On 8 May 1996, en route to Elizabeth's desert film set, I was staying in a hotel – La Roseraie in the Val d'Ouigagne – that had few communication facilities. I wrote to Catherine, 'I am writing this in a hotel in the middle of a mountain which has no fax – no outside phone line, in fact. So I am giving this to the driver of the local minibus, who goes into Marrakesh in the morning, and have bribed him to fax this to you.'

But was I always a reliable narrator? Again and again, the letters from my thirties portray the mental state of somebody who seems at different times acutely and genuinely sensitive, depressed, melancholy, anguished. Yet that is somebody I struggle to recognise.

So much of my angst was to do with the fact that I remained rootless in LA, away from Upton Cressett; and my unhappiness grew as I left my rustic Hollywood Hills vineyard home for a small suburban two-bed house in the Valley where I hosted my thirtieth-birthday dinner.

On 16 September 1996, two weeks after my birthday and now back in England at Upton Cressett (I returned to LA for another three largely wasted years), I wrote again to Catherine after 'tramping for miles' through Shropshire cornfields. The letter began cheerfully enough: 'My dearest C, Glorious Maximus September afternoon. Peacocks swaggering lazily around the moat and garden fanning their late summer aquamarine tails.' But the memory of that birthday dinner was still sore: 'I am sick of dreading birthdays, Christmas, Thanksgiving, etc., because my life is such an appalling mess. I haven't felt like celebrating a huge lot recently.'

I regard myself as being one of life's optimists – somebody with an overactive imagination, perhaps, but rarely prone to depression. But that is not the impression that comes over from the letters; I am often a moody misanthrope. My relationship with Catherine lasted for two intense years of highs and lows, ending after a final personal crisis and serious breakdown following my trip to Morocco. The end of our tortured love affair plunged me into a suffocating darkness of despair.

In 1996, I met a young English actress called Louise King. She became another Binder Box girlfriend. We had first met in London a month or so before she flew to LA, as she wanted some advice on expat life in the city. Within a month or so, she had moved in. The letter to Catherine about life being a 'long walk' that I wanted to end in my oak-panelled bedroom was also the one in which I told her I couldn't see her any more. I told her that I was now seeing Louise, whom 'I may marry'.

Then my LA friends started slipping home. Elizabeth's shepherd's pie suppers stopped. When she started earning serious money as the face of Estée Lauder, and played opposite Mike Myers in *Austin Powers*, she moved into a series of grander houses and sold me her old car, a throaty black Volkswagen GTi with a dent on the side. Later, I upgraded to a Saab Turbo but financial pressures had me selling it on to a son of John Le Carré, who was working for the *Independent*. After the Saab went, I drove a battered old Audi that even valet parkers were reluctant to have outside their fancy restaurants. My friends, like Henry, had given up on the LA dream and were all returning to England, usually to get married. But, as ever, I clung on.

To help pay the rent in LA, Louise decided to set up a catering company to the stars, called Velvet Rope Cuisine. But the venture failed. We had one booking and that had been a free trial dinner. I didn't even get a tip. Louise then returned to England to take up a place at the Oxford School of Drama. I stayed on.

Every year or so, while living in LA, I wrote to Tom Wolfe in New York asking how he was getting on with his new novel. Each time, I received back a typed letter, the signature usually more floral, saying he was still trying to finish the book. One letter said: 'God knows when that's going to be.'

It wasn't until 1998 that I finally got to East 79th Street. Yes, the Man in the White Suit lived in exactly the sort of apartment with a marble entrance floor that 'goes on and on' and thirteen-foot-high ceilings. Just like that owned by Sherman McCoy, bond trader protagonist of *The Bonfire of the Vanities*: 'One of those fabled apartments that the world, *le monde*, died for!'

On arriving at Wolfe's building, I was ushered into a mahogany lift by a doorman who frowned at the ripped shopping bag I was carrying under my arm. Like in the 'co-op' owned by McCoy, Wolfe's doorman wore green livery, like somebody from the nineteenth-century Austrian court.

As the lift jerked to a stop in a vestibule entrance on the fourteenth floor, I was greeted by a grey-haired Wolfe looking like Beau Brummell. He was decked out in full ceremonial armour – an eighteenth-century-style three-piece, double-breasted suit and a white shirt with burgundy stripes fitted with a stiff white collar that almost resembled an Elizabethan white ruff.

As I pulled my disintegrating shopping bag behind me, Wolfe's strobic blue eyes zoned in on the object sliding across his marble hallway floor, as if to say, '*WhyinnanameaGod* is this Brit bringing his *shopping* here at 9 a.m.?'

I explained that the proof manuscript of *A Man in Full* was so large it would not fit in my briefcase. The weight had broken my bag.

'Heavy reading?' he said.

We sat down in a sprawling drawing room decorated with canary-yellow sofas and cream armchairs. We could have been in Virginia. When I asked why it had taken so long to write his follow-up novel, he replied, 'Mr Cash, I find it hard to write if I have any money in my bank account.' His advance, when he'd signed his contract with Farrar, Strauss & Giroux in 1989, was $7.5 million. He said he began 'wallowing' in the success of *Bonfire*. 'A foreign publisher would invite me to some country I'd never been to,' Wolfe said, 'and I'd go and have a wonderful time. It became a disease.'

Wolfe had no secretary, no computer, and told me he had 'no idea' how to 'surf' the Internet. 'I think it's one of the great time-wasters for writers of all time.' He still did all his own 'reporting' using a notebook and pen. He was an old-fashioned letter-writer and we continued to correspond, usually by fax. After two hours, when I asked him to sign my battered copy of *Bonfire*, he half jokingly wrote in his black jellyfish scrawl: 'To William Cash, who knows my work better than I do.'

'Are large advances bad for writers?' I asked, as I put the book into my briefcase.

'Yes,' Wolfe said. 'Writers who strike it big probably shouldn't have as much money as they get. But don't tell my publisher that! Being pressed was what kept Dickens going full-tilt.'

As much as I should have found his words comforting, I didn't. Back in LA, I wasn't just falling between the canyon cracks metaphorically but also physically. My time was nearly up.

The end came when I had a 'very nearly fatal' accident after a dinner party at the Laurel Canyon house of John Irvin, the British director of the original BBC series of *Tinker Tailor Soldier Spy*, along with many films. As I had walked towards my car after midnight, I slipped on some makeshift concrete steps and fell into an empty pool. I wrote to Louise: 'I don't remember anything about falling. I was out cold for around eight minutes . . . When I finally came round, I thought about you, my darling . . . and you are right, I have been living here too long . . . I love you with all my heart.'

It was time to leave. The other reason for returning home was that I had decided to get married. But, first, I had to finish another book, so I moved into the Gatehouse at Upton Cressett to write a biography of Graham Greene (with the Greene estate giving permission to quote from Greene's private letters) that examined his lengthy affair with the American society beauty Catherine Walston, which inspired his 1951 novel *The End of the Affair*, and the creative debt that literature owes to adultery. The book came out just before the release of Neil

Jordan's 1999 film adaptation starring Ralph Fiennes. I dedicated the book 'To Louise with Three Years' Love.'

I proposed to Louise on a cold and misty evening in the garden of a Benedictine abbey in the middle of France after we had attended vespers. It stood next door to a little three-star hotel with a good restaurant. We had stopped to stay at the hotel en route to England from a holiday.

I can't recall the name of the abbey. I kept a half-used box of the hotel's matches that I picked up as a melancholy memento mori and kept for many years with my cufflinks. The beauty of the moment in the abbey gardens in the chilly dusk as the monks' incense burned in the candlelight prompted the spontaneous proposal.

Louise said yes, and we had a happy dinner in the hotel looking forward to our future together.

But then God reversed the charges. The next morning at breakfast, before I had even had a chance to call her father, Louise asked if she could 'think about it' before any announcement. I waited for a few weeks. Then, as the weeks turned into months, and I was still waiting for an answer, I met my first wife Ilaria in a café in the Bibendum building at South Kensington's Brompton Cross.

III

7

Before the Wreck

I proposed to Ilaria Bulgari – with a ring this time – after a whirlwind romance of barely two months. I had first met her for coffee after a financier friend, Jonathan Bailey, who knew Ilaria from New York, put us in touch. She was looking for a job in London's publishing world. I said I'd introduce her to my agent, the late Gillon Aitken. The next thing I heard, Gillon had offered her a role as his assistant (a job she never got round to starting).

I wanted to propose to Ilaria at Upton Cressett as I was very much hoping it would become our family home. Around 11 a.m. on Sunday morning, 21 October 2001, I led her through the damp morning mist towards the famous Royal Oak in an overgrown Shropshire field not far from Boscobel House. This was the Royal Oak tree that the future Charles II had spent the night hiding in while fleeing for his life in September 1651 after defeat at the Battle of Worcester. There was nothing left of the original tree – it had been hacked away by souvenir hunters – but a leafy successor, seeded and grafted from the original oak, now grew near where the original had stood. It was a symbol of family rebirth. The only snag was that the tree had recently been hit by lightning, so it looked burned and shell-shocked.

Standing under what summer leaves remained, I turned to Ilaria and produced a vintage 1970s Bvlgari diamond ring out of my pocket. I had recently bought it at Sotheby's, with the help of store manager Philip Baldwin. He had befriended me after Ilaria had pulled me into the store on Bond Street one afternoon and started asking to see 'some rings' in the private room.

'That would be $450,000, sir . . . and this very fine and suitable diamond and sapphire would be $650,000,' Philip had said as he set the rings on a table.

As I had heard these figures, whispered into my ear sotto voce, a small river of sweat flowed down my back each time she picked out a new ring and put it on her engagement finger. I was getting the message. By the time we left the store, my suit was soaked and I was panicking.

Understanding my dilemma, Philip had tipped me off about a vintage Bvlgari diamond ring coming up for sale and said he wouldn't bid against me (the family were buying back rings for their museum in Rome). It was one of the first auction sales after the 9/11 Twin Towers attacks in New York, in which my friend and LA neighbour Berry Berenson (Rupert Everett had rented her house for a time) had been killed after being on the hi-jacked American Airlines Flight 11. Her 9/11 murder, aged just fifty-three, had shocked me.

The New York attacks had resulted in a nearly empty Sotheby's saleroom. There were few bidders but I felt little guilt. Once I had secured the vintage ring at reserve, I secretly flew out to Rome to see Ilaria's father, Nicola, for lunch.

Nicola agreed to meet me at the Grand Hotel on the via Veneto. We had met a couple of times before for dinner at Wilton's and at his heavily guarded country estate in Tuscany's Val d'Orcia, where armed guards with guns had raided my bedroom in the middle of the night. I was put in a stable block away from the main villa reserved for drivers and staff – they hadn't realised that my nocturnal 'intruder' was Ilaria in her pyjamas.

The family had good reason to be security-conscious. Ilaria's handsome uncle Gianni Bulgari had been brutally kidnapped by masked men in Rome in March 1975, with a reported $2 million ransom paid by the Bulgari family. This had been two years after oil tycoon John Paul Getty had reluctantly paid the Mafia a $2.7 million ransom for the release of his kidnapped sixteen-year-old grandson after they sliced off his ear and sent it to a Rome newspaper. When I had stayed with Ilaria that summer at the Tuscan seaside resort of Punta Ala, she had two full-time bodyguards outside her house (when I was there alone, they disappeared).

Nicola had an imperial presence at six-foot-four with a senatorial Roman nose, bright and intimidating aqua-blue eyes, a high Greek forehead (the family were originally Greek silversmiths who moved to Rome) and a politely gruff, diffident manner. He could be moody and reserved but I usually found him warm, funny and engaging so long as you stuck to subjects like American films from the 1950s and Buick cars (he had a collection of several hundred cars, stored in America and Rome). He was a true Anglophile and an English history and politics buff. Like his older brother Gianni, he exuded powerful charisma. I liked Nicola but was a little scared of him (I noted that he had newspaper articles about John Gotti Jr pinned up around his study desk).

Lunch was at 12.30 p.m and so I had a few hours in the morning before my rendezvous. I was happy to be a tourist. I stood in the ground arena of the Colosseum where so many had been killed. Walking away into the hot sun – I was wearing a wool suit – I had never felt so alive. No ruin I had ever visited contained a stronger sense of emotional communion, or Spirit of Place. Picking up a warm handful of dusty and gritty sand, I thought of how lucky I was. I was in love with Ilaria and I felt as if our stars and fates were aligned. Aged just thirty-five, my Wheel was finally turning.

I walked along the Sacred Way towards Palatine Hill and then along the Via dei Fori Imperiale. This vanity project road by Mussolini was opened by him in 1932 (cutting the ribbon from his horse) after eight years of digging that had disinterred and destroyed much of the most important parts of the ancient forum. I remembered my Uncle Jonathan regarding this vandalism as one of the greatest of modern 'archaeological crimes'.

Yet as I headed for my lunch with Nicola, I felt curiously unmoved. It's strange what the memory hangs onto at life-changing moments. I recall how incongruous the potted shrubs were in the modern tree tubs that lined the 'Imperial Way'; and the fact that the Colosseum tour guides claimed to be 'Italian' but were clearly Czech or German.

At lunch, Nicola and I were the only two people dining in the enormous fancy ballroom-sized restaurant. He was wearing a trade-mark navy-blue double-breasted suit, white shirt and tie, and looked like Marlon Brando in a starched bib. A small army of waiters fussed around him as if he were the Pope. As we had lunch, we remained almost the only two people in the place with even more waiters emerging and hovering around us, making the uneasy formality almost unbearable.

When I finally got around to asking if I could marry his daughter, my future father-in-law said, 'Bravo, William, this calls for a celebration,' and ordered a bottle of champagne. He then picked up his mobile to make a call. I presumed it was to Ilaria's mother, Anna, from whom he was estranged.

My Italian has always been poor, but I had to grab his phone from him when I heard him just about to congratulate Ilaria. 'She doesn't know yet!' I said, worried that my proposal – planned for Shropshire

– would be blown. 'Could you wait until Sunday as I haven't actually asked her?'

Nicola pulled a puzzled Brando-esque face, that I interpreted as: 'You haven't *proposed* yet?'

'I'm going to ask her at the weekend,' I said. 'I just wanted to ask you first.'

I wasn't sure such formality was the norm in Italy, but he happily gave his blessing and I caught a taxi back to the airport.

As we stood under the Royal Oak that Sunday, I recited the opening lines from an unpublished Graham Greene love poem to Catherine Walston that I had found in a spidery handwritten letter from the early 1950s in an archive box in Georgetown University library:

> *I can only believe in love that strikes suddenly*
> *Out of a clear sky;*
> *I do not believe in the slow germination of friendship*
> *Or one that asks why?*

Ilaria accepted immediately, dissolving into tears as she slipped on the ring, which I had hidden in an old sock. As we crossed the River Severn on the Bridgnorth road – just a mile from our single-lane turning to Upton Cressett – we passed under the railway bridge just as a Severn Valley steam train was crossing in a magnificent cloud of billowing coal smoke, its 1930s whistle at a deafening full blast. 'Can you hear that whistle?' I shouted with delight. 'Driving under a moving train is good luck. But a whistling steam train, that's an even better omen!'

A few months later, on a cloudless August afternoon, we wound our way up the road above the bay of Portofino to visit the Hotel Splendido. We were in a high state of excitement. We were due to be married in London on 12 October and I had already provisionally booked the famous Italian hotel – whose guests have included the

Duke and Duchess of Windsor, Richard Burton and Elizabeth Taylor, and Madonna – for what I thought would be the perfect honeymoon.

Half an hour later, I was speeding back down the drive with a sense of relief. Thank God I'd checked it out. There was nothing wrong with the hotel; the problem was that all the other guests seemed to be young (under thirty) British and American 'honeymooners'. The prospect of a week closeted with a hundred smug newlyweds was not our idea of fun.

Back in London, I hurriedly booked a walking tour of the Bavarian Alps. It would probably rain most of the time, but what the hell? We could cosy up after lunch in our romantic hunting lodge with a large whisky, then retire to bed.

Unfortunately, when 13 October arrived the person sitting across the log fire nursing a tumbler was not my new wife but my best man, Bugatti racing driver Charles Dean. The hotel management were convinced that we were a trendy gay couple who had just got married under new German laws.

I was forced to ramble around Bavaria with my best man because our wedding had to be postponed due to the demands of some whose approach to our marriage did not coincide with that of either myself, Ilaria or the two Catholic priests who were marrying us.

'You've paid for the hotels and all you're going to do is mope around and get depressed in London,' said Charles, when we went out for a curry at the Noor Jahan, our regular haunt close to the Gloucester Road. 'I'll come with you. We'll try to have fun and forget about it all.'

'But I've booked *honeymoon* suites in several castles,' I protested. 'That means double beds.'

'Then let's hope the beds are very large and comfortable,' Charles said.

On the last day of the 'honeymoon', having tramped around various castles and abbeys with Charles, I came down to breakfast in the dining room of the Bayerischer Hof Hotel in the medieval harbour town of Lindau. The restaurant was empty, save for a solitary German with a large moustache and bib eating a hard-boiled egg. When Charles sat down opposite me at our window table overlooking the lake, he looked towards the grey October drizzle and said, 'William, I hate to say it, but this place has "failed love affair" written all over it.'

Ilaria and I were married four months later on Saturday, 8 February 2003 at Farm Street. This time the invitations were by handwritten letter. The service was celebrated by Dom Antony Sutch, headmaster of Downside School, who had taught me as a teenager. As I waited with my best man Charles for the bridal horse and carriage to arrive, my father observed an elderly Jesuit priest shuffling slowly up the east transept. He tapped me on the shoulder. 'Do you know who that is?' my father said. I had no idea.

It was Father Robert Wingfield-Digby, SJ, who had baptised me in the very same church on 17 September 1966 – some thirty-six years earlier.

By 2003, the stage set of my life was becoming increasingly public. *Hello!* reliably informed readers that as we 'walked up the aisle it would be hard to beat the couple in terms of pure joy'. *Tatler* reported from the wedding lunch at a Mayfair club that 'the usual customs were observed – heavy drinking from the British and talking over the speeches from the bejewelled Italians'.

'Over the years, William and I have done many things together,' began my best man Charles Dean. 'We've rented a castle in Umbria, driven around Morocco, were in Prague for the Velvet Revolution, travelled to Iceland by cargo boat from Grimsby, drove from LA to Miami and back . . . and we've even been on honeymoon together.'

This got the eighty guests baying with laughter. Bruno, the maître d' and incidentally a former communist, brought more wine for the tables. Even the cross-table-talking Italians began to sit up and listen. That was all in the past now.

The Graham Greene poem I had recited to Ilaria under the Royal Oak was printed on our wedding matchboxes. It was called 'After Three Years' and had appeared on page 69 of my Greene book so I came to call Ilaria 'My Page 69'. It was our secret code for our love.

'I should let you know, sir, that we have a minimum order of 1,500 match-books,' the managing director informed me.

'That's fine,' I said. 'Enough to last a lifetime.'

Or so I had hoped before the marriage went up in flames just before my fortieth birthday.

We lasted just three years.

When Ilaria's elegant Italian mother Anna had come to our flat to watch the wedding DVD, there had been an unfortunate incident that set the tone of the farce that was to follow as our marriage later unravelled.

'I think you will enjoy the beautiful film,' I said, as we sat on the sofa in our sitting room. 'Especially when Ilaria arrived at the church in a horse-drawn carriage.' I pressed the button on the DVD player.

To my horror, up flashed a writhing group sex scene in a grand four-poster bed and the credits rolled for a triple-X-rated film called *To The Manor Porn*.

'Fuck! Oh, my God!' I said, as I stopped the DVD.

Anna looked at me in disbelief.

I had forgotten that I had been commissioned by the *Evening Standard* magazine to write a profile on the Hon Jasper Duncombe, Britain's most unlikely porn baron. He was the heir of Lord Feversham and had stood to inherit a £35 million estate in Yorkshire before launching relishxxx.com films. As I had left their Fulham offices, Jasper had given me a disk of his latest film, shot at a friend's stately home.

'You'd better take a look,' my editor had said. 'It would be great if you can recognise the country house.'

After I explained to my mother-in-law that the DVD was 'research', we all had a good laugh and watched the real wedding DVD.

Still, I had known what I was getting into before the marriage.

'Life isn't *fair*,' her family's lawyer had told me on the phone after our original London wedding date was 'postponed'. He was a condescending Etonian. 'Don't you know that yet, William?'

Nor will I forget his sense of timing. The night of my fortieth birthday party remains welded in the memory bank as the night Ilaria did a runner. The party was a few days before my actual birthday. Just as I emerged from my bath, with tables set up for around thirty friends in our flat near Hyde Park, I noticed she was missing.

I had seen her arranging the lilies and the *place à table* at 6.30 p.m. but, by the time I had put on a dark suit for dinner, she had vanished. I had to make a speech thanking my wife for the party but apologising to my guests that 'our hostess' wasn't present. She did reappear, the following day, and I managed to spend my actual birthday with her at the Drunken Duck pub in the Lake District. For two days, I tried to persuade my wife that our marriage was working and that I loved her. Shortly after we returned to London, two spotty youths in badly fitting suits approached me in an alleyway outside my publishing company's offices in Notting Hill Gate.

It had been the lawyer who had arranged for me to be served with divorce papers by these two pimpled 'notaries'. I had mistakenly thought they were bailiffs serving my fledgling financial publishing company with a summons for an unpaid bill. When I saw that they were divorce papers, I felt as if my world had collapsed.

Ilaria and I had made plans only that morning to have a romantic dinner together that night at the Lanesborough Hotel, close to Hyde Park, where we had been staying for two nights; I was reviewing the hotel for *Spear's* after a makeover. Just as I left our room, I remember Ilaria asking me – twice – what my diary was for the day.

'See you at dinner – meet back here at seven-thirty?' had been my last words before kissing her.

'Yes,' she said.

Instead of walking back into my offices after opening the envelope, I fled, practically in tears, across Hyde Park. When I entered our empty hotel room, all her clothes, wash bag, make-up, pyjamas and suitcase had been removed. Her mobile number was disconnected. No voicemail. It was just dead. This was excommunication.

My stage exit appeared to have been ruthlessly planned. I heard it rumoured that her family might have wanted me out of the way before selling the family business (which they sold to LVMH). Ilaria had been installed in Claridge's with a security guard outside her room. I was still deeply in love with her and I thought that this was entirely over the top. Until the Lake District, we had never – perhaps tellingly – had a proper discussion about the state of our marriage, as she had pretty much moved to New York to be close to her expensive Italian-American doctor. Our marriage had been far from perfect but it was not beyond rescue as we loved each other. Being apart was not the solution.

But it was not to be. For weeks afterwards, I was followed around the clock by two goons who reminded me of the private investigator Mr Parkis, who followed Sarah Miles around London in *The End of the Affair*. Wherever I went – on the Tube, in restaurants, in banks, nightclubs and investor meetings – I was watched.

But I was too busy trying to launch *Spear's* (as my flagship magazine later became) to make their reports especially interesting. Things came to a head late one afternoon when I was having a drink in a pub near Liverpool Street station to discuss the digital launch of *Spear's* with my old friend Deirdre Brennan, who was in London with a New York media delegation invited by the Mayor of London. As we sipped our vodka and tonics, I suddenly saw Ilaria – flanked by two security guards – heading towards me. The next thing I knew she had slapped Deirdre's face.

Ilaria's lawyers were being paid too much not to deliver a decree absolute. She told me that she only waited until after my birthday to serve me with divorce papers as she 'didn't want to humiliate or embarrass me' in front of my friends at my party.

I remember spending much of the launch party for *Spear's* at HSBC Private Bank in St James's, standing in a corner of the lobby on my own, talking to Ilaria in New York, trying to get her to call off her legal attack dogs. Twice I had to tell the violin quartet I had hired to 'quieten down', and finally, 'Please *stop* playing,' so I could hear what Ilaria was saying. It was farcical.

There are so many Binder Box letters from myself to Ilaria – with most to the Mark Hotel in New York where she was then living – that it's hard to know where to start to give a flavour of my dejection. As I was launching *Spear's* to the media and advertisers, I was privately a wreck. I wasn't even sure Ilaria was reading or receiving my faxes.

The Mark Hotel, New York – April 2006

> *I am in a terribly dark and lonely place and am praying for God's mercy and grace that we can be reconciled to give our marriage a final chance. I never knew it was possible to be so broken and distressed. I want to start again away from everybody, and London, and lawyers and everything that is crushing me at the moment.*

It was not until at least a month later that I finally heard from Ilaria, a call late at night just a few days before Easter. The next morning I was on the first plane to New York, laden with bags of Fortnum's Easter eggs. My hastily written note said:

> *I am so glad you called me last night. Some of the darkness lifted when I heard your voice. I am not a good telephone person, so I am flying out to New York this morning in the hope you will*

at least see me for a few hours this evening and tomorrow. I am
hoping the truth will set us free to do whatever God has planned
for us . . .

I rarely used headed stationery when writing my Binder Box letters. I preferred to write on postcards with drawings or pictures that had some meaning. After our wedding was postponed, I had walked to the Courtauld Gallery to see Turner's bleak 1841 watercolour known as *Dawn after the Wreck*. The picture depicts a lone mongrel dog standing alone on a deserted Margate beach just as the early sun is breaking at dawn. I had always seen this picture as a symbol of a new dawn and rebirth. Whatever I had said must have had some resonance.

After the original wedding had been postponed in September 2002, I had no idea where she was for at least a month.

When, after weeks of silence, I finally saw Ilaria again at a country-house-style 'private retreat', I received the most beautiful handwritten letter from her in response to my Courtauld postcard of the dog howling alone on the dawn beach. It repeated what she had said to me when we had our first hour alone together before I took a taxi home. I had walked there on a cold but dry Sunday morning, 29 October 2002, from South Kensington, nearly five miles away.

The joy she felt at seeing me could only be described as a coming home 'to my other missing piece'. She said that her soul was filled with answered prayers when we were alone in the Gothick drawing room, where a coffee machine sat in the corner, along with a fish tank.

'William,' she said. 'I have prayed every day since I left in September. I can't go into what happened, or why the lawyers did what they did, but let me just say that my heart was torn in two and breaking more and more each day. But now seeing you in front of me, smiling back at me, fills my heart with such love. I can only say I know my prayers were answered . . .'

'I feel the same,' I said. 'The lawyers should never have been allowed to get between us. The important thing is that we think of today as a new dawn. That's why I sent you the Turner postcard. There wasn't an actual wreck. It's about a new start.'

'It was beautiful,' she said. 'Will you forgive me for all the pain I have caused you? My life has been almost unbearable since I left you. I have felt such a deep sense of loneliness and darkness without you.'

'So have I.'

'I was just telling the people who are looking after me here, it was as if a hole was carved out of my soul and I was left with a shapeless dream. You are the only one for me. I know that now.'

Alas, this was a theme that was to feature heavily in my Binder Box files, and so often capricious Fortuna had the last smile. It was not to be. After I was served with divorce papers by the lawyers (Ilaria told me that even her father complained over the size of the final bill), we did reconcile for a while by spending a week along the Amalfi coast in Italy in June trying to repair the damage. But Ilaria's father and the lawyers had other ideas and continued to send me what I regarded as 'petty and aggressive letters' on an almost daily basis.

They won. Their legal crucifixion machinery cut me into pieces financially, emotionally and physically. By 29 June, I was writing a hurried letter on Claridge's paper in the lobby of the hotel where we had begun our life as husband and wife in her suite.

'Will you deliver this to Ilaria Cash?' I asked a man behind the front desk.

But by now, the head concierge – a short, burly Irishman in full livery – was starting to recognise me. He took the letter. I was beaten and I knew it. I left another note later that evening:

I now realise we have no real chance of a future; that it is now best that we part as husband and wife. I loved you and I am sorry we never made it. You were my p. 69. The end of our marriage

should never have happened like this but I will always think of you
whenever I walk past this hotel of broken dreams.

I don't think we will be seeing each other again. So goodnight
and goodbye.

Your husband

I angrily crossed a line through the word 'husband' and replaced it with my initial 'W'.

From the Binder Box letters to Ilaria it is clear that divorce was something I never wanted, and tried to fight against to the end, which often makes for the most painful type: the legal equivalent of being garrotted while the heart is still alive.

8

Last Guests at the Savoy

I met Vanessa Neumann at a friend's birthday party at Annabel's nightclub.

I have never been asked to fill in a Proust Questionnaire asking when and where I was happiest, but certainly the early days of my first few months with Vanessa was a happy period of my life.

One morning in December 2007 stands out in the memory bank; we were the last guests to stay in a suite of the Savoy Hotel – empty of all guests, except for ourselves.

'A dirty midweek in town,' Vanessa had called it.

I had been woken at 7 a.m. by the noise of a team of builders demolishing the 1930s bathroom next door. Vanessa was asleep.

The hotel was closing down for a major £100 million refurbishment, and I had been invited to write an account for the Savoy as the 'last guests standing' – *Titanic*-style – before it was ripped apart and rebuilt by teams of architects and decorators.

The strangest thing about our hotel suite on the sixth floor was that every item – from the pale-blue curtains to the huge red damask sofa and the mirrored double bed – had Bonham's lot label numbers hanging off it. The Savoy had the feel of a once super-luxurious 1920s transatlantic liner that was about to depart for a last voyage before the scrapyard. A highlight was the marble bathroom with a plaque by the bath that said, 'Warning: Bath Water is Extremely Hot'.

The timing of our stay at the Savoy suited my mood just fine. I was ready for a new voyage of the heart. Just as the hotel was having a giant clearance sale so, having shocked both ourselves and our friends by falling madly in love, Vanessa and I were undergoing similar clear-outs of the heart; or, at least, a major 'delete' exercise on our mobiles when it came to 'clarifying' things with a variety of exes and other romantic stragglers – New York to Notting Hill – from our former single lives. Vanessa called it 'weed-killing'.

Although I had enjoyed aspects of being a single man-around-town for a year, I was relieved to be giving up my bachelor life. I had not enjoyed the experience. It was one reason I had flown out to Burning Man in the Black Rock Desert in August 2007 to celebrate my forty-first birthday on my own, having given the builder instructions to gut Upton Cressett in my absence.

Whenever I groaned to my friends about the misery of divorce, they told me to stop whining and find a new girlfriend. 'It's not as if there's any shortage of girls in London,' I recall one married hedge-fund-manager friend saying to me over dinner. 'Frankly, I'm jealous of you, William. You're single, have no kids, no luggage. I mean, what the hell are you moaning about? I'd start dating a new girl every night right away.'

A married former It girl – a member of Richard Kay's social cast – warned me not to be naïve when it came to dating foxy young (she meant under thirty-year-olds) girls in London. 'What you guys don't get is that girls will sleep with slightly older, richer guys – especially if they're a notch on the bed-post – but when they're with their girlfriends, they'll mock you. And if you think you have the upper hand when it comes to a bit of casual fun, you don't realise that the last laugh is on you as they move on to the next guy. Girls are much better at doing "cruel and casual" than guys.'

The closest I got to actually going out with any of the girls I 'dated' was with a beautiful, bestselling Turkish novelist (she had an art-dealer day job), called Selin Tamtekin, whom I met at an art-party dinner given by dealer Simon Lee in the private downstairs room at Automat. Selin, the daughter of a Turkish diplomat, was a gorgeous Muslim and was under daily attack in the Turkish press for writing a sexually risqué exposé of London's nightlife scene.

After the summer, when she was in hiding in Turkey, castigated as an 'upper-class whore' and portrayed in the media as Turkey's answer to Salman Rushdie, we began seeing each other when I lived in a rented flat on the Cromwell Road. But the affair fizzled out after she told me that she 'loathed the English countryside', didn't like making plans, and 'frankly preferred cats to men'. She never made it to Upton Cressett. She married a hedgie.

The truth is that Selin was simply more than I could handle. I finally knew this after a night out at Annabel's with her when my friend Fritz von Westenholz called up the *Spear's* office the next morning and left a message with my assistant saying that he had seen me out the night before and that what he had witnessed was 'pathetic'. 'William was following some beautiful girl around the club like a puppy on heat and he was well out of his depth. He needs to get out before he gets hurt.'

Part of the trouble with being divorced was that it was all too easy to let dating standards slide. Divorce, I knew, was bruising, painful and expensive. Until I met Vanessa, the last thing on my mind, having just escaped from one marriage – left homeless, sleeping in 'traveller' dormitories in Bayswater and financially scarred – was to start looking for another wife to repeat the pain. 'You have to go through a phase of sleeping with a lot of girls – often several in the same day,' my Belgian private-equity friend Frederic (also divorced) had advised me. 'And then you find somebody and you can start your life again.'

One invitation I got was from my old friend and *Times* colleague, author Rachel Kelly (married to Sebastian Grigg). She decided that they knew so many single friends that she would give a sit-down dinner for sixty singles at her Notting Hill house, where she gave a famed Christmas party every December with guests who often included Boris Johnson, David Cameron, George Osborne, every editor in London, and several bestselling writers.

If her Christmas party was a status anxiety ordeal then her 'singles only' version was much worse. When I arrived, some of the more glamorous singles in London were there, including Caroline 'Pidge' Spencer, ex-wife of Princess Diana's brother Charles Spencer, along with a raft of wealthy and eligible bachelors. Guests had to wear name badges and everyone's mobile numbers were scrawled on a large blackboard. A giant table stretched all the way through the garden, kitchen, and then dog-legged left along the hallway – all heaving with lust, laughter, Italian plonk and blind hope. But I got nowhere. Others were more lucky. 'Three couples were dating within a week,' Rachel told me after. 'And one couple headed off to a hotel that night!'

I found myself slowly being sucked into an ever-decreasing social circle of fellow divorcés, or old bachelor friends with socially deviant habits. It was all too tempting to go for the easy, semi-casual, no-commitment option when it came to girls rather than seeking something serious, which risked more tears, emotional punishment and rejection. I couldn't face being crushed again. Not yet at least. Divorce had made me jaundiced. I was wary of more heart stamping.

At least, that was how I felt until I met Vanessa. So the obvious solution in my year of being single was to 'hedge' and keep my options open. You multi-date until you're sure; you don't have time to spend six months dating somebody before you decide whether or not you really like them or are suited to each other. Hence the need for the relationship 'weed-killing' that Vanessa had wisely suggested we both do.

So, I handed my mobile phone to my assistant at the *Spear's* office and asked her to go through it and delete any names and numbers in my 'contacts' that she wasn't sure about. I found – to my embarrassment – that when she asked me to clarify the actual name or surname of at least a dozen women, I hadn't a clue who many of them were.

'Who is "Boujis Anna"?' my assistant asked.

'No idea.'

And, worse, when I told my assistant to ring a number listed as, say, 'Boujis Anna', the said Anna – or Karin, Sara, or Natalia – had no idea who I was either.

Another piece of advice I'd been given by a veteran of the London scene was that clubs like Annabel's, Boujis and Tramp are the very last places you go to *meet* girls. 'They are places you take girls,' he said. But, in the end, it was Annabel's that came through for me. If I hadn't met Vanessa at the bar and spent an hour drinking champagne, six months later I might have been feeling as unloved as the faded-blue striped curtains being auctioned off in our hotel suite.

I remember opening our Savoy curtains, looking out across the darkly glimmering Thames stretching out ahead of me in the crisp winter dawn. As the December sun slowly rose above Waterloo and Charing Cross Bridges, making them stand out from the river shadows, I was thinking how lucky I was that my life had changed so quickly again.

After my divorce from Ilaria, I was getting another chance in life after walking into the birthday party for our mutual friend Giulia Costantini in October 2007. Vanessa and I had known each other slightly during my first marriage, but had never met properly until we found ourselves together after dinner. Can one fall in love over a dish of bitter-chocolate ice-cream? I had found Vanessa at the bar and ordered the famous club ice-cream, which arrived in a silver dish with two spoons. Nobody knew what made it so special (it was rumoured the secret was a teaspoon of black treacle).

We danced and returned to the table. I had been telling her of my Burning Man adventures in the desert and how I was glad not to be sleeping on a sofa in the Pink Pussycat camp.

'Could you imagine getting married again?' she asked.

I looked at her.

Pause.

'I could see myself marrying somebody like you,' I replied.

It wasn't long before we were driving up the M1 to the Lake District in my old BMW for our first romantic weekend. As the wipers scudded against the windscreen and winter rain, I called my car insurance company to have Vanessa's name added to my policy. We were on speaker-phone in the car. 'Would that be additional temporary or permanent insurance cover?' a female Newcastle call-centre voice asked.

'Permanent,' I said, without any hesitation.

Then Vanessa winked at me. Right eye. Her bright hazel-green eyes smiled. 'Your certainty came like a bolt from the blue,' she later said. 'I knew I had my man.'

As I was to discover, she was a zealous winker. In a witty column she wrote for *Spear's* ('Eye'll Have You') once we were engaged, she explained the advantages of being a serial winker, which for her was a lost art form with its own powerful seduction code. 'I am a winker,' Vanessa wrote. 'I wink often and with many. Despite being about to marry, I wink with men I meet on the street. I have even enjoyed good winking with women. Why? Because winking often gets me what (or whom) I want. It got me my husband.'

Upton Cressett Deserted

Not long after our shared dish of Annabel's ice-cream, I had invited Vanessa home to Shropshire for the weekend to show her around the architectural salvage-yard that I hoped would be our family home.

It was November and we arrived late on a dark, wet and foggy night in Shropshire with the rain making it impossible to see anything of the deserted house. There were no outdoor lights – what looked like a few broken headlamps hung off various walls. The only way to see anything was by torch or by switching on the lights in the house with the windows acting as a rudimentary beacon. Ever since my Liverpudlian builder had completed his demolition work over the summer, the house had become a haunting symbol of how my life had become a romantic wrecking yard.

As we drove past the turreted Gatehouse, it had no shape other than a shadowy outline in the drizzle. There was nothing especially inviting about the approach to the house, reached at the top of a steep hill after a two-and-a-half-mile winding single-track lane.

The wrought-iron entrance gates had been removed. The pair of Portland-stone balls from a broken-up estate in Scotland were lying in a corner of a barn. As we drove in through the back entrance, where a rotted wooden gate lay on the ground, it looked as if we were arriving at some muddy Shropshire farmhouse. It certainly didn't look like the moated English manor that had once decorated the cover of *Country Life*.

'I'm camping next door,' I said cheerily, as we walked into my temporary Coach House digs. 'I've got various builders lined up and have a great architect with a beard and lots of initials after his name, called Trevor, and a horse-mad project manager called Belinda, who you'll love. She can introduce you to the local hunt.'

'This was the old Coach House?' asked Vanessa, as we walked in.

'Well, the tack room.' I warned Vanessa that the house was not at its best. 'It might look like a bomb has hit it but I hope to have moved back in within six months.' I showed Vanessa the photos of the derelict house, with tumbledown chimneys and pigs inside. 'The panelling was ripped out by vandals in the Sixties and was replaced. The flagstone floor comes from a house that belonged to Anne Fleming, wife of Ian.'

Many of the rooms contained odd bits of orphaned house bric-à-brac that had not made it to my parents' storage barn where the family oil paintings and furniture were stored under tarpaulins covered with peacock shit. On a window sill stood a Staffordshire pottery figure of a cricketer, his bat missing. An enormous pile of dusty green stacks of *Hansard* stood in a corner.

My builder's pick-axe and sledgehammer had combined to make the old Tudor kitchen seem especially unloved. The giant medieval fireplace was being used as a concrete mixer. Rubbish and abandoned building materials lay everywhere. My mother's white Formica kitchen was one part of the house I was truly glad had gone. But that morning, as we continued our house tour, I was beginning to realise the scale of the task I had set myself.

Walking up the stairs, we turned right into a room with huge arched, braced beams made of ancient oak that Pevsner called the Chapel Bedroom. This was the original fourteenth-century Great Hall, with a carved crown rose in the middle of the central beam. It was the oldest part of the house.

'We call it the Bat Room,' I said. 'They are a rare protected species. If we poison them, we can go to jail.'

We moved to the corridor and inspected a few bedrooms before we passed my father's old dressing room, small with mullion windows looking out on to the front lawn. 'This will be the chatelaine's bathroom,' I said. 'This place is going to have hot water like the Savoy! It will be like an American hotel.'

'Sounds great,' said Vanessa. 'I'm a New Yorker, so the freezing-water English-bathroom thing isn't what I most love about this country. Scottish houses are even worse.'

We ended in the panelled bedroom. Several huge oak floorboards had been 'lifted' by my plumber as he had drilled (for two hours) through the giant beams that lay under the floor. In my parents' day, we had just had a few electric night storage heaters and slept in dressing gowns and sweaters. When it was really cold at Upton Cressett, we resorted to ski outfits.

The beautiful panelled room that had lodged in my subconscious was now empty. Only a gilt mirror still hung on a wall, looking lost and naked. Above the fireplace, an oak overmantel bore my mother and father's initials carved into two sections of panelling, with 'AD 2000' in the middle; a carved portcullis under the Staffordshire knot symbolised my father's parliamentary connections to Stafford as an MP.

The carving was a present from my father to my mother to mark thirty years of living at Upton Cressett. He loved engraving their history into the house, just as Richard Cressett had done back in 1580 when he had a carpenter carve his own initials in the panelling above his bed. I had long wanted to add mine, along with those of my wife. We stood by the cobwebbed window and looked out towards the half-dead trees beside the Gatehouse. 'You see those Spanish chestnut trees across the lawn?' I said. 'Two are dead. They were planted to mark Wellington's victory at Waterloo.' I looked towards Vanessa. 'One day I'll replant them,' I wanted to add, 'to celebrate something special, like a child,' but held back. We had only been together a few weeks.

'What's happened to the paintings and furniture?' Vanessa asked.

'What my parents didn't take with them is stored in the barn,' I said. 'But I'm hoping to get some back soon. There's an important Christie's sale coming up.'

'OK, hon, that sounds great,' she said. 'I've got a load hanging in New York that might help to fill the walls.'

The paintings never left New York.

9

Meet the Cressetts

Back in April, I had heard that a number of important Cressett family pictures and furniture were being disposed of by an elderly member of the Thursby-Pelham family of Sussex. They were the last twenti-eth-century descendants of the Cressett family, who had become Pelham-Cressett in the eighteenth century when they lived at Cound Hall, the Shropshire sister house of Upton Cressett.

My father had been in contact with the last of the Thursby-Pelhams for at least thirty years. The two last surviving lineal relatives who had been born Thursby-Pelham – direct relatives of the last Cressett, who had died in 1792 – were now, through marriage, Ellinor Bird, and her sister, who lived in Australia.

'My naughty aunt wants to sell off her heirlooms,' Deirdre Thornewill, daughter of Ellinor Bird, told my father on the phone from her home near Yeovil. 'So we've decided to sell. My mother is nearly ninety-five and we put her in a nursing home in March. Since you've always shown such an interest, I wondered if you'd like to pop down to Little Cookhams and take a look before it all goes to the saleroom.'

Would you like to *pop down*? That was a bit like asking Howard Carter if he fancied 'popping down' to the Valley of the Kings where there might be some old Egyptian items of interest. A letter soon followed, which explained more. The family were selling all their Cressett paintings and furniture, some of it original to Upton Cressett from the Elizabethan age. As a family, we could hardly believe our luck.

Much of the furniture had been photographed for a *Country Life* article published on 21 April 1923, entitled 'Mr Thursby-Pelham's Collection of English Furniture', which described how, shortly before the outbreak of the Great War, Augustus Thursby-Pelham had moved his entire inheritance of furniture and paintings, including early Tudor furniture, into his large house in a Chelsea garden square.

Number 55 Cadogan Gardens, or simply 'Number 55' as the Bird family referred to the house, is just around the corner from the Peter Jones department store. My father had tried to visit in the 1970s and '80s but had been rebuffed by the buzzer. The collection had been moved into Cadogan Gardens when the family had left Cound Hall in 1910. A noted collector, Thursby-Pelham had turned Cadogan Gardens into a private museum, housing what the *Antique Collector* had described in 1938 as a 'a distinguished collection of art treasures'.

Highlights included 'the Oak Room', which was covered with oak panelling, 'and is thus the room that gives the best idea of the appearance of Upton Cressett'. A 'rare and fascinating piece untouched, save for the canopy top, is an oak cradle', originally at Upton Cressett as it 'has a running frieze of dolphins, a characteristic ornament of that mansion'. The 'Cressett Cradle' was photographed in Brackett's *An Enyclopaedia of English Furniture* in 1927.

There was also a portrait by the young court painter Wilhelm Wissing of Sir Francis Cressett – steward and treasurer to Charles I – in ceremonial armour. My father and I were hoping that the oak chair on which Charles I had supposedly written his 'spiritual biography' (*Eikon Basilike*) in Carisbrooke Castle might still exist at Little Cookhams. It was well documented in Crown records that Francis Cressett was among those who had tried to rescue the King from Carisbrooke Castle in 1648, and we'd heard that something called 'the King's Chair' used to exist at Upton Cressett. Francis was codenamed 'A' in Charles I's coded secret correspondence to him. The plan – executed with Sir Henry Fairbrace – only failed when the King found that he could not squeeze through the bars ('for my Boddy is too much thicke for the breadth of the Window').

When Charles II was restored to the throne, Francis Cressett was one of the first back in the King's service. On taking up the throne, Charles remembered the loyalty of Francis to his father, although he was unable to pay Francis back the £1,455 'lent and expended to his late Majestie out of his own Moneys'. Ouch – that was over £180,000 in today's money lent to the boss.

But as we turned into the drive at Little Cookhams, only one question was on my mind: how much of the famous Cressett collection still existed? How much had been already sold off to pay for school fees, houses in Australia and the rest?

Deirdre Thornewill and her husband Digby were charming people. We were offered tea and cake in a comfortable chintz drawing room, then led into various bedrooms and corridors that had paintings stacked on beds and lying against the walls, like in an auction house.

'I want to show you some larger pictures that are going to be too big for us to keep,' she said. 'And some original furniture to Upton Cressett.'

First, we were shown a carved oak settle, dated 1679, of which the catalogue claimed the provenance was Upton Cressett. Only the carved initials didn't appear to fit any Cressetts living at the house in the late seventeenth century. Beside it was the Cressett Cradle. Kneeling, I could see the moulded sides with carved sea-dragons exactly as described in the *Antique Collector* article of 1938. They were almost identical to the carvings of Upton Cressett's celebrated lost 'dragon frieze' panelling. When my mother peered inside, she noticed the bottom of the cradle was lined with lead. 'Looks like it's been used as a log basket,' she said.

We were then shown boxes full of various Cressett seals, leather-bound books and an assortment of other family memorabilia, including genealogical pedigrees. There was no sign of any 'King's Chair'.

'I'm not an expert on the seals,' said Deirdre. 'But my mother told me one of the seals is a pardon from Queen Mary I to Thomas Cressett in 1553.'

The portrait by Wissing of Sir Francis Cressett, holding a black armour helmet, looked to be the prize piece to return to Upton Cressett. It had the Cressett family crest in the top left corner along with the words 'At age 49' in Latin. Historically, Francis was one of the most important of the Cressetts. In addition to having been steward and treasurer to Charles I, he had been one of his most trusted secret agents. While Cromwell had the King incarcerated at Carisbrooke, Francis had smuggled out secretly coded letters and messages to his Catholic friends in Scotland and France whom he hoped might raise an army.

As Deirdre left us to inspect the sale items and rummage around in the bedrooms, it became clear that there was only a handful of original Tudor or seventeenth-century furniture pieces left from the huge Thursby-Pelham collection at 55 Cadogan Gardens; the rest must have been sold off already or were not being consigned to the sale.

The larger portraits included a three-quarter-length portrait of Robert Cressett with Cound Hall in the background and another entitled *Portrait of Miss Cressett*, standing in a blue apron, a spaniel at her side. This was Elizabeth, the heiress who owned the family Shropshire estates of Upton Cressett and Cound Hall, which were inherited on her death in 1792 by her maternal uncle Henry Pelham (who changed his name to Henry Pelham-Cressett). This was the same Pelham family that had produced two prime ministers.

'The last of the Cressetts,' I said. 'Wouldn't it be wonderful to see her back at Upton Cressett?'

'David Waller will be bidding for her,' replied my father.

He was referring to the new owner of Cound Hall who, along with his American wife Nancy, had recently restored the Grade I Baroque mansion built by Richard Cressett in 1703 as a family home (it had previously been broken into flats), having gained permission to build a group of luxury executive homes on the edge of the estate. David was a very affable property developer, part-time antique dealer and another paid-up member of the restore-a-wreck club.

As we stood in the hallway of Little Cookhams, saying goodbye, Deirdre came up to my father and gave him a small cardboard box with various papers inside. 'These are some old family letters relating to Upton Cressett. They won't be going to Christie's. I thought you should have them. You might find some of the contents interesting.'

The Oak sale was on 5 November 2007 at Christie's, South Kensington. I had been counting down the days to this 'treasure sale' as my relationship with Vanessa was gathering momentum. Meanwhile, the restoration of Upton Cressett was coming together and I had started ordering curtains and other fabrics.

Founded in 1940, George Spencer was my favourite of all the fabric design shops. It was staffed with pretty girls under a delightfully camp front-of-house manager called Dudley. The first time I walked in he had a large plaster across his nose and a badly grazed face (I didn't like to ask). I was taking the advice of James Hervey-Bathurst, owner of Eastnor Castle in Herefordshire and former president of the Historic Houses Association. James advised members never to buy cheap curtains. 'You will only regret it. Money spent on the thickest and best curtains is always money well spent – and use the lightest of blinds to stop them fading.'

James went so far as commissioning bespoke curtains from Watts of Westminster for the stately Eastnor library and billiard room. But then Eastnor had a turnover in seven figures. When I took over Upton Cressett in 2008, the house's commercial activities were limited to some holiday lettings, house tours and a choice of three postcards at 50p each.

I made progress with the 'soft furnishings' side of the restoration before much of the building work was begun, let alone finished. When large wallpaper tubes marked 'GSD' (George Spencer Design) started arriving in Shropshire, with large quantities of thick biscuit linen to be edged in dark-claret silk velvet for the master bedroom curtains, I had to stash them away from my mother. She was already worried that I wasn't controlling my budget.

To help me with the decoration, I had rehired my friend Nikki Atkinson – formerly with Colefax & Fowler and now operating from her house in Little Coxwell in Oxfordshire. She had decorated Ilaria's and my Bayswater flat and had been supportive through the hell of my divorce when I had been homeless for a while as I tried to launch *Spear's*. I had slept on the office sofa, in Elizabeth Hurley's nanny's bunk bed and various Bayswater 'Muslim traveller' hotels before finally moving to an overpriced rented flat on a noisy part of the Cromwell Road.

Nikki and I would go into George Spencer at lunchtime and, after a half-hour gossip and chat with Dudley, we'd emerge with our arms full of exquisite chenille and hand-blocked samples of Copper Gilt Florentine or Dark Plum Flocked wallpaper.

On 7 September – just back from the Burning Man festival in the Nevada desert – I had brought together my renovation team, which included architect Trevor Edwards of Hawkes, Edwards and Cave in Stratford-Upon-Avon; project manager Belinda Edwards; and decorator Nikki. They were to be helped by Kathy Hanley, my housekeeper, who was doing painting and wallpaper stripping. The other member of my team – and no less important – was Darren, my part-time gardener and handyman, who wore thick Eddie the Eagle-style glasses and hardly spoke. He was a friendly soul and enjoyed the peace of working in the garden after a divorce from a brief marriage. He could have walked out of a Tom Sharpe novel. He had a fishing friend called Nathan, with the teeth and tattoos of a pirate, who used to help him cut logs, spray weeds and build bonfires.

My mother, meanwhile, had volunteered to work as Belinda's deputy project manager, supervising the parade of builders, plumbers, glazers, electricians, joiners, plasterers, burglar-alarm technicians and so on who came to give quotes. I was ready to get started but, by mid-September, we still had no written quotes from any local builders. 'I cannot help feeling that everything is getting a bit bogged down this end,' my mother wrote to me. She went on to suggest that I ship a team of Polish builders up from London. She had had a long conversation with somebody called Peter, who was the owner of Polish Subcontracting Ltd. His team could sleep in sleeping bags around the house and get the job finished in a few months working around the clock. 'He is from Ukraine but speaks perfect English – he was at Oxford! They are not amateurs. They are doing a listed house at the moment, matching everything to the old . . . Everything seems to come from China.'

Did somebody say 'Made in China'? We were straying some way from William Morris's SPAB manifesto and the notion of the independent artisan craftsman here. I politely told my mother that I would continue to search for a local English builder.

'No sign of Waller,' I whispered to my father, as we sat down in the Christie's auction room and surveyed the competition.

David and my father had met a couple of times to discuss Cressett family history – they also shared the same political views. Our families got on well but the battle for these pictures would be personal.

I was interested in Lots 362–5, which were described in the catalogue as 'The Property of a Descendant of James Thursby-Pelham'.

The auction room began stirring with excitement after the bidding for an oak refectory 'single plank' table belonging to Shakenhurst Hall in Worcestershire went above £25,000. The hammer finally came down at £34,000, which was £42,500 after 25 per cent commission. There was money in the room.

Many walked out as soon as the hammer came down. It was now only around a third full, mostly provincial dealers, some well-dressed interior decorators in suits and a few saleroom private buyers, who looked like country-house dreamers.

'Now Lot 362,' said the auctioneer. 'A matched pair of English walnut caned armchairs – late seventeenth century.'

These were the oak armchairs with 'squab' needlework cushions that looked identical to the pair of Daniel Marot armchairs photographed in the 1938 *Antique Collector* magazine. 'They would do honour to any national collection,' the magazine had stated.

The estimate for the chairs was £1,500–£2,500. As the hammer went down to me at £1,300 before commission, I was relieved. While I placed great emotional value on them, nobody else seemed remotely interested. That was the first lot coming home.

I relaxed.

Now for the Cressett Cradle – not exactly the Cressett Ark, but as close as I was going to get to it on a November morning in South Kensington. The estimate was £1,000–£1,500.

'Lot 364 . . . an English oak cradle,' began the auctioneer. 'Do I have a thousand pounds?'

Maybe it wasn't even going to reach its reserve. I stuck my paddle up.

There was a quick rally of bidding in the room. A few people dropped out as it reached the higher estimate. I couldn't see who was leading but it appeared to be somebody in a trilby seated towards the front of the room.

'I have fifteen hundred pounds against you, Sir.'

I stuck my paddle up.

And had to keep it up as the bidding slowly crept up in increments of £200, £300 and then £500.

I had been told by an auction-house friend that 'brown furniture' was almost valueless. Nobody wanted it. But the bidding was rising sharply and aggressively above £3,000.

As it reached £3,500, I looked at my father with an expression of mounting concern. Then panic. I was now in a bidding war for a carved oak cradle-turned-log basket. It couldn't be a family member. Who was it? And why was he ruining my morning?

'I now have four thousand pounds in the room,' the auctioneer said. Looking towards me, he added. 'I have four thousand *against* you, Sir.'

The bid was now four times the estimate. One thing was certain – the market for brown furniture hadn't just woken up. It was roaring that morning.

Gritting my teeth, I stuck my paddle up again. I couldn't lose it. But I was reaching my limit. I could feel my hand shaking.

'I now have four thousand, five hundred pounds with the gentleman at the back.'

There was a painfully long pause. The saleroom had become quite animated by this unexpected battle over a cradle.

'For the last time, at four thousand, five hundred pounds . . .'

Then the hammer came down. We had it – but it had been a painful victory. I was so shell-shocked by the price that I wimped out of the next lot – the 1679 oak settle from Little Cookhams that might once have stood at Upton Cressett. I had to keep some funds back for the Cressett portraits. The settle sold for nearly £6,000. I walked out in a funk and sank a whisky in the pub across the street.

After the sale ended, I introduced myself to my rival. He was in his sixties, wearing a crisply striped shirt and a grey suit with a polka-dot pink silk square in his breast pocket. I guessed he was a London dealer with a shop on Pimlico Road or at World's End.

'I noticed you were bidding for the oak cradle,' I said.

'Yes, such a lovely thing,' he said. 'It has such fine moulded carving.'

'Were you aware it belonged to the Cressett family?'

'No,' he said. 'Are you family?'

'I live in their old house,' I said. 'The cradle is now going back to its former home in Shropshire.'

'How nice.'

'Could I ask what your interest in the cradle was?'

'Oh, yes,' he said, smiling. 'I thought it would make the perfect kennel for my cat.'

Did I hear the word *cat*?

'I'm sorry to have disappointed your cat,' I replied, and marched out.

By the first week in December, when the Cressett pictures were being offered for sale at Christie's, I was in a very different sort of collector environment – the contemporary art-world circus of Art Basel Miami. Since I was in America, my father was bidding on my behalf.

'The likelihood is that Waller and you are the only people really interested,' he said. 'We're talking about Wissing here, not Warhol.'

The next morning, I prodded hash brown and eggs in our hotel while I awaited a call from my father in London as to how the Cressett sale had gone on Wednesday, 5 December.

'I did a deal with Waller before the sale,' my father said. 'In the pub opposite.'

'What sort of deal?'

'He wouldn't bid for Sir Francis Cressett if we didn't bid for Robert Cressett and Miss Cressett. David was always going to outbid you for the Cound pictures. He was just as keen to get them as we were.'

'So what happened?'

'Sir Francis is coming home to Upton Cressett. Just over reserve.'

That was a relief.

'You also have another painting for the drawing room. A peacock still-life.'

Another painting? I hadn't agreed to any other bidding.

'Yes, your mother fell in love with another lot later in the sale. It's a large still-life of a peacock in a country-house setting by the Dutch court painter Pieter Casteels. You know how your mother loves her peacocks.'

A *peacock*? I gulped.

I quickly looked up the lot in the catalogue in front of me.

Peter Casteels III (1684–1749) was a Flemish painter and engraver who lived in Richmond from 1708 and was best known at the English court for his flower pieces, game and exotic bird scenes that celebrated the country house – his clients included many courtiers, aristocrats and royalty.

I looked at the lot description: 'A peacock by a basket of upturned fruit, rabbits and a monkey, by an urn and hollyhocks, a formal garden and country house beyond.'

I loved it. It was a beautiful Flemish Old Master still-life that celebrated the harmony of the natural world in a country landscape. And the memory of beautiful peacocks fanning their aquamarine feathers as they paraded around the grounds took me back to my childhood at Upton Cressett when my mother bred them. Even better, I hadn't paid a silly Art Basel Miami price.

Vanessa and I spent Christmas at Upton Cressett – lunch in my parents' tithe barn as the house was still a building site – and I gave her a matching pair of Tanner & Kroll red-lipstick suitcases for our 'life's travels'. The smaller case fitted inside the larger one like a Russian doll. Clearly, I was thinking of my family dream.

As I dreamed about what I was hoping would be our idyllic life at Upton Cressett, I concocted a series of ambitions – having twins, writing bestselling thrillers, buying two borzoi puppies, importing wild boar to roam around the medieval wood and peacocks for the garden, flooding our medieval moat, learning to cook, paying my credit-card bills each month in full and, most importantly, building a much-needed bedroom extension to my one-bed London flat.

I had already decided after two months that I wanted to marry Vanessa. I had also decided I would propose to her in Mustique, where she had been partly brought up thanks to her grandfather. A few days before Christmas, I rang her friend Assia Webster, wife of the jeweller Stephen Webster.

'I need a ring, Assia.'

'For Vanessa?'

'Yes. An engagement ring.'

'Wow. That's such great news. When do you need it by?'

'Tomorrow.'

Assia suggested that I presented Vanessa with a 'stand-in' cocktail ring to give her on holiday when I proposed and then we would get Stephen to make up the proper ring on our return. I arranged for my friend Mowbray Jackson – a veteran member of my 'Ushers Club' – to collect the cocktail ring from Assia's Mayfair shop on Christmas Eve and to meet me at Victoria station when Vanessa and I were en route to Gatwick on Boxing Day. The ring-box was buried in a Boots plastic bag full of sun cream.

I had never been to Mustique before. Vanessa showed me around her old family's villa of Point Look Out, designed by Thomas Messel. We had picnics on Macaroni Beach and went for drinks at Mandalay, the house of millionaire publisher Felix Dennis. The first time she had been to Mandalay, when she was sixteen, David Bowie had owned it. Mick Jagger had also been present. That was the first time they had met, although they were not to start dating until 1998.

Vanessa also led a tour of the island via golf buggy for novelist Jay

McInerney and his wife Anne, with whom we had dinner just after Vanessa had accepted my proposal. We had discussed novels-in-progress. At dinner, I remember Jay saying to me, 'William, there are two types of book: the type you put in everything you know, and the type you leave out everything. Make sure you know which yours is before you start.'

As he said that, I thought, There is also the type that never gets written. Part of my misery on reaching both my thirtieth and fortieth birthdays had been to do with the fact that the books I had promised myself – and kept promising to myself and others – had not been written. With my marriage to Vanessa, I was now determined to end this creative entropy. The island was full of friends and it was a happy time. Elizabeth Hurley had also been at the Firefly restaurant when I had just proposed to Vanessa. She was one of the first to congratulate us.

By the time we were on the flight back to London, via Barbados, the news of our engagement was already in the *Daily Mail*. A reporter from the paper had managed to reach us on the island. 'When it comes to affairs of the heart, the path of true love has not run smoothly for William Cash,' I read in a copy on the plane. Following my divorce, I was apparently 'contemplating a bleak romantic future'. But that pessimistic outlook had now been overturned, with Vanessa being quoted as saying: 'It is amazing when two pieces click together . . . It was a revelation – we fell in love so easily.'

10

Racetrack Lodge

The plan was to move into my one-bed bunker of a Holland Road flat before we were married.

'Nice place for parties,' said Vanessa, when I first showed it to her. 'But where would the children sleep?'

When I had bought it, the last thing I was thinking of was a family home. The only reason I had made an offer was because of the rear 'large garden', with an entrance off Addison Crescent, and I'd thought I could get permission to build an extension for another bedroom.

'I know we're going to be living under a dual carriageway to start out,' I said, taking Vanessa into the basement bedroom. 'But once the extension is built, we'll have a lovely bedroom upstairs overlooking the garden.'

'Garden' was an optimistic term. The flat was in a house officially named Acacia Lodge, after the six half-dead acacias that populated the garden. With the ever-present noise of passing traffic, I called it

Racetrack Lodge; lorries, buses and builders' skips thundered daily past my triple-glazed ground-floor windows.

The problem was that, to build our bedroom extension and car park area, two acacia trees needed felling and their roots digging out. I had found a tree-surgery company and given them £500 to remove all the trees and stumps one Saturday morning.

Around 9.30 a.m. my mobile had rung. I had decamped to a café on Kensington High Street.

'We have a problem,' the East European voice said. 'My man was just starting on your tree when the council sent an enforcement team. A neighbour must have informed them.'

It turned out there were conservation orders on the two surviving acacia trees.

If I couldn't get them removed, I couldn't build my extension, and my marital life was doomed to continue in a tiny, windowless basement bunker of a bedroom under the A40.

I consulted my builder. Digging a small trench around the tree with a spade, he inspected the roots of one of the trees. 'A mixture of diesel and industrial Roundup,' he said, 'applied liberally for around two weeks should do the trick.'

Death by poison or chainsaw? A tricky choice. I told him to wait while I considered my options. I didn't want to break the law but those tree stumps were ruining my life.

Not long before we were married, my builder called me to say the ceiling in the hallway had fallen down. A few days later, he called again to say he had fallen through the floor into the basement neighbour's flat while he was watching football on TV.

As our wedding day in June approached, the flat remained a work-in-progress, with no blinds or curtains, no carpets, half-painted bookcases, an unfinished study, a TV that didn't work in the basement bedroom, and – my particular bête noire – secondary glazing that didn't fit over the huge sash windows in the reception room past which the west London traffic roared. The double glazing was six inches too short. Another layer of glazing was added.

Still, Vanessa remained upbeat and we laughed a fair amount. When I explained that the protected trees saga meant we might be living in a basement bunker a little longer than originally planned, she said, 'A friend of mine got married and couldn't afford to move to a bigger house, so they kept the baby in a drawer of a desk for the first few months.'

Since the Chelsea Register Office was about 150 yards from the *Spear's* office on the King's Road, I dropped into work for an hour in the morning, walked across the street and tied the knot with Vanessa in the Rossetti Room (cost £150).

One of the best things about a register-office wedding is that you get to choose the readings and music you like. Anything religious, or which so much as hints at there being a God, is strictly *verboten*. So I spent a fortune with iTunes trying to come up with a suitable 'wedding song'.

I thought I had the perfect track when I started downloading Matt Monro singing 'On Days Like These', the 1969 theme tune from *The Italian Job*, telling Vanessa over breakfast that this song – beautiful red Italian sports car speeding along the mountain roads – was 'just perfect for us', only to see a pained look flash across her face when the lyrics began: 'On days like these when skies are blue and fields are green / I look around and think about what might have been . . .'

What *might* have been?

We settled for Billie Holiday singing 'The Very Thought of You' (Vanessa's choice) as we signed the register.

One of the dilemmas facing anybody getting married for a second time is whether or not to ask the previous best man to step up again. I had discussed this dilemma with Andrew Roberts, historian (and fellow divorcé), only the week before at a party and he had admitted that he thought it was beyond the call of duty to ask somebody – however close a friend – to get out their old notes and recycle a wedding speech. His determination to find a replacement best man was confirmed when he attended a divorced friend's wedding in which the best man had been recycled; in his speech he kept referring to the new wife by the ex-wife's name. I asked my friend William Dartmouth to be best man.

In my speech, I commended Vanessa for not only being bold and beautiful but for her range of skills, which included calligraphy – she wrote all the invitations herself – speaking German, and winning my heart with a single wink on that drive up to the Lake District.

I might have read the signs better. A trip to St Moritz in February to celebrate Vanessa's birthday and to present her with her engagement ring (a yellow sapphire with the interwoven initials 'VW' in diamonds on each side) ended up with us returning to London with the ring cut into pieces.

It was delivered to our hotel by Mowbray Jackson. I had paid for him to catch the first flight to Switzerland with the box the moment it had been finished in the Stephen Webster workshop. He then joined us for a few days' skiing.

It had been Valentine's weekend – a few days from Vanessa's birthday. After too much wine at lunch up on the slopes with my friends Zoe and Sven Ley, I had chosen to ski down fast with Sven rather than take the lift with Vanessa. She had spent most of her winters in Mustique and semi-professional scuba diving was her preferred winter sport. It was a silly thing to do on her birthday.

But this incident was followed by another more unfortunate episode. The yellow sapphire engagement ring turned out to be a size too small and was cutting off the circulation to her finger, which was turning a nasty blue-black. So bad did the situation become that the ring had to be sawn off by an expert Swiss surgeon in the town's Klinic Kut. We laughed about it but it was not how we had planned our trip to end. The ring returned to England and the Stephen Webster workshop. It wasn't the best omen.

It all sounded so glamorous – a house in Shropshire, a flat in Holland Park and Vanessa's apartment on Park Avenue. But the reality was painfully different. The cracks were becoming impossible to avoid. Not long after we returned from Switzerland, we went to a colourfully glitzy but strange dinner at the Dorchester Hotel organised by *Spectator* editor Matthew D'Ancona and my Italian friend Guilia Costantini to launch Boris Johnson's campaign to become Mayor of London. I wasn't quite sure what the point of the dinner was as most of the guests were socialites married to Non Doms, or London hedgies rather than serious politicos. Women certainly seemed to like him, which was very much part of his electoral appeal.

The very last thing London's Euro-financial classes wanted in May 2008 – when the mayoral election was held – was to see 'Red Ken' Livingstone returned to City Hall. Vanessa (who was then writing for *Diplomat* magazine) was a keen Boris supporter and somehow had his mobile number and email. She wanted to interview him as she reserved a very special dislike for Mayor Ken Livingstone, who had done a 'discount' oil deal worth around £15 million to subsidise cheaper diesel for London buses with her political nemesis, Venezuela's president Hugo Chavez. Hardly a week went by when Vanessa wasn't writing some excoriating public attack on Chavez – or appearing on *Newsnight* – for having exploited and ruined her home country, as well as having seized vast swathes of land and companies from her family and friends. She was one of the Venezuelan Government's number-one irritants as an anti-Chavez public intellectual.

I didn't know Boris well. I had only met him a few times at parties. There was something theatrical and larger-than-life about him. He certainly enjoyed, or craved, attention. At one party I'd been invited to by Toby Young at the *Spectator's* offices in Doughty Street, Boris jumped up onto the editor's desk to make his speech. The mahogany partner's desk juddered under his weight. I couldn't imagine Dominic Lawson (the magazine's best editor I worked with) playing the 'editor-showman' in such a way, and I guessed that my strait-laced great-uncle Wilson Harris – who was both MP for Cambridge and editor of the *Spectator* (1932–1953) – would have choked to see the editor's famous desk used as a stage prop.

Under the glare of the Dorchester's lights, champagne glass in hand, Boris and I said hello and chatted amiably. Like me, he had started his career in journalism as a graduate trainee at *The Times* – although he had preceded me by few years and ended up getting fired.

My parents often used Upton Cressett as a political salon for fellow MPs and journalists, inviting them to stay en route to party conferences in Manchester or Birmingham. This was after my father had led the Maastricht Rebellion in the early 1990s when Boris was building his caustic and colourful reputation as one of the few leading political journalists happy to throw javelins at Brussels and expose the EU for its profligate and anti-democratic excesses. In this he was a natural political ally of my father – dubbed the 'St John the Baptist of the Eurosceptic movement' by the BBC – and he would have been welcomed at Upton Cressett. That my father and Stanley were friends from their Oxford days also helped bring him into my father's confidence.

According to Sonia Purnell's *Just Boris* biography, Boris came to the house one weekend in the autumn of 1995 and his stay landed him in some trouble with the *Telegraph*. As Purnell relates:

> *One notorious occasion during the Conservative Party Conference that year, Boris disappeared for longer than usual. He could not be found anywhere but was needed to write an emergency leader on the death of a prominent politician. He did not answer his mobile*

*phone – a capital offence for most journalists – and had not booked
into his hotel. In the end, he was found at the eleventh hour but
again it went right up to the wire. It transpired he had spent the
weekend staying with the Eurosceptic politician Bill Cash at his
house in Shropshire.*

When Boris came, my father would have pointed out the brick border edging the front lawns that had been laid in the 1970s by Colin
Lucas, Boris's own historian godfather. Colin was also godfather to
my brother Sam as he had been close college friends at Oxford with
my father as well as best friends with Stanley Johnson, father of Boris.
Colin and Stanley had both been at Sherborne School and many of
my father's closest friends were from this set. Indeed, my father first
met my mother Bridget (known as 'Biddy') in Oxford in the early 1960s
after the group went to see a Shakespeare play at Stratford. My father
ensured that he sat next to my mother in the RSC theatre; and then
drove her in his sports car back to Oxford (where she was at Beechlawn
Tutorial College, about a decade before Tina Brown).

My father had been at Lincoln College and Stanley Johnson was
at Exeter, which was opposite on Turl Street, so they all used to drink
together at 'The Turl' pub. My father recalled one 'classic' Stanley
moment when he attempted to head off by motorcycle and sidecar
(travelling with two friends) to follow the trail of Marco Polo, setting
out from Oxford to Venice, before biking across India and Afghanistan.

'It was an adventurous thing to do and we opened some champagne
to see Stanley's expedition off but just as his huge motorbike and
sidecar roared off, a lorry pulled out in the Turl and Stanley had to
suddenly hit the brakes. He kept revving the engine as his dramatic
college exit was ruined. We all thought it was hilarious.' But, like
Boris, behind the bravura showmanship, there was a steely and
impressive classical intellect and writing talent. (In 1962, Stanley
won the prestigious Newdigate Prize for Poetry.) It was later because

of Colin Lucas – who later became knighted and vice-chancellor of Oxford University – that Boris had been sacked from *The Times* after he concocted a fictitious quote relating to the archaeological discovery of a royal palace belonging to King Edward II. 'Dr Lucas' was quoted as saying that the monarch had cavorted there with his 'catamite' lover Piers Gaveston in 1323. Colin was annoyed that his godson had got his facts sloppily wrong just when Colin was running to be Master of Balliol; Piers Gaveston was beheaded in 1312.

But by 1995, Boris's ability to skewer the EU emperors was such that my father was uninterested in such minor literary crimes against his former flat mate. Indeed, at that time, Bill and Boris were so closely aligned that during one lunch (they usually went to an Italian restaurant in Crown Passage, St James's, called Il Vicolo) Boris had agreed to be the official keeper of my father's papers and secret diaries in the event of his death. 'I just said over lunch "I think it might be a good idea if you were my literary executor, and have access to my political diaries" and Boris said, "Yes, that would be a good idea."'

Boris was to be given exclusive access to my father's hoard of political papers, including his diaries going back to 1984 and his confidential archive of letters and memos from Margaret Thatcher. Although it was his Brussels posting that made him a journalistic star, Boris's position was actually far from secure. My father was also friends with *Telegraph* proprietor Conrad Black and Jimmy Goldsmith, both ardent Eurosceptics (Jimmy once told my father privately that he was prepared 'to spend $100 million' to take Britain out of the EU). Conrad confided over one dinner with my father that he regularly had to 'protect' and 'defend' Boris from the pro-EU leaning Max Hastings, editor of the *Telegraph*. After being pardoned by President Trump, Conrad was to continue defending Boris against continued attacks by Hastings, declaring in the *Spectator* that Boris was 'more reliable and trustworthy' than his former *Telegraph* editor, whom he called an 'ill-tempered snob' and a 'coward and a flake.'

'I used to talk with Boris a lot, going back to the early Nineties,' my father said. 'Boris always understood the European question. He knew his way around the Brussels undergrowth. I gave him stories. At the time, he was just a colourful and bright young journalist who I used to lunch with. He was good company. It never occurred to me in the 1990s that he was interested in entering politics himself. He never mentioned it. What he did tell me was that he played some rugby with the Oxford Greyhounds, the university second XV, and that did surprise me as I never thought of Boris as any sort of sportsman athlete.'

When Boris had been to stay at Upton Cressett in 1995 he had just been a political journalist and family friend looking for copy. Amusing my mother with Brussels gossip over poached salmon, washed down with several bottles of Tanners wine, he was regarded by my father as 'on side' for having done much to help make Euroscepticism less of a fringe movement and more an intellectually respectable cause for his wing of the party.

'How's that Elizabethan house in . . . Where is it? Shropshire?' Boris asked me at the Dorchester dinner.

Our conversation was friendly and non-political. I told him that my parents had moved out, the builders were shortly moving in and that Vanessa and I should be installed shortly.

'Lovely house. Lucky you. Love to Biddy,' he said, referring to my mother.

Little could either of us have imagined how our lives were later to become entangled.

Credit Crunched

By our first Christmas my marriage to Vanessa was in trouble. The London flat was still far from being finished. The main building works at Upton Cressett had still not started.

Then, on Valentine's Day, Vanessa had a riding accident.

'You had better collect her straight away,' Phil, who kept her horse, said on the phone. 'She's in pain but I think she'll be OK after a hot bath and a glass of whisky.'

After I went to collect her in the early afternoon, we thought it judicious to go to A&E at Telford's Princess Grace Hospital. After waiting for two hours with no sign of being examined, we decided to give up. It was Valentine's Day after all and we were expected for dinner at a friend's house near Much Wenlock.

We had a bad row on the drive home. Vanessa packed up her stuff and flew to New York, where she was giving a party for her birthday on 18 February. We had been married for six months and were now separated.

I had been seeing a therapist at the Priory in Roehampton during and since my divorce from Ilaria. She had suggested it might be useful if I drew up a list of what I wanted out of my marriage, why I was committed to it, and why I was going to 'fight for us', whatever the pain and cost.

But it was already too late.

I hadn't expected the axe blow but I felt its full force when I opened the *Daily Mail* on 26 February. Richard Kay's latest tabloid instalment of my marital soap opera certainly spoilt my breakfast:

> *They are going through a difficult time. Vanessa says she is very sad and William has been left devastated, although both of them are still hoping it won't be the end.*
>
> *But after their whirlwind romance . . . friends say Vanessa never settled into a life that revolved around a country home in Shropshire . . . and their London apartment.*
>
> *Things were not helped by the properties both needing building work. 'Vanessa found herself pretty much living with her mother-in-law, which was not what she wanted from married life,' says the pal.*
>
> *Vanessa was also desperate to start a family. 'She has always*

spoken about how much she wants children. She was becoming
frustrated by the idea that their living situation might make that
impossible,' says a friend.

A New York pal tells me, 'Vanessa decided she had to get some
space. She is still hoping there might be a chance for reconciliation.'

Might be a chance for reconciliation?

I booked a flight to New York. It was her fortieth birthday.

Vanessa ended up cancelling her birthday party on the day after her
New York doctor had said she had a 'herniated disk' from her riding
accident. I got the call from her at Gatwick just as I was about to check
in. Glumly, I headed back to London, feeling particularly low as I sat
on the Gatwick Express, watching Brixton, Clapham and the graffiti-
scrawled railway escarpments of south London slip past for the second
time in two hours.

I flew out a week or so later, at the end of February, and our marriage
was painfully dissected over dinner, leaving me little hope. 'I came
here to New York wanting to fight for our love but I realise I lost the
fight some time ago,' I wrote to her from a diner around the corner
from her Park Avenue apartment.

Looking back, it read more like an obituary than a love letter. I had
lost the battle.

For everything I have done to hurt and disappoint you, I am sorry.
I need to go back to England and be true to myself; I think that
one reason you did marry me is that somewhere, deep in my being,
there is an artist and a decent good man with the spiritual and
other values that we both share, waiting to come out. But for too
long I have been like Caliban, stuck in my cave, not being true to
myself – and I can't be true to myself writing garbage hackery, or
even publishing Spear's, or actually doing any journalism. I saw

*you as my way out of the cave but now I will probably have to do
it alone. . . .*

As I sat drinking cup after cup of watery black coffee in that Upper
East Side diner, my mood was resigned. Vanessa would never be the
chatelaine at Upton Cressett. Under UK law, one has to wait at least
a year before divorce papers can be filed. Can words or prayers really
rescue or save a relationship? Or win over a woman? I certainly
spent enough time praying in St Patrick's Cathedral on that trip to
New York.

Two days later, I was back in the Coach House on my own, feeling
like a condemned man – with the executioner's blade set to fall in
June. I had imagined that we would be happy simply because Vanessa
had made me so happy in those first exhilarating months. I wrote to
her with those sentiments, trying to fathom what had gone wrong:
'I always loved you very much – what happened was like one of those
huge waves on Macaroni Beach; it just knocked us over; and I became
intoxicated on our happiness and thought the love and the dreams and
the talk were enough.'

11

Answered Prayers

By May 2008, while I was writing, not drinking, and searching for a builder for Upton Cressett, something wholly unexpected happened. Vanessa was back in England and wanted to try to make the marriage work. My visit to St Patrick's Cathedral in New York had resulted in a miracle.

Better news still was that the building works looked set to start in July. One afternoon, Vanessa headed off to Telford to learn how to operate CAD architectural design software. She had also arranged quotes for the shipment of some of her art collection from New York. The house *had* worked some magic.

To pay for the works at Upton Cressett, I had arranged to take out a hefty mortgage ('home improvements', I had written on the form) and had been busy interviewing builders. One fled the house after I led him up the newel staircase to show him the works that needed doing in the Great Chamber – the former Chapel Bedroom. The wallpaper had been stripped back and bare oak floorboards were exposed. Where a sink had once stood only bare exposed pipes could be seen.

'We may be revealing a Tudor fireplace in here,' I said, entering the room. 'Have you done that sort of work before?'

When I looked around, the builder was nowhere to be seen. I peered out of the window and saw him running towards his van. I shouted to him through the window, 'Hey there . . . where are you going?'

He stopped and shouted back, 'This is way, way too big a project for anybody. Good luck, mate!' And with that he accelerated down the drive.

I had a lucky break finding my builder Dom Crowe, from Much Wenlock, when I happened to be driving by his house after a walk on Wenlock Edge. Dom lived just a few hundred yards from the National Trust car park. Seeing he had a huge pile of local Wenlock stone for sale, I stopped to enquire. I needed a supply of local stone for our perimeter wall.

When he said he was a builder, I invited him up to the house to give me a quote. I ended up choosing him after noticing that he had a National Trust membership sticker in his car window. At least he loves old houses, I thought. And I was right. I later discovered that Dom had recently repaired the Norman church of St Gregory in our local village, Morville. If he was able to restore the tall western tower of the Grade I church with its twelfth-century stone walls, flat buttresses, fine early Norman chancel arch, nave arcades and long chancel, he was ideally suited to Upton Cressett.

Dom worked as part of a building team with Martin Reidy, who lived in the old 'butler's house' at Monkhopton. Martin was in his fifties, had trained in the Irish army and was from a building family based in Manchester. He had a precociously academic daughter called Megan, who was showing great promise at school. Martin was a joiner and 'craftsman' builder who had an artisan's eye for detail and could take a brass lock apart as quickly as a rifle. He had formerly worked for

Love at first sight. Upton Cressett as it looked in 1970.

The Gatehouse in 1970. Wild pigs were in residence on the first and second floors. The ground floor 'porter' rooms were used to store farm machinery.

St Michael's in the late 1960s. The Norman church had been closed since 1958 when it was designated Grade 2 due to its derelict condition.
(Peter Lea)

The Gatehouse in August 1909 as photographed by the Scottish philosopher and mathematician John Edward Steggall on a cycling holiday. *(© University of St Andrews, Special Collections)*

By the late 1960s, the ivy had been cleared but Upton Cressett still resembled a farmyard with sheep in the grounds, and the Hall inhabited by pigs and chickens. *(Peter Lea)*

(*above*) Ornamental plasterwork in the Gatehouse in 1970. This is the room in which Prince Rupert was said to have slept during the Civil War.

(*right*) The same room after restoration. It is now known as the Whisky Suite after Lady Thatcher's visit in 1994.

Bill and Biddy Cash around 1962. This was taken at Oxford where Biddy was at Beechlawn and Bill was at Lincoln College reading 'history and cricket'.

In the mid-1960s, Biddy worked as a 'garden room' secretary at 10 Downing Street. She gave up the job after my birth and was soon house hunting for a wreck to restore.

Bill Cash mowing the lawns in the 1970s with my brother Sam and myself getting a ride.

My sister Laetitia in her late teens.

My mother in her rose garden in the 1970s.

Searching for Shropshire hill forts aged around eight.

Sitting in a JCB during restoration of the Gatehouse.

My uncle Jonathan Roberts staying on an 'archaeology holiday' in the 1970s.

The fourteenth-century Chapel Bedroom in the 1980s with its pieta. Now known as the Great Chamber or the 'Bat Room'.

Margaret and Denis Thatcher outside the Gatehouse during their stay in 1994.

The Viles at play. A typical lunch party with the ex-pat LA set in the early 1990s. Elizabeth Hurley is on my right, Bond girl Maryam d'Abo is opposite, next to designer Celia Wise.

Holly McConkey in England in 1991 after I met her at the Cannes Film Festival.

With Binder Box girlfriend Philippa in Australia in 1994.

'The Baron', Clem von Franckenstein, in trademark *Miami Vice*-style dress and Binder Box girlfriend Louise King.

Racing driver Charles Dean and myself at Sudeley Castle in the 1990s. He was the founding member of my Best Man Club.

Screenwriter Allan Scott, Philippa's father and my LA 'Uncle Alan'.

Binder Box girlfriend Catherine Jordan, LA editor of the *Gault Millau* guide.

My dear friend Christina Knudsen, who died in 2016.

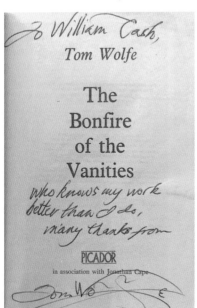

Tom Wolfe's octopus signature.

Sharing gossip with my *Telegraph* boss Conrad Black at a London dinner in 1998. *(Dafydd Jones)*

Formula 1 boss Ron Dennis in the London area but had decided he preferred life in Shropshire. His wife had been a teacher who went on to work in a Bridgnorth funeral parlour.

Meanwhile, I was learning the language of conservation building. I understood about 'double-beading' on the new oak doors and the difference between medieval and modern methods of plastering. I was spending my evenings rubbing special Jacobean oak stain (to match new studded Gatehouse doors) from the Period Shop in Shrewsbury into the oak panelling until it shone like polished leather. Some of the technical language might as well have been High German, but I was happy; life had thrown me another chance.

An Unexpected Sale

In July, I found myself confronting my marital past, and my inability to let go, in a way that proved fatal. Out of the blue, I got a call from a secretary who had worked for Ilaria when we were married. 'Ilaria is selling the Jilly Sutton sculpture you gave her,' I was told. 'Lots Road auction house this Sunday.'

It had been a present for her thirty-fifth birthday in 2005. After I had seen the carved wooden portrait of Poet Laureate Andrew Motion in the National Portrait Gallery, I had decided Jilly was the artist to capture Ilaria's creatively fragile, impulsive but loving nature. As a surprise, I had driven Ilaria to her Devon studio on the River Dart. Jilly was one of Britain's most celebrated wood sculptors and we had stayed for two days in a local ramshackle hotel while Ilaria had a plaster mask made of her face; this was followed by a few sittings in the studio.

Jilly created an exquisite larger-than-life wooden sculpture of Ilaria's head on a specially made aluminium geometric stand. Her work is well known for its veneration of the human head in a style that she describes as touching the serenity of the 'life embodied in every tree', which then lives on in the 'still living nature' of her portraits. In other words, her work was about the defeat of time.

I was surprised – and distressed – to find that the sculpture had been sent to the Lots Road saleroom but then I doubted her lawyer had any idea who Jilly Sutton was. It didn't especially bother me. But I thought I would trek down to Lots Road and take a last look at the portrait before it was sold.

There it was – incongruously upstairs with the battered old antiques, partners' desks and fake Louis VIII chairs and chandeliers. It made me sad to see such a fine piece of art sold off without so much as the sculptor's name attached. The last time I had seen it was in the marble hallway of our London flat where I had held my fortieth birthday dinner – *sans* Ilaria.

As I ran my hand softly along the contours of her carved head, I had mixed emotions. As my fingers felt the heavy grain – moulded from the plaster life mask made in Jilly's studio – I felt that Jilly had been right. The wood still contained some element of Ilaria's living and loving spirit. Certainly, as I ran my hand along her grainy face, I felt something. It was a melancholy combination of love, regret, pain and sadness.

Shortly after seeing the head in the saleroom, I wrote to Jilly Sutton, expressing my dismay that her *Head of a Girl* had been put on the block. 'I just wanted you to know that Ilaria sold your wonderful bust of her at the Lots Road auction house, of all places. Seems such a shame – still, they got over £7,000 for it so at least you clearly have admirers . . .'

What I wasn't expecting, however, when I walked into the main auction lot showroom was to see almost the entire house contents of our Bayswater home being offered for sale – with price tags on everything. It really was a clearance sale – eerily like the bedroom I had shared at the Savoy back in December 2007, with Bonham sale price estimates on everything.

The yellow-gold silk curtains that had hung in our sitting room were there, and the framed poster of the Goodwood Revival historic racing festival in 2003 where we had begun to fall in love. There was the framed still from the 1966 French film *Un Homme et une Femme* that I had given her as a present, our fireguards, the beautiful blue crystal chandelier that had hung in our hallway . . . It was a complete boot sale of the three years of our life together.

Then I saw it.

Out of the corner of my eye to my right, next to the kitsch lights and unused mattresses wrapped in plastic. There it was! Our marital *bed*, with a royal-blue velvet headboard and valance and our V-Spring mattress from Harrods. It had been stripped and stood forlornly next to a cheap pine bed wrapped in plastic. I hadn't spoken to Ilaria since our divorce but I felt outraged that at some time on Sunday afternoon *our* bed was to be auctioned off anonymously for a few hundred pounds.

This sale of Palace Court's contents troubled me . . . and I couldn't understand why. Why couldn't I let go? I had moved on with my life. I had had no contact with Ilaria since her lawyer had told me to communicate only through his office. But I didn't like the idea of a stranger in our bed or my curtains lying crumpled in the corner of the Lots Road saleroom.

I bought back my past (except for the bed). The sale date was mid-July 2009. My life with Vanessa was dissolving, and my default setting in such a situation was to engage reverse gear. To make a claim on the past, which was the only certainty I knew.

Bizarrely, I was attending a charity clay-pigeon shoot at a shooting school in Berkshire when I got Vanessa's call. I was standing by my fellow team members with hundreds of shotguns firing off at the same time. I felt as if I was watching a firing squad, only with pump-action shotguns not rifles. Bang. Bang. Bang.

It was swelteringly hot and I had sweat running down my forehead from the exertion of shooting clays in the July heat wearing sunglasses and a checked open shirt. It was a sport I hated. I was only doing it as *Spear's* had been invited and I was under pressure to schmooze with CEOs of leading banks.

'What's going on, hon?' she said. 'Why do we need a chandelier and these old curtains right now? I thought you didn't have any money.'

All around me cartridges were flying out of their automatic ejectors. Bang . . . bang. I could smell the cordite and my ears were ringing with the deafening gunfire of champagne-refreshed City men in their Ray-Bans and suncream.

I could have lied to Vanessa and said I was just picking up some furniture and curtains for Upton Cressett but I didn't. I told her I hated the idea that my old 'stuff' was being flogged off without reserve. As I drove home, waiting for an unhappy Vanessa, I felt like a man on his way to turn himself in.

By the end of July, Vanessa had left for New York, this time for good.

12

A Truth Universally
Acknowledged

To paraphrase Jane Austen, I was a single man in possession of a good house – and still in need of a wife. Above all, I wanted the house to become my family home. I saw the restoration as another chapter in the house's worn history, with myself just a small actor on its stage.

When Upton Cressett became my responsibility, I felt as if I had been handed an old chalice that needed some bad dents removed and a good polish. The house offered a form of communion with the past, perhaps even a chance of absolution for my marital failures. A re-stringing. An opportunity for renewing my spirit and sense of who I was, or what I had become away from it.

Having already had two non-British wives, I was nervous about auditioning more American or European candidates to be the third

Mrs Cash. It is a truth rarely admitted that the reality of living in muddy and freezing Shropshire is rather different from the dreamy world of *Town & Country* or *Howards End*.

After Vanessa had left for New York, I decided it was time to throw my energies into the rebuilding of Upton Cressett – and myself. I was looking for a healing Arcadia. In setting out to restore Upton Cressett, I wanted to retreat into the familiar to establish a break with my past.

As I contemplated my second divorce, I reflected on how the English have a very different relationship with old buildings from other Europeans. For me, Upton Cressett was more than just a building project. Our nation's relationship with buildings is often more emotional than economic. That is why you can still buy a crumbling palazzo in Italy or a French château relatively inexpensively, while in Britain a 'romantic wreck' will be sold at a premium as a 'historic character' property.

The Germans, French and Italians don't understand the British Cult of Restoration – restoring an old manor farmhouse, mill or ruined abbey until we are driven into the financial grave. It relates to our national obsession with the past and how our best domestic architecture – from castles to cottages – gives character and identity not only to our towns and villages but also defines who we are.

When we take on a neglected or romantic wreck we aren't just looking for a family roof over our head. We want an emotional connection. To buy or restore such a wreck is an act of faith. We don't just invest financial capital but also considerable emotion and spiritual capital. In many cases, we invest our very souls in the stones and walls of the past.

This was, indeed, why William Morris and his architect friend Philip Jebb, heavily influenced by the writings of John Ruskin, had founded the Society for the Protection of Ancient Buildings (SPAB) in 1877; their intention was to ensure that houses and churches were restored in a way that was in keeping with the 'living spirit' of their evolution and – in any repairs or renovation – to keep that spirit true to its original architectural purpose.

Morris abhorred how ancient buildings, especially churches of medieval and Tudor origin, were being ruined and defaced by 'the strange idea of Restoration', which stripped a building of its very history and soul – 'of its life that is' – in the name of conservation and authenticity. The result was often a faked imitation of the past.

In his *Seven Lamps of Architecture*, Ruskin speaks out against the destructive cult of 'restoration' of old buildings, which in his view robs them of their beauty and character. Ruskin calls restoration 'a lie from beginning to end' because it sought to change the essence of an old building – 'erasing the evidence and record of its true history', as the SPAB puts it. The SPAB's founders, led by Morris and Webb, took up Ruskin's ideas and translated them into a new architectural conservation cause.

The Society railed against attempts to improve on, or fake, the original. It believed that the right sort of renovation preserved the original materials and thus the 'soul' of a building.

As I embarked upon the task of reconsecrating the past at Upton Cressett – and distancing myself from my own – I wanted to do it in a way that was true to the living spirit of the Elizabethan house, not the derelict 1960s place my parents had acquired. Part of the challenge I set myself was to adapt the aesthetic and architectural moral principles of William Morris and Ruskin to my own life.

Like a building that had been sabotaged by ignorance, I needed some grounding philosophical principles, not just for the building work ahead but also to help restore my own self. I needed to be scraped back to my core and sandblasted. My rotten wooden casements would be replaced with new stone, and any faux late twentieth- and early-twenty-first-century additions raked out. The social tinsel that had mutated inside me for twenty years would be ripped out and tossed on to a garden bonfire so I could breathe again. I needed my very own English Renaissance makeover along SPAB 'restoration and repair' guidelines.

Ruin Lust

Thanks to the architectural vandalism of the Reformation and the Civil War, we are a country of rebuilders and restorers. Whereas other countries may prefer to demolish and erect new edifices, we often prefer to put old stones and bricks to fresh purpose. Our houses – and our rebuilding – reveal much of who we are, not only as individuals but also as a nation. The story of England, indeed, is the story of our buildings and ever-changing architecture. As Kenneth Clark puts it in *Civilisation*, 'If I had to say which was telling me the truth about society, a speech by a Minister of Housing or the actual buildings put up at the time, I should believe the buildings.'

Before they had started on their two-decade restoration of Gwydir Castle in North Wales, a friend of Peter Welford asked him why he and his wife, Judy, could possibly want to switch a comfortable enough life in London for a damp mattress in a remote, flood-prone, haunted and semi-ruinous Welsh castle. Peter replied, 'To live there, of course.'

Restoration is, alas, a costly business, emotionally and financially. Often even more expensive than the house itself. There is a poignant moment in the film *In the Gaze of Medusa*, directed by Gavin Bush, about the restoration of Wenlock Priory. Speaking softly to camera, turned to one side, De Wet says that there were times when the gas bill arrived and he had to kneel at the twelfth-century abbot's altar to pray for a way to pay it. This is a common enough experience among the restore-a-wreck brigade, especially those who have branched out into the 'punter trade' to pay the bills or for the next phase of works. By the way, a 'phased' restoration means 'we ran out of money' before we could continue.

My friend Caroline Lowsley-Williams runs Chavenage in Gloucestershire, which is used by the BBC as the Poldark family house of Trenwith. She only half jokes that she'd like to spend less time looking for two-for-one deals on Tesco brand loo paper. 'Can't I just have Andrex for once?'

My financial situation became even more precarious in the late summer of 2009 when a consortium, led by American private equity house Nectar Capital (run by Scott Rudmann), bought *Spear's* before it was sold off at auction by the Bedford Row liquidators. I now owned the majority stake again but that meant even less money was available for George Spencer hand-blocked wallpaper. If I ever got to that stage of the restoration.

Still, one has to start somewhere. I couldn't keep living in the Coach House. German scholars use the expression '*Ruinenlust*' (or 'Ruin Lust', as Tate Britain titled their 2014 exhibition on the subject) to describe people who are swept up in the mournful euphoria of broken old ruins and buildings, fantasising about restoration and re-creation; the romantic English quest for houses whose walls, stones and bricks are still alive with their original soul of place, or what the classical poets called *genius loci*.

In the process of restoration, we hope to restore not just the stones of the past but often also something (both creative and almost spiritual) within ourselves. So we buy (or try to buy) property we can't afford, property we don't need, property we have no real modern use for. Property we can't afford to keep up, even if we do somehow pull off the renovation miracle (if divorce or bankruptcy doesn't get the deeds first). What a property is really worth is not the guide price of an estate agent or the online guesswork of a Zoopla search but something much harder to value: how much the place is worth to ourselves and our family, to whom the mortar of memory is encrusted.

In *Sissinghurst*, Adam Nicolson's 'unfinished' biography of his family home in Kent, which his grandmother Vita Sackville-West had bought as a wreck in 1930, he writes that 'the broken romanticism of its condition was one of the things that drew her here'. Harold Nicolson, her husband, had considered it 'big, broken down and sodden' and had doubts. But Vita – who was paying the £12,375 for the estate – had her way. 'I fell in love; love at first sight; I saw what might be made of it. It was Sleeping Beauty's castle; but a castle running away into sordidness and squalor; a garden crying out for rescue.'

The Gatehouse at Upton Cressett has been compared to the Tower at Sissinghurst, which was built around the same time with similar ambitions. Both are almost perfect expressions of the English Renaissance architectural spirit, embodying a sense of place whose melancholy brick music somehow survived the decay, farm use and ivy-clad ruinations of time.

That is certainly what my parents heard in 1970 when they saw the broken twisted chimneys and scarred sixteenth-century diaper work. For my parents, restoring Upton Cressett wasn't just about leaving north London and finding a new family home in the country to raise me, my brother and sister. It became a forty-year quest to reconsecrate Upton Cressett's spirit of place after the vandalism of the post-war years when much of its original panelling was ripped out and studded oak doors stolen.

One source of much regret in my parents' phase of restoration in the 1970s and 1980s was over the fate of the 'lost' Cressett family brass. Its removal in 1959 by the Hereford diocese was a source of much sadness to my mother, in particular as it showed the Cressett family together at prayer.

My parents regarded their forty years of restoration work as incomplete until the beautiful Cressett Brass had been fixed again to its rightful place in the Cressett family chapel. Their wish to return the memorial brass was an ongoing drama. I only realised on taking over the house myself that its return was a symbol of what most restoration projects are really about – a restoration of spirit and the natural order.

IV

13

Searching for Rex

Phase two began with my housekeeper Kathy stripping my mother's blue Tudor Grotesque wallpaper (printed by Cole & Son in the 1970s) in our one and only large guest bathroom. On her second day, we made a dramatic discovery behind the walls – large areas of magnificent, brightly coloured sixteenth-century murals.

All works had to stop immediately. This discovery of vibrant and rare extant Elizabethan murals – the most vivid being a dapper Sir Francis Drake figure in armour slashing away with a sword in an Arden-like forest background – was the equivalent of funding an expensive movie on location, then having to pay the entire crew every day while the star lay in bed with 'flu. The murals had probably been hurriedly covered with limewash when Cromwell banned churches and private houses from displaying walls with rich and symbolic decoration.

This was all going to hold up the works, bankrupt me – when I needed funds for my divorce – and would probably mean that one of my guest bedrooms would resemble the Pizza Express off Oxford High Street; it is famous for having the 'Golden Cross Grotesque' preserved behind a glass wall of what used to be the Cross Inn, set in its own medieval courtyard.

The fragmented images in the north-east wing of the main house contained elaborate black-and-white *antickework*, as well as strikingly clear blue-and-white battle scenes, hunting scenes, naval scenes, with other grotesques and multi-vines that bizarrely bore a resemblance to the torn 1970s wallpaper on top. At the time, my mother had no idea that real Tudor murals lay under the wallpaper.

My uncle, Mark Roberts, was sent for from his Nottinghamshire studio on the historic Welbeck estate. He was one of Britain's leading art conservationists, having begun his career as one of the *angeli del fango*, 'mud angels', rescuing and restoring frescoes and paintings in the Florence flood of November 1966. The only good thing to have come from the flood – the worst in the city's history since 1557 – was that it led to pioneering new methods of fresco conservation and restoration, and my uncle's career was born. He went on to restore Old Masters, from Titian to Stubbs, working for major museums and collectors.

After studying the wall paintings, Mark declared them the work of sixteenth-century artisan muralists who painted generic scenes, typically of hunting and battles, usually in tempera with only a few colours. The dry pigments were then 'tempered' with a binding glue, which might have been made from eggs.

'You need to think of these murals like we do wallpaper today,' he said, as he shone a torch on the work. 'After a while they got filthy from smoke and grime and were just painted over.' Tempera fresco painters, Mark added, were not to be confused with the 'painter stainers', who belonged to a different guild. Such murals were very common in grand Elizabethan houses, but most examples have been lost. 'So these are very rare and will invite curiosity,' Mark said, as he sipped a glass of wine after his inspection. 'I suggest you cover the fragments quickly with dry plaster board and wallpaper over. They can be restored later.'

Instead of restoring a jigsaw of old mural fragments in a family bathroom, I decided to find my own neo-Elizabethan muralist. A master alchemist in the mixing of casein distemper paints and somebody who could give Upton Cressett its Tudor Revival, using casein cartouches and decorative friezes to cover the walls and ceilings in a cathedral of Elizabethan colour, gilt and my own private love secrets.

But where to find the right muralist to make the house come alive again, with a riot of rich colour? The painting of decorative walls, ceilings and Great Staircases was a lost art.

My inspiration for the role of 'house artist' was the pre-war muralist Rex Whistler, whose work I had first seen at Port Lympne House in Kent, built by the 1920s politician and society host Sir Philip Sassoon. While touring the dilapidated building in 2006 with casino manager James Osborne, who had lived there, I had been seduced by the Augustinian brilliance of Whistler's Tent Room mural painted in the 1920s.

My introduction to Whistler led me to his more famous 1939 mural for the sixth Marquess of Anglesey's family at their home, Plas Newydd, on the coast of Anglesey in North Wales. This magisterial Claudian fantasia is as golden and elegantly crafted as a Scott Fitzgerald novella. Whistler takes scenes and vignettes from the Anglesey family history and mixes them into his own romantic autobiography. The first marquess had been a hero at Waterloo in 1815, where he was second-in-command to Wellington and had his leg blown off. Whistler interweaves past and present to create an Arcadian Golden Age fable – set in a Venetian-style lagoon – that is also something deeper and more unexpected, a lyrical study of an artist's own romantic tide drifting out towards the horizon.

The mural – at fifty-eight feet long – lays a strong claim to being Britain's longest unrequited-love canvas. Whistler painted the mural when he was in his early thirties and deeply in love with Lord Anglesey's beautiful eldest daughter Lady Caroline Paget – sister of Rex's friend Henry – who was often staying at the house when he was working on the mural. But even though he painted an arresting nude of Caroline, his love for the elusive sister of his friend was not reciprocated. His letters suggest she tortured him.

On the left-hand side of the mural there is a self-portrait of Whistler dressed as a gardener and carrying a broom. But he is brushing away not autumn leaves but rose petals; the entire mural is a metaphor for the sweeping away of his romantic hope for an aristocratic beauty, who was out of his reach.

Whistler knew his love for Caroline was doomed; the letters show she regularly 'chucked' him, having agreed to a dinner or other date as he was finishing the mural in the winter of 1937/8. In 1939, he was sent to train as a tank commander in the Welsh Guards. He painted a half-smoked, burning cigarette on a step close to Caroline's fawn pug and told the family he planned to come back and finish the cigarette after the war.

He never returned. His unit wasn't sent to France until 1944. On its first day of active service in Normandy, on 18 July 1944, Whistler's Cromwell tank was caught up in some broken telephone wire and he was blown up by a mortar. Later, Evelyn Waugh used Rex Whistler (who had designed a book cover for him) as a model for the artist-soldier Charles Ryder in *Brideshead Revisited*. He was killed just five days after my grandfather, within a few miles of each other. Both had been educated at Haileybury School.

I needed to find my own Rex Whistler.

Fortunately, I knew the very man – my friend Adam Dant, winner of the Jerwood Prize of 2012 and, like Whistler, an artist whose intellectual and imaginative energy was inspired by the Hogarthian spirit of the eighteenth century. The *Guardian* described Adam as nothing less than the Hogarth of our age when I sponsored an exhibition of work he had done for *Spear's*, satirising the New Golden

Age of London's financial world in a show called *The Triumph of Debt (Observations on the Credit Crunch)*.

The November 2008 exhibition was co-hosted by Dutch art dealer Helen Macintyre at her Duke Street gallery in St James's. She had a cosy office on the top floor and shared a chartreuse-green velvet upholstered dining room on another floor with gallery owner turned *Celebrity MasterChef* winner Derek Johns. Helen, known as 'Miss Maastricht' at The European Fine Art Fair (TEFAF) in the Netherlands, exuded 1950s Parisian glamour and spoke several languages. She could be found sitting at a table outside Franco's restaurant in Jermyn Street, dressed in Dior, with a cigarette in hand and her two dachshunds – Monty and Carlo – snuggled on her lap inside a dark fur coat.

Helen was way out of my league as a potential girlfriend (she had a very rich Canadian property-developer boyfriend, Pierre Rolin, who flew her around on a private jet) but was a good friend and confidante. She had a sharp dealer's eye, was sceptical of the real 'value' of much overpriced abstract contemporary art and shared my enthusiasm for Dant's work. She saw him in the tradition of great British eighteenth-century draughtsmen, like Rowlandson.

All I knew about her private life when I first met her was that she was friends with people like Andrew Neil and close to Mayor Boris Johnson (for whom she was unpaid 'art adviser' at City Hall) and lived in a large townhouse in Belgravia, with a chef, butler and chauffeur. She had won her car – a mint-green Mini Cooper S convertible, with a private numberplate, that she kept garaged at the Cavendish Hotel – in a raffle. She lived a strange life; when she once invited me to dinner at her house – Pierre was nowhere to be seen – the butler wore white gloves and a rare vintage Château d'Yquem was served with foie gras. We sat about fourteen feet apart at opposite ends of an enormous polished mahogany dining-table. Before dinner, she had asked me to choose some wine.

'Help yourself to some from the rack,' she had said. 'I'm not drinking'. This was unusual.

When I bent down to grab a bottle I noted her kitchen rack did not contain the usual Waitrose or Tesco finest. It was piled with dusty £500 bottles of Latour, Pétrus and the like. She was an enigma, wrapped in mink, and belonged in a Thackeray novel.

Then I got a call from her and Helen said she wanted to meet me at The Wolseley on Piccadilly for a drink. I sensed it was urgent. We told each other everything. She had that effect.

'I'm pregnant,' she said. The baby was due in November.

'Congratulations,' I said.

'It's not straightfoward,' she said. I sensed she wanted to tell me something.

'Pierre's like a nomad,' she continued. 'I was on my own so much of the time. However glamorous the planes, the yachts and the holidays sounded, I was pretty lonely as he was hardly around. He rented a yacht in the South of France for two weeks last summer and I found myself sitting on deck most of the time with just the captain and crew. It was so boring I had to ship my mother and stepfather over to keep me company. Something wasn't right. I couldn't work out how my life had ended up like this. And then I got pregnant.'

Adam and I had become close friends after he had done every *Spear's* cover for me since our first issue in May 2006. I knew that he was a virtuoso illustrative artist of the same brilliance as Rex Whistler. His work was bought by the V&A, the Metropolitan Museum in New York, and some of the world's top collectors, including HRH The Prince of Wales.

Was he up for becoming Upton Cressett's house muralist?

'Oh, yes,' he replied. 'I began my career as a fresco artist when I was studying at the British School in Rome and frescoed the entire ceiling and walls of my big bedroom there. The director was shocked when he walked in and saw it. I think they had it painted over as soon as I left, which I thought was a bit foolish. The inspiration was Doria Pamphili; and the paintings in the Villa Borghese – very different from Elizabethan painted ceilings.'

This was encouraging.

What about William Morris? Did Adam identify himself with John Ruskin's notion of the self-sufficient artisan craftsman?

'You could say I'm some sort of disciple,' he said. 'I'm very aware of his designs and his writings, and also the domestic nature of his work. I will try to invoke the same spirit at Upton Cressett.' It turned out Adam had participated in an exhibition of his work at William Morris's house in London. He had even read – or at least started – Morris's *News from Nowhere*, his Utopian novel about retreating to a rural idyll to live and create artisan craftsman art.

So, I was hiring a Morris champion. Adam added that, like Morris, what attracted him to taking on the Upton Cressett commission was that he was 'updating' and re-interpreting the Elizabethan art in the house. 'I'm going to be drawing on William Morris, the traditions of Tudor domestic painting and even twentieth-century Rococo revival stylists, like Rex Whistler himself. It's a commission for an English country house, isn't it, which has evolved over hundreds of years? So you get to dip in and out of various aspects of English history. That's the fun part.'

Although Adam would be using techniques of medieval gilding, and was going shopping for dozens of packets of gold leaf from Stuart Stevenson's gilding shop on the Clerkenwell Road before he arrived to start on 14 January, he stressed that the new work would not be to a grand scheme. 'It will very much be about the workaday decorative techniques of the Tudors. The mural your housekeeper discovered was not designed for a royal palace.'

To get him started, I had first commissioned Adam to make a large ink drawing to hang in the Great Hall dining room called *Upton Cressett: Time Present and Time Past*. This was to feature the

Hall and Gatehouse populated with a figurative gallery of the house's reputed historic visitors and owners enjoying themselves in the house and grounds in their respective period costumes. The list included Edward V (the Prince in the Tower), Prince Rupert and the Thatchers walking through the Gatehouse arch, a medley of peacocks, family dogs, my parents in the garden, my brother Sam, sister Laetitia and then myself standing in front of the house holding a cricket bat.

My exes were also to feature. In a nod to Whistler's autobiographical weaving of his ill-fated romantic relationship in the Plas Newydd dining room canvas, I asked Adam to include 'the chatelaines who got away' – my two ex-wives – in his architectural tapestry of time present and time past. The head of Vanessa's horse Noblesse had been drawn bizarrely under our family crest.

'It is important to get the look on Vanessa's face right,' I wrote to Adam on 31 December. 'I want it to have an almost Pre-Raphaelite feel – the dream that got away; the dream that is part death and part life. Needs to be beautiful . . . One for the art critics to mull over – is she coming back or galloping off?'

The drawing was almost finished by the first week in January when Adam and his family came to stay for a few days. On 4 January, Adam emailed to say he hoped to have the picture finished shortly and would then be sending it to his framers. After that it would be impossible to add anything into the picture.

A few days later I rang him. 'Would it be too late to add another figure?' I asked.

'It's a bit late for changes,' Adam said. 'Are they important? I've included everyone on your original cast list.'

'It's my new girlfriend,' I said.

'Oh,' he said. 'How new?'

'A month or so.'

'And you want her in the picture? Are you sure?'

'I'm in love again,' I said. 'It's serious, Adam.'

'Well, if you insist. What's her name?'

'Laura.'

'Send me some photos of her overnight and I'll work her into the picture. Let me think now . . . I'm presently drawing you on the front lawn. How about if I draw her sitting on the Gatehouse wall as the recipient of your gaze?'

'Give it a go,' I said. 'I'd hate for her not to be in the drawing.'

'I'll delay finishing for a few days,' he said. 'If I'm going to include Laura it might be an idea if you can bring her to the studio. We can't have her disappointed. But for God's sake, William, *slow down* . . .'

14

Gainsborough Glance

By January 2010, I was in love again. I had my former *Spear's* CEO Alan O'Sullivan to thank, an Irishman who ran various royal polo events and magazines. If Alan hadn't been owed a considerable sum of money by a restaurant owner for some unpaid advertising, I might never have met Laura.

'The guy is paying me in Italian dinners,' said Alan down the phone. 'He's just opened up a new restaurant in Belgravia.'

It wasn't an invitation to refuse. It was October 2009.

Our table of eight was there to provide some social decoration and padding to the elegant room in the first few critical weeks of its opening. I was seated next to Laura. She was a close friend of Alan's 'executive assistant' (read party organiser, fixer and PR) called Emma Wigan, who had previously worked for me at *Spear's* before we had bought the company back from the administrators.

'I know all about you,' Laura had said, as she turned to me.

The first thing I noticed about her was that she had such classical features – the pale cream complexion and slightly rouged English beauty of a Gainsborough portrait. As she glanced at the menu – as if she already knew what she was going to order – she sat up straight like one of his eighteenth-century society beauties in the National Gallery. Her essence belonged to a more formal age. She would have heard about me from Emma, known as 'Wigs'.

'What mischief has Wigs been telling you then?' I said, trying to keep things light. Wigs knew pretty much everything as she had been my assistant until Alan had poached her.

'Nothing through Emma,' Laura said. 'Aren't you the guy who keeps coming into George Spencer and buying our wallpaper and fabrics for a house in Shropshire that your decorator says is still a work-in-progress?'

'How do you know *that*?'

'I work at George Spencer,' she said. 'Downstairs. I'm the girl who sends you your invoices.'

'Ah, yes . . . to Money Pit Manor.'

Laura laughed. I was referring to an article I had written about my credit-crunch struggles to restore Upton Cressett while married to Vanessa.

'Yes, everyone in the office saw that article. Dudley thought it was hilarious.'

'Why did he have an enormous bandage across his nose when I first met him?'

'Dudley fell off his bicycle,' she replied. 'He ended up in the A&E.'

At that point the waiter asked for our order.

'Veal Milanese with fries,' said Laura. I ordered the same. It was her favourite dish.

Is it possible to fall in love because of a voice? That first dinner had been enough. The moment I turned towards Laura, trying to think of something to say, I was blinded by her natural style, charm and laughter. What I most remember was her Georgian crystal voice . . .

or was it more vintage Lalique? It was like sea-music (Norfolk coast, as it turned out). From the first second of hearing Laura, and seeing her profile, I was smitten. I was captivated by her beauty and spirit of life.

But would she have dinner with me?

I was only too aware that the Cash stock had taken a bruising since my second marriage had failed. But as I sat captivated by Laura – her topaz eyes shining brightly – a voice inside mocked me for daring to imagine that I could persuade such a twenty-six-year-old beauty even to have a drink with me, a financial publisher, past his prime, going through his second divorce.

I didn't ask for her number. A week or so later I saw her again, however, with a group of her friends, including Wigs, at Nikita's Russian restaurant off the Fulham Road. Alan had organised it and texted me to come along after dinner; the Belgian royal family were having a late-night karaoke party. Sounded fun.

The evening at Nikita's ended badly after Alan's group started doing vodka shots from an ice sculpture on the table – something I have never been able to do, even at university when I could never get through a 'bumper' dinner without having to run out towards the Gents. But I was chasing a London beauty who had many admirers. I was meant to be worldly. I had to go for it when handed the half-full tumbler. As the vodka hit my throat, I knew I was in trouble. Was there a pot plant at hand? An ice bucket?

I had a millisecond to find my target – an invitingly half-open Hermès Birkin bag hanging off the back of a chair on the table behind me. Fortunately, everyone was having a rollicking time and didn't see me swivel around. Apart from Laura.

'I can't believe you've just been sick into that woman's bag,' she whispered in my ear.

I couldn't quite believe it either. 'I think it's time to leave,' I said.

'Vom and run?' said Laura.

'Yes,' I said cravenly. 'I've got form.'

Not long after that night, we had our first dinner and, by November, I had taken her to the theatre, Annabel's and even the Elton John Winter Ball. Eventually, we drove up to Shropshire to spend our first weekend away together. I was still living in the Coach House but at least the building works were now under way.

When I told Laura that I would be moving in to the Big House within six months, I really believed it.

Map of the Heart

Before Adam worked Laura into his picture, I sent him a few photos in which she was wearing a red military-style tunic and had her dark hair up in a bun. She was smiling at me in the foggy grounds of Wenlock Abbey ruins, which we had visited one weekend before a fireside pub lunch at the Talbot in Much Wenlock. She had been to stay in November and December while I was living in the Coach House. Laura had cooked a roast chicken one night for my father as my mother was away.

'Bad pictures, but they'll have to do,' I told Adam. 'Make it subtle,' I added. 'I don't want Laura thinking I'm moving too fast – she's only twenty-six.'

'Ah.'

But things were warming up, despite the thick snow that had fallen in both London and Shropshire making travel almost impossible. On 6 January, Laura wrote to me after I had taken her to the theatre the night before: 'I wish you had given me the keys to your flat this morning as I could have snuck into your house and cooked us some dinner . . . ohhh . . . next time.' She also wanted to know what my middle initials, RP, stood for, and if anybody had shown up to the *Spear's* offices despite the snow.

The 'new offices' were my Holland Road flat where I had moved the entire team into the double reception room while I raised investment finance and looked for new premises. I wrote a note to Laura, saying: 'Loved seeing you last night. Can't wait to take you to the theatre again. Unbelievably everybody turned up to work but it's a bloody battle here, I can tell you.' By the 'bloody battle' I meant the company's survival if we didn't raise significant investment funds – fast.

One person had chosen not to make the transition from our (now seized and padlocked) offices in Chelsea to my Holland Road flat: my head of sales Wendy, a feisty Greek in her mid-fifties who was no stranger to the company of cosmetic surgeons (I noted the magazine began appearing with various beauty enhancement ads). As the vultures had circled over *Spear's*, she had defected to a rival firm. In many ways I was relieved. She had an annoying habit of coming into the offices at four in the morning and rifling through people's desks looking for invitations to parties. She would then invite herself. She also used to intercept the office mailbag and sort it, looking for envelopes that contained such. She was in search of a wealthy husband ('I'm looking for a rich teddy bear. Age and looks don't matter.')

I had been in the country to see how the Upton Cressett works were progressing. On 11 January, the day I was meant to be taking Laura to Adam's Shoreditch studio, I had opened my Coach House door to find two feet of snow piled outside. Normally, I loved being snowed in but not when I had a date in London with Laura.

That morning, Darren and I spent two hours digging out the snow and putting down grit. The delivery van with the specialist casein paints for Adam had to drop off the delivery with a local farmer. I wrote to Laura: 'Darren had to walk with the brushes and paint all the way from Meadowley Hill – about two miles!' Laura replied: 'I like Darren's dedication to his job but I hope it doesn't mean you can't get out.'

In the end, I walked to the end of the two-mile lane in my snow boots and took a taxi from the local pub to the station. By 6.30 p.m. on 11 January, the Upton Cressett picture was finished. After Laura arrived at 7.00 p.m., Adam unveiled the drawing in his studio, depicting her waving at me from the Gatehouse wall. He had portrayed her wearing the red tunic coat that she had worn on our visit to Wenlock Abbey. We opened a bottle of wine and Adam began to talk.

'This used to be a sweet shop and, before that, a minicab office,' he said. 'I like the studio because it's cheap and just fifty yards from my home.'

Laura laughed. It was a real Dickensian artist's studio and she seemed to enjoy its eccentric bohemian spirit.

'The artist's studio is what lies behind all great art,' said Adam. 'I like to think of it as the captain's map room on the *Golden Hinde*. Still, I mustn't get too attached as my landlady wants to sell to a developer.' He explained he had bought the concrete-splattered oak floorboards from two unlikely-looking Irish labourers, who had wandered into a Mayfair gallery he had once worked in. 'They were nineteenth-century and had been ripped out of a bank that these builders were turning into a Bond Street handbag boutique.'

The studio comprised a Belfast sink, a bath, a Calor Gas-fired kitchen, various salvaged features and a parquet floor that had been rescued from a skip. 'See the piece of Japanese rough silk covering that chest?' said Adam. 'I rescued it from my gallery's rubbish bin after the head of watercolours spilled coffee all over it.'

'I love it,' said Laura. 'It's always been my dream to have a studio of my own.'

'Do you think the right studio really makes a difference to your art?' I said, as I examined the wonderful large drawing of Upton Cressett that was standing on a huge easel.

'It must never be too comfortable,' said Adam. 'Give me a dream studio and I'll never make another decent drawing. When Picasso painted his chilly Blue Period paintings, it was so cold most of the studio chairs were thrown on the fire. I promise not to do that.'

'I'll make sure Darren keeps the fires going for you,' I said.

He had just been out for a drink with his friend Alistair Brotchie, the chief set painter who had decorated the Globe Theatre and was the backcloth painter at Drury Lane. Alistair had lent him his library.

'He's sorting me out with sixteenth-century recipes for mixing casein paints and other techniques,' said Adam. 'The Egyptians were the first to skim milk solids with child's piss, which is really ammonium, and that sets the process off. It dries very solid. But it's water-based so you can add any pigment you want – like pig's blood.'

His studio was certainly not a bustling human factory of assistants and mass production, in the manner of Andy Warhol or Damien Hirst. The space was sparsely furnished with a plain wooden desk, rickety old chair, electric fire, strange William Morris scarlet wallpaper on the ceiling and a wooden ladder leading up to an attic. Rare books on eighteenth- and nineteenth-century architecture, borrowed from the London Library, were piled on a desk in a corner. The studio had the feel of an unheated eighteenth-century tailor's cutting room, the type of place one could imagine a young Blake or Hogarth renting.

'Shakespeare wrote his plays close to here,' Adam added. 'His theatre at New Inn Yard is now a multi-storey car park.'

Adam believed that the fabric and energy of a building, beyond its 'physical history', had an 'eternal' element that allowed travel through time.

'So buildings live on?' Laura said.

'Yes, as will this studio after it is bulldozed,' said Adam. 'Our streets and buildings are always being dug up and reordered. But as long as we live, they exist in whatever form we care to imagine them.'

'A map of the heart?' I said as I looked closely at the Upton Cressett drawing on his easel.

Vanessa was writing on a note-pad under a hammock tree close to St Michael's church. Ilaria was some way off in the distance, reading Graham Greene poems under Boscobel's Royal Oak tree. As Adam had said, Laura had been woven in and was waving happily at me, sitting on a brick wall on the Gatehouse lawn with my parents, dogs and peacocks behind her.

'So, Laura, do you approve of the drawing?' asked Adam.

'Oh, yes!' she said.

The next day, 12 January, Laura wrote that she had to go home to Norfolk for the weekend as she was having her portrait painted by her artist cousin. 'Better get it out of the way, then you can have me the other weekends . . . I have been thinking of you all day.' We had been seeing each other for around a month and I was incredibly happy.

The Girl Stays in the Picture

Adam Dant was to spend nearly ten years painting his series of murals at Upton Cressett. He usually stayed in the Gatehouse and went about his work in all conditions. Before he started, I was told to order a supply of Farrow & Ball casein distemper in Strong White; F&B strainers in 100ml tins in black, raw umber, yellow ochre, burnt sienna, red oxide, lime yellow, blue and red; a box of flat brushes (six-inch, four-inch, three-inch and one-inch); and protective gloves for handling the paints.

'And rags,' said Adam. 'Old, frayed cotton shirts work well. Preferably from Jermyn Street, a hundred per cent English cotton.'

His first mural scheme – a painted gilded ceiling for the Great Hall dining room – was begun on 14 January 2010 and took him several months. The use of lime plaster in the fabric of the interior at Upton Cressett meant that he had to use 'sympathetic painting materials' and employ Tudor techniques – non-porous modern paints were 'useless' for application on the breathable lime plaster.

By way of studio assistants, Adam had Darren – gardener and handyman – to hold the wobbly ladder, make him coffee, carry trestle boards around and drive him to town if necessary. Darren's friend Nathan was also around most days – if he wasn't fishing or shooting rabbits. I had hired him to clean all the house panelling (mired with centuries of dirt) with soapy water, then treat them with Sheraton beeswax polish. Kathy ensured Adam was provided with daily lunch and other meals if I wasn't there. Adam was working *in situ*, often on his back, in freezing conditions as the main house did not have any working central heating at this point. We used log fires and Calor Gas heaters.

The use of casein paints allowed Adam to work in a more fluid and intuitive fashion. The only trouble was that they stank of ammonia and had to be hidden in the attic or the old dairy whenever Adam returned to London to see his family. On one occasion when he was away, Nathan rushed up to me in the kitchen and said, 'There's a dead rat in the attic, I think – there's just such a vile smell. It's spreading all over the house. Shall I call my rat-catcher mate?'

When he dragged me up to inspect the smell, I noticed that Adam's paints were sitting just inside the old attic stairs. 'It's not a dead rat, Nathan,' I said. 'It's Adam's paints. Why don't you remove them to the barn?'

It was typical of the Upton Cressett restoration project that the mural paintings came before the major building work was finished. But at least other work was now going on around Adam. My carpenter, Martin, was busy with the joinery, which included laying down in the Gatehouse oak floorboards reclaimed from historic Compton Verney in Warwickshire. I had found a huge stash of them at Ditton Priors Reclamation after a tip-off from project manager (and racehorse trainer) Belinda, who lived close by.

I was now managing the restoration myself. With funds severely stretched because of my divorce and also having to pump money into keeping *Spear's* going, I had to pay my final bill to Belinda with surplus oak panelling.

In preparing for his mural scheme, Adam consulted the libraries and collections of the Victoria and Albert Museum, the Geffrye Museum and various wall paintings. This included a trip to Knole in

Kent to draw the murals on the Great Stair, where he had to 'sketch' as they refused to let him take photographs. Other sources included murals in the Tower of London and Homerton Hall in Cambridge.

The painting scheme in the dining room ceiling features an alternating red-and-blue tracery design adapted from Kentish Tudor wall painting and imitates a coffered ceiling with timber lattice. Each coffer design incorporates 24-carat gold leaf.

'The Tudor decorators would most likely have executed their design freehand,' he explained. 'The work wasn't polished like in the age of Pugin. If somebody important was coming to stay, they might cover it and paint new designs to make it look fresh and vibrant. Smoke had a way of layering the walls with sooty grime.'

One can buy medieval earth pigment paint at Cornelissen's, a specialist artists' supplier in London. 'The Tudors had a limited palette as they didn't have modern Dulux paint-mixing machines. So, no purples. But they loved bright colours, which was similar to the medieval age they identified with. They used earth colours, often botanical colours. They had blood red and a woad-like blue.'

One difference, however, was the background music. While painting, Adam generally liked to listen to Radio 3, which also suited Martin Reidy just fine. Although not a member of the SPAB, Martin might have been as his instincts were to repair whenever possible ('I don't do fast' was one of his catchphrases). It came as no surprise to me that Adam and Martin's musical tastes were aligned. I'd often hear some Gregorian chant or plainsong emanating from the paint-splattered Sony radio that Adam would have turned on. He often painted just from the light of a single halogen bulb hanging from a beam.

But Darren and Nathan could not be in the same room as any medieval music.

'It is very strange,' said Adam, at dinner one night. 'If Nathan and Darren walk in when there is a canticle or some early music playing on the radio, they put their fingers in their ears and leave the room. It's as if it was a form of cruel and unusual torture.'

Still, Nathan recognised that Adam was a famous artist and he wasn't going to waste an opportunity to benefit from their working association in those freezing winter months when Adam was often alone in the house, *sans* car or much to do in the evening.

'Nathan has been trying to befriend me,' said Adam one night.

'He asked you out to the pub?'

'No – he asked me if I wanted to go lamping one evening.'

'You mean shooting rabbits in the headlights of Darren's car?'

'Yes. I declined the offer. But you know what he asked me next?'

'To go fishing on the Severn?'

'No. He asked if I could design a large tattoo he wanted on his body!'

'In Grotesquework? Or more of the "Nathan loves Sally" variety?'

'I'm not sure there is a Sally,' said Adam. 'I think he wanted a pike along his spine.'

'A pike? Like a medieval weapon?' I said.

'No – he wanted his back decorated with a two-foot-long freshwater pike with a pointed snout and teeth to match.'

As Adam Dant painted for hours in the early weeks of January, he kept me informed via pictures on his iPhone of how he was proceeding with his Cressett mural opus. Upton Cressett's walls and ceilings were starting to rub their eyes after a four-hundred-year sleep and awaken to rich, bold Elizabethan colours. He even sent me an email with a photo of Darren up a ladder with a paintbrush, entitled 'Follower of Dant'.

On Friday, 21 January, I had lunch with Alan O'Sullivan at Rules restaurant in Covent Garden. I wanted to thank him for introducing me to Laura. I only ever went to Rules when I had something to celebrate. It had been Graham Greene's favourite restaurant and was where he had first taken Catherine Walston to lunch in 1949.

'I must bring Laura here,' I said. 'She loves anywhere that's still back in the 1950s.'

'I'd never thought of you and Laura as a love match when I first sat you together,' Alan said, across the starched white tablecloth. 'But the more I see you together, the more I think it really works. She's very aesthetic and creative and likes a party as we all do. Similar friends and family backgrounds. But she's really a country girl from Norfolk who likes her pugs. I could see her liking Shropshire. How long have you been seeing her?'

'Five weeks. I saw her yesterday.'

'You proposed to both your previous wives after six.'

'Don't remind me, I know. But I'm not even thinking of that yet.'

'My advice is to play it cool. Take her away on a nice holiday. But don't rush in like a maniac and scare her. Don't pressure her. She's only twenty-six.'

'You're right.'

I was in London that Saturday as I was going to my cousin Isabella's wedding at the Brompton Oratory. I emailed her: 'Dearest Laura, I would love to see you tonight after my family wedding – let's drive to Shropshire in the morning. I can't wait to see what Adam has done in the dining room and I want to go for a long walk on Wenlock Edge. I send you my love this rainy morning from Holland Park . . . xx.'

I changed for the wedding and kept checking my phone to hear back from Laura. During the wedding, I prayed feverishly that Laura would drive up to Shropshire with me. It wasn't until the middle of the wedding dinner at around 9 p.m. that I heard back. She was having a drink with a friend called Zita at a bar off Ladbroke Grove called Montgomery's. Did I want to join them at 10.30 p.m?

Almost as soon as I arrived at the bar, her friend left. I ordered some cocktails and it wasn't long before Laura got to the point.

'I am not sure I'm what you're looking for right now, William,' she said bluntly. 'I'm not ready to settle down with anybody. I'm only twenty-six.

Everything is going too fast. You proposed to your last two wives after six weeks or so and we're now in week five. That makes me nervous. I've had a lovely time with you, but I can't give you what you want right now. Sorry, but this relationship is going nowhere. I'm just not ready for the sort of relationship you seem to want.'

I was stunned. Poleaxed. Had Alan been teasing her that I was going to propose according to past form?

I was being 'chucked', to use Rex Whistler's phrase after he was left hanging by Caroline Paget.

This was a knife to the heart.

'Can you order a taxi?' Laura added calmly.

We might as well have been driving back to my Holland Road flat in an air-conditioned coffin. Not a word was spoken. I just gripped the plastic door handle and stared blankly ahead. This was a summary execution I hadn't seen coming. As the taxi turned into Addison Crescent, all I could think of was the cautionary words of my older female friend when I had found myself single again after my unwanted divorce from Ilaria: 'Girls are much better at doing "cruel and casual" than guys.' I'd forgotten about that.

I said nothing as I got out of the cab when it pulled up outside the back entrance of my flat. There were no departing words. I just slammed the black cab door shut with all the force I could manage. Had Laura's long artist's fingers been in the way . . . I could not recall ever being so angry.

I turned briefly to see the cab driving off. It was now raining, and I stood under the gloaming streetlights. I walked up my back steps and past my overgrown rear garden with its two half-dead acacias, now struck with conservation orders. The council were still refusing to acknowledge their terminal condition and allow removal. As I looked back towards those sagging, leafless, ugly trees – symbols of my own half-murdered self – I could have sworn they were sneering at me.

Minutes later, I was lying on the bed in the dark in my dank, basement crypt of a bedroom and contemplating my future. I didn't sleep that night. I left for Shropshire as dawn broke on Sunday morning. I needed to be at home. All I had to hope for was that the sight of Adam's new mural might lift my spirit.

On the Monday, I rang Adam.

'The painted ceiling looks magnificent,' I said.

He was coming back to Shropshire later that week to continue with it.

'How's Laura? A lovely girl.'

'Laura is no more,' I said abruptly. 'We've split up.'

'Oh, I'm sorry,' he said. 'You seemed so happy.' There was a pause. 'What do you want me to, er, do about her being in your picture? It's not at the framer yet. I can make some final changes.'

'What do you mean?'

'I can still remove her.'

'You mean erase her?'

'Yes. I can paint her out. Take her off the Gatehouse wall.'

'What's she doing on the wall?'

'Waving at you.'

'Keep her in,' I said. 'Laura can join the gallery of exes. Memento mori.'

Another ex, another broken dream.

15

Going Dutch

If I was ever going to find a chatelaine for Upton Cressett, I needed to move into the house. No more next-door camping. The year 2010 marked the fortieth anniversary of my family living there, which seemed a good time to kick-start the major works.

The days of phased restoration were over. If Upton Cressett was going to be called 'Money Pit Manor', I might as well start shovelling cash at it. At least I had enough to get to the end of phase two.

Another reason for my change of restoration gear was that I wanted to enter Upton Cressett for the Hudson's Heritage Awards, the Oscars of the British 'heritage tourism' world. I had twelve months to get the house finished and open for business. And whether I had a girlfriend, chatelaine, mistress or wife was irrelevant. I was single again and moving into the house was now the only thing that mattered to me.

But not for very long; about a fortnight after I had stood in the freezing rain watching the red tail-light of Laura's taxi turning right down Addison Crescent and out of my life, I was standing at the traffic lights on Brompton Cross in South Kensington. I recognised the car and the woman behind the wheel. It was the mint-green Mini Cooper S convertible of my art dealer friend Helen Macintyre.

As the car stood at the lights, I tapped on her window. It was around lunchtime.

I can't remember what I said, but it was something along the lines of 'are-you-free-for-lunch-need-to-talk'. Helen parked her Mini close by and we headed for a little restaurant on the street behind. It does not exist any more but it was close to the Coco de Mer luxury sex boutique.

I ordered a bottle of Provence rosé with lunch. I told Helen that I had split from Laura; she also had some major news. I spilled out the glass splinters of my heart to her and she did likewise.

Who knows why two people suddenly become more than friends? I had never forgotten my first meeting with Helen in the lobby of the Grosvenor House Hotel some two years before. It had been the May bank-holiday Monday before my June wedding to Vanessa and my editor at ES Magazine had wanted me to interview a Qatari 'playboy' prince, Sheikh Khaled, who was having an exhibition of his photographs – desert sunset shots with falcon hunters on horseback and so on – at a Mayfair gallery. From what I could gather, the Qatari royal family were involved, and the show was all part of the Qatari national charm offensive with the UK.

I didn't want to write what sounded like a dreary interview with a minor Arab royal and I wasn't in the best of moods to be working on the bank holiday only a week before my wedding. But contracts are contracts and I dutifully showed up at the lobby on 26 May 2008 to meet the organiser of the show – Helen.

A peculiar thing happened when Helen breezily came into the hotel lobby at 9 a.m. and introduced herself, then her mother

Wilhelmina, to me. That was a first. What was Helen's mother doing at the interview? Helen wore a cream piped Chanel suit, her bright Delft-blue eyes flashing when she said, 'Hello,' in a disarmingly frank, open way. She smelt of Dior and Silk Cut. I guessed she was early thirties; no engagement or wedding ring.

The first instant I met Helen's eyes, a fuse blew inside me. I could hear myself asking banal questions about the interview when another dialogue altogether was going on inside my head – how odd life is, I thought. I was deeply in love with Vanessa and was thrilled at the prospect of becoming her husband in a week's time. But out of nowhere – like the bowshot of an arrow from a forest – came the most irrational thought: if I wasn't engaged to Vanessa, and marrying her in a few days, I'd marry Helen, or at least try to. I know this sounds absurd but it's true. I wrote as much to Helen, some two years later, in one of my first Binder Box letters to her:

> I did believe you that evening in your kitchen. And I knew then, just
> as I did when I met you for the first time at that silly interview at the
> Grosvenor, that if I wasn't getting married the next week, I would
> try and be with you.

Of this woman in a cream Chanel suit whom I had just met in a hotel lobby, I knew precisely nothing. Although I gathered that her attractive and elegantly dressed mother – with the same piercing blue eyes – was Dutch, I had no idea her father had been a celebrated Scottish artist and writer who had died suddenly from a heart-attack when she was a teenager. Nor did I know the full details of other tragedies in her family upbringing. But I felt there was nothing unusual about my attraction to her. It seemed perfectly normal. But I was happily marrying Vanessa.

I sat opposite Helen and her mother on a Grosvenor House Hotel suite sofa, lobbing soft questions to her Middle Eastern minor royal, from his collection of pet falcons to his garage of Hummers. Still, the magnetic current I felt drawing me to Helen did not go away. This was all within less than an hour of meeting her on a wet bank-holiday Monday in late May.

But back to our lunch – nearly two years after that first meeting – in that little restaurant off Walton Street. We talked and lost all track of time as she explained how her circumstances had changed since I had visited her at London's Portland Hospital after she had given birth to her daughter Stephanie. She had been on a drip but we still managed to share a glass of champagne as she showed off her baby daughter, a pretty bundle with a shock of blonde hair the colour of wheat flax. There was no sign of Pierre, and the baby looked nothing like him.

Then, after I'd ordered a second bottle of rosé at our lunch, she dropped a mortar bomb into our conversation. 'Pierre and I have split,' she said. 'In fact, I've moved out of South Eaton Place and have taken a house in Chelsea where I'm living with Stephanie.'

'I'm sorry to hear that,' I said.

'Pierre's in trouble,' she said. 'He hasn't been around. He's always travelling. Things have been falling apart for months. He's under investigation. People were showing up to the house. Administrators were knocking on the door. I don't know exactly what's going on but Stephanie has to come first. That's all that matters.'

Helen had every right to be scared. The assets of Pierre's property business were being frozen by lawyers acting for a Middle Eastern client – his main client – wanting to know what had happened to tens of millions of pounds deposited in his property fund.

Her new house was just a hundred yards from the famous old Pheasantry building (now Pizza Express) where her father had painted some Cavalier-themed murals on the façade that exist to this day.

I felt awful for Helen. She had become involved with a man whose financial dealings were opaque, at best. In the same month that she had given birth, she had had no option but to flee her Belgravia home.

Two months later, when the story of Pierre Rolin's imploding property investment empire became the subject of a *Daily Telegraph* investigation, the headline confirmed what I had been shocked to hear. The *Telegraph* journalists did not spare any details: 'Administrators have seized £850,000 of valuable art from the home of a London property adviser, Pierre Rolin, amid claims that his collapsed firm managing $6.5bn (£4.25bn) of assets for a key Middle Eastern client had been making "unauthorised payments".'

Rolin later denied all the allegations and told the *Evening Standard* that he was working to 'resolve misunderstandings' with his former investors in the Gulf. 'We had a commercial dispute,' he said. 'We tried to resolve it, and we weren't able to resolve it. When you're hit hard, your life changes and you have to start from less than zero'.

The reversal of fortune was such that it wasn't long before a £100,000 library built by artisan designer Rupert Bevan was broken up into bits on a skip outside the house. No wonder Helen – with a tiny baby – had had to find a new home, fast. But Helen seemed to be taking the Rolin drama in her usually optimistic stride. 'Pierre was always on a plane doing deals or sitting on another charity board,' she said. 'One moment he was in New York as a trustee of New York's Museum of Contemporary Art, the next flying into the World Economic Forum in Davos.'

At the mention of Davos, Helen took a gulp of wine and looked away.

I wasn't expecting what came next.

'You know that Pierre may not be the father,' she said.

I nodded.

'Pierre is dark, like you,' I said.

'The identity of Stephanie's father cannot get out. He was calling me at the hospital'.

'Does Pierre know who it might be?'

'He has an idea.'

'How did he take it?' I asked.

'He's having a paternity test. We both knew our relationship wasn't working, in fact it was over, so it may not have come as a complete surprise.'

So long as her infant daughter and two glossy dachshunds were safe and secure – and she had a roof over her head – that was all that seemed to matter to her. She was used to dealing with whatever life threw at her. She had had a triple family tragedy – her two sisters, Enid and Stephanie, and her father, had all died within a few years of each other when she was growing up in Kent. At the time, she was one of the only girls attending St Edmund's boarding school in Canterbury. 'I was in the CCF and carried a rifle,' she told me. 'I was the only girl and was called Lance Corporal Macintyre.'

While her life collapsed around her, Helen showed steely resilience and never lost her self-deprecating and witty good humour; she had been there before. Besides, her unfortunate situation with Pierre bore no comparison with the tragedies of the past. What was a little financial wobble compared to her daughter coming into the world? As I later wrote to her: 'You have been through much worse things and just stay strong and focused . . . I love you very much and am here if you need me for anything at all, W xx.'

What I liked about Helen was her combination of optimism and intuition. You could tell her anything. Nothing surprised her. She usually had her own quirky insight into any subject – people especially, or a work of art. She also had an almost total lack of reserve or guard when it came to talking about men, love, authors, politics and sex. She loved risqué texts and louche Paris clubs and casinos. I later came to understand that this almost Scandinavian libertarianism was a Dutch thing. But at the time, I had never met anybody else of such disarming candour.

Lunch in the little restaurant off Walton Street lasted for at least two hours. I walked her to the Mini. As she stood by the car, I kissed her beside a parking meter (yes, she had a ticket). There felt nothing surprising about this. When she grabbed the ticket, she laughed and walked towards her new home, which was less than a few hundred yards away off Jubilee Green. As she waved back at me, I knew another chapter in my life was about to begin.

Seeing Helen at the Brompton Cross traffic lights and having that spontaneous lunch off Walton Street in late January 2010 had set something entirely unexpected in motion. I soon became madly in love with Helen and had some of the most extreme highs and lows of my forties because of her. That kiss at the parking bay led to dinner soon after, and it wasn't long before I was spending much of my time at Helen's cottage off the King's Road. I was happy again; the grim midnight memory of lying on my bed staring up into the ceiling of my dark bedroom – feeling like I was in a damp coffin – was forgotten.

The truth is that I had known for some time that Pierre might not necessarily be the father. But there was never any sense of dishonesty about her. She was true to herself. I remember quoting her a line at dinner from the narrator of John Le Carré's A Perfect Spy. 'Betrayal is like imagining, when the reality isn't good enough . . . Betrayal is love, as a tribute to our unlived lives.'

In my Binder Box for Helen there is a receipt for a lunch at Mark's Club in Mayfair where, back in 2003, I had had my wedding lunch after marrying Ilaria, and where I also had the wedding lunch that followed my civil marriage to Vanessa in 2008. Throughout this voyage into memory, so many of my choices for meetings and lunches were never simply random. Although I didn't think of it at the time, I'm sure taking Helen to the club where I had hosted two wedding lunches was both deliberate and symbolic; it was an attempt to erase the past and divorce my marital ghosts.

We sat down in a dark-red, velvet upholstered booth in the club's dining room and I ordered a bottle of Chablis. 'It feels so strange sitting here again with you,' I said. 'I remember sitting over there,' I pointed towards the garden area, 'after my wedding with Ilaria and saying, "This feels like sitting on an Orient Express train about to set off on a romantic journey," which was what the beginning of my marriage felt like.'

Freud said that all dreams about train journeys were either about sex or death. Twice now, my marital journey had become derailed; in Vanessa's case, almost before we had unpacked our luggage. Now Helen and I were together, I wondered how far our journey would get.

'I feel as if I'm leaving the station again,' I added, after we'd finished pudding.

Helen smiled. 'Shall we go to the terrace for a cigarette?' she said.

I didn't smoke but joined her. I can tell this Mark's Club lunch was significant in our relationship as it was long and ended with two glasses of Courvoisier on the terrace, with Helen smoking her Silk Cut. The receipt is in my Binder Box marked 'H', with her initial also circled in blue ink on one corner of the printed cream invoice. I think it may have been on the empty terrace when she dropped her 'B' bombshell.

She never moaned about how she had been let down, or how life was unfair. As she spoke about how things had ended with Pierre, it was clear that their relationship had broken down many months before the bailiffs were knocking on her front door. Although I knew rumours were circulating around London about the identity of Stephanie's real father, she had been steadfast in saying nothing to me – or to anybody else, as far as I knew.

'I never even got to see a rough cut of my wedding video to Vanessa,' I said. 'We did send out a wedding announcement card with a photo of us but that was it. I never saw a wedding present. It was over that quickly.'

'I was engaged once.'

'Who to?'

'A young Frenchman from some ancient titled family. I was in my early twenties and was too young. He opened my eyes – to Paris, its clubs, everything. But I broke it off. I wasn't ready for marriage.'

'We seem to be pulling out of the Gare du Nord,' I said. 'I'm enjoying the view.'

'This could work,' said Helen. 'I'd never thought of "us" before.'

'Did I ever tell you that the very first time I met you at the Grosvenor House Hotel, I thought, If I wasn't marrying Vanessa, I'd try to marry you?'

'Careful now.' She took a pull from her cigarette. The smoking terrace was empty. The electric heaters glowed above us in the gunmetal winter sky. After a hovering waiter left, Helen continued, 'William, I think there's something you should know. About the father of Stephanie.'

'Yes.'

'Nobody else knows other than my family. This has to stay *absolutely* between us and you cannot tell anybody.'

'No secrets then,' I said.

'It's Boris.'

'*Johnson?*'

Helen had the entire Johnson oeuvre of books – from his comic political novel *Seventy-Two Virgins* to collected journalism – on a shelf beside her bed.

'I've known him for years. I'm an art adviser to the mayor's office. He's smart and funny. One day he may even be prime minister.'

'Fuck!' I gulped. 'Do you think?'

'Knowing Boris, yes.'

'You know him. My father does. I don't. What's he really like? Did you love him?'

I hadn't wanted to use the present tense.

'I'm so torn, William. He texts me the whole time but I never know what's coming next.' I didn't ask many more details. She was always discreet. I certainly wasn't one to judge. Although initially blown over by the revelation, I quickly came to terms with what Helen had told me. In the school playground of my contemporaries, Alexander Boris de Pfeffel Johnson was probably the one person you wouldn't want as a *rivale d'amour*. Boris was two years older than me and a heavyweight champion when it came to conquests.

I felt as if I had inadvertently been pushed out into the hot glare of the Circus Maximus sand to fight against a popular and seasoned champion with a string of prize conquests notched on his leather belt. Boris was a veteran swordsman and super-hack paid £250,000 a year for one column.

While I had been relatively ancient, in my mid-thirties, when I got engaged to Ilaria, Boris had got engaged while still at Oxford in the mid-1980s to Shropshire aristocrat Allegra Mostyn-Owen. The marriage had lasted a few years before she left him for embarking on an affair with barrister Marina Wheeler, a childhood friend, and later second wife, with whom he had four children. I knew that Marina was a formidable woman who put her children above press and politics, and would not give up on her marriage easily, or at least not unless Boris refused to change and continued his 'Eastern' (as Petronella Wyatt once described them) ways when it came to women.

I was simply relieved that the father – if it wasn't Pierre – was somebody Helen wasn't seeing any more. That much was certain – at least, I sincerely prayed it was. That Boris may have been Stephanie's father didn't bother me – at least, not while his identity remained a secret. It only started to become a problem when the calls and texts and rumours started to cramp my relationship with Helen. I had no problem with Boris, who had known my family for years.

It was all too easy to see why Boris and Helen had plenty in common. Apparently they had first met many years before at the theatre in Watlington of all places. Indeed, I'm pretty sure it was for his witty writing, charisma and amusing company, rather than any political skills or views, that Helen was attracted to him. She was never that interested in world or even domestic politics. She liked the backstage; human politics behind the curtain. She found politicians – as people – interesting, but not necessarily because of their politics. Helen was more interested in the ethereal, sublime and aesthetic – the eternal – rather than the drab minutiae of select-committee politics and news.

I had nothing against Boris personally. I saw him as a hugely ambitious celebrity politician who – if he smartened up his political act – could become a Conservative Party Teflon version of Ronald Reagan, with cross-party appeal as a showman/MP. It was said in Westminster that the closer you got to Boris, the more difficult it became to like him. But I never got that close. He was certainly more intelligent than most politicians I knew, and I was also jealous of the hold he had over Helen.

I knew nothing of his marriage to Marina (whom I had met at a few parties) other than that he had previous 'form', which his wife had suffered with dignity but angry exasperation. While the tabloids would doubtless throw Boris to the lions, should he be exposed, I was fervently hoping this would never happen.

All I wanted was to be with Helen and if that meant bringing up Stephanie as my own daughter – preferably as her stepfather – then I was 100 per cent fine with that. With his Pericles-like political ambition, I thought, the likelihood of his leaving Marina was remote.

What was critical, as I told Helen's mother, was that everyone in the tight family circle who knew the truth of Stephanie's father had to be bound by a strict code of *omertà*. Nobody could talk about it – not even so much as *hint* about it. For myself, I feared being burned alive by the firestorm that would destroy anything, or anybody, within its range if the news were to break. Including my relationship with Helen.

What we couldn't control, however, was what Pierre said, especially after the results of the paternity test were known.

Within a month or so, I had pretty much moved into her house in number 16 Markham Street in Chelsea. Sixteen was her lucky number – it was also her birth date. It was the number she liked to back in a casino. *Spear's* was no longer operating out of my Holland Road flat and, until I had built the bedroom extension, I was much happier living with Helen when not at Upton Cressett where the restoration works were moving along well. Another perk of living with Helen was that Pierre had gifted her some very fine wine.

From the outset with Helen, I never made any secret of the fact that I wanted to start a family with her. If we had our own children, nobody was going to know (or care) that the eldest had a different biological father. Helen did not seem averse to this idea. She was a brilliant mother and clearly loved her new role. As Helen opened up about her unconventional life after losing her father and two sisters, I understood why she was so close to her mother, and why Wilhelmina had been at our first interview at the Grosvenor House Hotel. I always knew Helen was much stronger than me. As I wrote later:

> *There have been some moments when I have begun to understand who you are and why I have loved you more than any woman in my life – and why I will always want to marry you. . . . For all of your talk of bourgeois upbringing etc – the truth is that you are right: you have never fitted in; never really at school where you were the only girl and not at Edinburgh . . . There really is nobody who has been through as much as you and emerged on the other side with such true spirit and strength.*

After such a long wait and so much wasted time with other wives and women, I told her I felt that 'I had found somebody whose nature I loved enough in itself'.

The other good news was that as the works proceeded at Upton Cressett, Helen started to get involved with them, as the person I was hoping would – finally – be its future chatelaine. I had taken her up to Shropshire within weeks of us starting to see each other. She had a natural decorator's eye – her mother had run an antiques shop in Kent after her father's death – and was soon helping with sourcing a potential six-leg refectory table from Christie's in Amsterdam and other items for the house.

To get us started, her mother had given us a lovely set of six Delft-blue china mugs from the V&A. Instructions soon followed from Helen for buying a complete set of Fissler cooking pans (in Harrods' sale), *only* Miele dishwashers and washing machines and so on. I was happy to do anything that led to us moving in together. I introduced her to my decorator Nikki Atkinson over breakfast in London; thereafter, she was copied in on all emails regarding the house.

On 29 March, I was writing to Helen to say that I had the electrician booked in to do the 'final fix' before moving in. 'I'm buying some very sexy pewter "vestry" wall lights, which will make various rooms – including the master bedroom – seem like a fifteenth-century monastery and I already know the effect that ruined abbeys have on you . . .'

This referred to a visit we had made to Wenlock Priory, on one of Helen's earliest visits to Upton Cressett. I don't know what it is about ruined historic abbeys that make me act impulsively and trip my imagination. It wasn't just a coincidence that I had proposed to Louise in the gardens of an abbey in central France, or to Ilaria by the Royal Oak next to the ruins of White Ladies Priory.

It was a cold morning with a light crust of frost on the ground and Helen and I were the only visitors walking around the towering thirteenth-century abbey and topiary gardens. I knew them well. When my friend Mark had lived at Wenlock Abbey the yew topiary had been sculpted into the shapes of various animals. We sat on a wall behind what had once been a bird of paradise. Half of the branches were still dusted in morning frost.

In front of us was the abbey's 'Norman lavatorium', built in 1220. 'That's the communal washing area where the monks used to wash and shower naked before going to eat in the refectory,' I said.

'Must have felt cold on a day like this,' said Helen as she looked into my eyes.

The morning sun had still not fully lifted above the Chapter House and shards of sunlight were trying to break through the whitewashed clouds that bathed the picturesque scene in a mist of early-morning light. I kissed Helen. I could smell her Chanel scent on her warm neck. As she drew closer, brushing against the topiary, icy droplets of melted frost splashed against my face. In the medieval age, yew was regarded as a sacred symbol of salvation, change and transformation. I certainly felt reborn with Helen.

Helen and I learned we had something in common – ruined abbeys triggered some deep and atavistic instinct within us. I loved ruins, as I could walk away with the comforting feeling of being a survivor. The victor. While most historic houses I visited would still be standing as the stage set for future lives long after my death, ruins were different. With ruins, one felt one had the upper hand.

After only a month of seeing Helen, I was thinking of marriage. She seemed to love Upton Cressett, even if it was still mostly a building site. The only problem was that the rumours about the identity of the father refused to stop humming. After two months or so, it was decided between myself, Helen, her mother Wilhelmina and her stepfather Kerry Waite – a lawyer who was president of the Kent Law Society – that we needed to have a 'Boris Summit' and tell him of our intentions. The Boris boil had to be burst.

'You will have to meet him,' I said, 'and tell him about us.'

'Tell him what?'

'That I'm going to bring up his daughter whether people know the identity of her father or not.'

'Don't you think you should come as well?' Helen said.

'No,' I said. 'This is between you and Boris. Tell Boris that I'm in love with you and that I'm very fond of Stephanie and that I want to bring her up in Shropshire. He knows the house at least. And that within a few years or so, when we're married and have our own children, nobody is going to know that they're not all our own children. He can come up and stay at Upton Cressett whenever he wants to see Steph.'

So Helen went off – alone – to meet Boris at Brown's Hotel. As I waited at her house, I had a surreal vision of Boris becoming part of the extended Cash family, with long Sunday lunches washed down with rosé as he discussed politics with my father. Maybe he'd arrive in a bullet-proof Jaguar with a police detail. My father had also known, of course, that Boris was the father of Stephanie, but said nothing. He certainly didn't judge Boris in any way. Besides, who were we to judge? Despite being a Catholic family, my sister Laetitia (a highly qualified Oxford-educated lawyer who once appeared as the cover face of the *Sunday Times Magazine* as one of Cameron's female 'A list' candidates, photographed beside Theresa May) was a divorced mother with children by different fathers and I was twice divorced.

The 'Boris Summit' was a long meeting – worryingly so. Helen was away at least two hours. After the second hour started, I began to think I was a fool for having suggested a swanky hotel of all places for them to meet.

When Helen finally came back, she thankfully looked perfectly normal.

'Boris is fine with our plan,' she said. 'He's fine with you bringing up Stephanie.'

Boris told her he knew about Upton Cressett as he had been there. 'Biddy, I love Biddy. Will Biddy be there?'

'I told him that Bill and Biddy had converted a barn and lived next door.'

Boris thought Upton Cressett would make a perfect home for Stephanie, conveniently out of the London public glare. We were all going to be one glorious, extended happy family. I was already thinking of buying an engagement ring for Helen.

The only problem was the press; if the identity of the father got out, our plan was likely to blow up. So it simply could *not* get out. Which was why, when the rumour wires started up again in May (having started inside the *Spectator* offices many months previously), I decided to try for a High Court injunction prohibiting the disclosure of the alleged identity of the father. I took Helen to a top privacy lawyer, who sat us down at his twenty-foot-long mahogany board table in Bedford Square and went through the options.

'The problem, William,' he said, 'is that an injunction will cost you £25,000 and it will probably not be worth the paper it is written on. There may be a very strong case to be made by a newspaper that when it comes to an elected politician, in office, the public has a right to know.' This later proved to be the case in a 2013 Court of Appeal judgement.

By now Helen and Pierre had the results of the paternity test proving Pierre wasn't the father. He then began telling friends and reporters that he had been 'cuckolded' by London's mayor in a Davos hotel suite; and that he had seen a CCTV tape of Boris entering his Belgravia house when he was away on business. Pierre had also disclosed that 'his daughter' was going to have Lilian as her middle name, in honour of his mother, and that she would take the surname Rolin-Macintyre.

When Rolin finally vented his anger in an interview with the *Evening Standard*, he was unforgiving towards Boris, to whom he had given money as a Tory donor, including £80,000 towards a 400-foot-high tower for the Olympic Park. 'I think he (Boris) has no moral compass,' said Rolin. 'He thinks he is completely entitled and thinks he's above it all. I'm not on some rampage about him, but everyone is accountable . . .'

Against this background, our life often felt as if a slow-burning fuse had been lit under it.

We went away for a few weekends – to Elizabeth Hurley at her farm in Gloucestershire, to Helen's mother Wilhelmina and stepfather Kerry in Folkestone, and to Leon Max, my LA Russian fashion mogul friend, at Easton Neston, the Hawksmoor-designed stately home he owned. At lunch, with guests including Condé Nast chief Nicholas Coleridge, the subject of 'Who's the Daddy?' never seemed to go away. Helen never revealed anything.

The gossip and questioning continued wherever we went. Although Helen never disclosed the name of Stephanie's father, she was always being quizzed. Which was one reason why we flew to Jumby Bay Island, off Antigua, to celebrate her thirty-sixth birthday in late May 2010. We simply wanted to get as far as possible from the ferret run of media and political London. Wilhelmina kindly agreed to look after Stephanie for the week, along with Helen's nanny, Priscilla.

Helen had never been to Jumby Bay but had spent holidays in St Barth's and Antigua, including a New Year at a half-empty Carlisle Bay hotel where a wigless John Travolta had subjected guests to a running commentary through a screening of *Saturday Night Fever*. Her previous experience of Antigua had included a brief stay at the Sandals resort aged twenty or so, with her French 'baron' boyfriend.

'We came back to our room after the beach and found that we'd been robbed. Our money, cards – everything,' Helen told me on the plane, as we settled into our seats.

That was the final straw, and the excuse she needed to 'escape' from what she regarded as a Sandals 'holiday hell' (Helen was not an 'all-inclusive' beach holiday sort of girl) and move next door to a hotel in St John's called Coconut Grove. I found this anecdote intriguing, so one afternoon we went off-island to see if the beach-side motel where she had spent the rest of her holiday was still there. It was, and we had a few cocktails. I also learned a lesson about Helen – if she didn't like something, she would move on – or out – before you could say 'rum punch'.

On Jumby Bay we felt mercifully free from the inquisition. It was not the sort of place either of us was going to bump into anybody we knew. Until I went for a walk along the main beach at 6.30 a.m. on our first morning, only to encounter my old pal Piers Morgan with his teenage kids. He was on holiday for a week and was in the middle of negotiating his new contract with CNN to present a nightly chat show in New York.

'I can't believe we're marooned here with Piers Morgan,' I said to Helen at breakfast after our meeting. 'Just say nothing about Steph.'

When I heard about the volcanic smoke that had grounded European flights for the first time since the Second World War, and that Helen and I – and Piers Morgan – were going to be spending an extra three or four days on the island, I felt a Proustian kick of nostalgia for when I was snowed in at Upton Cressett and couldn't go back to school. I was delighted. But Helen was missing her daughter. She woke me up to say she had dreamed we had somehow arranged to travel back to London 'by train and boat via Marrakesh and Casablanca.'

What do you do in paradise when you can't leave the place? The first thing you do, of course, is throw an impromptu poolside party for those marooned on the island, which was what happened on Helen's birthday. The chefs made a delicious dark chocolate cake with her name written in white icing. In my Binder Box for Helen, there is a photo of an unshaven, tanned Piers – with a stubbly, oddly greyish beard – and Helen standing in front of him with a huge grin. Piers had come to my second wedding; I was already hoping he would come to my third.

Within a matter of hours, a guest list had been assembled, invitations photocopied and delivered by buggy, or on foot, to various villas and homes, and within a few hours half the island's residents were assembled around the bar drinking rum punch and champagne. As Helen blew out the candles, she couldn't have looked happier. I was secretly thrilled that the ash cloud had disrupted all international flights; it meant I had the extra three unexpected days with Helen on a tropical island that had no means of escape.

I had known Piers ever since we first met at the Eden Roc Hotel at the Cannes Film Festival in 1991 while stalking Madonna. We had been crouching together in the bushes outside the main entrance while he was working for the *Sun* and I was with *The Times*. Helen's birthday celebrations continued when Piers, Helen and I left the island on the ferry to Antigua for a very long lunch at Cecilia's restaurant, owned by a former muse of photographer Helmut Newton. Inevitably, Piers tried to do a grand inquisition – *Life Stories*-style – with Helen, but she never flinched. 'You will know him,' was about as far as she went. Every relentless line of questioning was met with a smile, a drag of her cigarette and 'No comment, Piers.'

16

I Liked Your Magazine
So Much . . .

It was a strange time of my life. I open the Binder Box for Helen and find a set of four black-and-white passport photos of us posing together at the Ark Gala Dinner of 13 May 2010 (at Waterloo station) hosted by French hedgie Arkie Busson and featuring the Killers on stage. In one of them, Helen rests her forehead on mine and I can see the little beauty mole on the right-hand side of her smiling mouth.

One moment I would be in a black Mercedes gliding along the Embankment towards the former Eurostar terminal at Waterloo to party with some of the richest people in the country; the next morning I would be walking in my long navy overcoat across Hyde Park to try to raise the much-needed investment to keep *Spear's* from going bust.

I was carrying some copies of the magazine and had just passed our original offices down an alleyway in Notting Hill Gate. That alleyway had been the scene of a farcical moment when Nicola Bulgari had arrived at our offices to decide whether or not he would invest in *Spear's*.

It was 9 a.m. on a wintry morning when I saw his black S-class Mercedes parking outside our alleyway. As I opened the door to welcome my father-in-law, I saw, to my horror, that a local tramp – just skulking away – had just deposited a freshly smoking turd on our doorstep. With the striding patrician figure of Nicola, vice-chairman of Bvlgari, dressed in an Anderson & Sheppard dark suit and polished Cleverley shoes, walking towards us, I shouted to my deputy editor, Sophia Money-Coutts, 'Can we please remove that huge shit on our doorstep! *Now.*'

Meanwhile, I jumped over the doorstep and blocked Nicola as the tramp's morning offering was removed. 'Before you meet the team, Nicola, shall we have a coffee first next door? An espresso?'

But the 2010 fundraising round was different. We were on the ropes. All the mortgage money I had drawn down was owed to the builders or other suppliers. I had to raise hundreds of thousands for *Spear's*, which I was pitching as Britain's answer to *Forbes*. As I pulled up the velvet collar of my trusty ankle-length overcoat, I remember passing a small coffee kiosk by the Italian fountains that was selling hot drinks to morning joggers and those walking to work. But I didn't stop for an espresso. I wasn't even taking taxis.

The presentation to my City grandees at Brown's went well. A couple of investors were very interested. In the end, I didn't need to raise any investment money. We sold the company instead to media mogul Mike Danson, who was on something of an acquisition spree. It was only when I was led by a secretary up to the waiting area of a swanky office building off Victoria Embankment, overlooking the Thames, and sat outside a huge glass boardroom that I thought I'd better Google him. I had noticed that the coffee-table bore not one copy of the *New Statesman* but a small pile of the latest issue. That was because he had recently acquired the magazine. He was a canny

Mancunian media entrepreneur and philanthropist who avoided interviews or the spotlight.

Mike, aged forty-seven in 2010, was ranked around halfway up the *Sunday Times Rich List* (in 2019, his net worth was estimated at £796 million). An Oxford-educated Manchester United fan, he founded Datamonitor in 1989 at his kitchen table, using four credit cards for £5,000 funding before securing investment from Reuters. He sold Datamonitor for £502 million to Informa in 2007, buying much of its business back for just £25 million in 2015. He was one of the earliest *Spear's* subscribers. It was a case of 'I liked the magazine so much . . .'

'We'll be partners together,' Mike had said, in his enormous glass boardroom. 'We'll build *Spear's* into a global company, with you at the helm, and we'll have the resources to roll the magazine out around the world.'

After sending me a one-line email while he was skiing, Mike soon owned 90 per cent of *Spear's* as well as the *New Statesman*.

I celebrated with Helen. I was retaining a 10 per cent stake and would remain as editor-in-chief and board member. *Spear's* was going to be the new *Forbes*, and I was going to marry Helen. At least, that was what I thought. I couldn't have been happier. I even agreed to buy a new car after she had been appalled at the age and state of my ancient (1990s) seven series BMW, whose leather seats had started to crack (her Mini was always immaculate). My *rota fortunae* – what the medieval world called the 'Wheel of Fortune' – was spinning favourably again.

Helen was as driven as if she had been an investment banker. I found her energy and fierce, fun optimism refreshing after the blows of my two divorces, which had drained me and left me half broken.

I remember once driving in her Mini past a red-brick apartment block on Draycott Place, near Sloane Square, and she pointed to a building. 'I lived in a flat there when I first moved to London. My rent was more than my salary.'

She was often on her BlackBerry under the covers in the middle of the night – with Dubai, Qatar, New York, Sydney. Having somebody typing away on their phone at 2 a.m. to do business with a client in Singapore might annoy some people, but it didn't affect me. I was in love.

Life was too short and precious to get worked up about a deal. It was only money. Her philosophy was simple: you had to know when to cut your losses and walk out. It wasn't so much about the money, or even the winning or losing. It was about moving on and not looking back. Helen lived for the spin of the wheel.

I'm not sure if Helen regarded love and relationships as a form of human roulette. She certainly had an all-or-nothing mentality at times but always tempered with good humour, win or lose. Certainly life with Helen was a roller-coaster ride; it was easy enough to see why men – many men – found her so alluring.

We didn't talk much about her previous boyfriends. With Helen, you had to take her as she was or you might get hurt. She once told me that she had been having dinner in South Kensington (at a window table) on her birthday with her last long-term boyfriend before Pierre – a property entrepreneur called Andrew – when, to her astonishment, another ex-boyfriend suddenly appeared at the window. As Helen sat frozen at her table, her ex-boyfriend produced an engagement ring, opened the box in front of her and said, or mimed through the glass, 'Will you marry me?'

That was the sort of effect Helen had on men. They could behave irrationally and impulsively. Everything was negotiable. Life was one grand auction. Whether it was a £10 million Picasso or a £10,000 drawing by Adam Dant didn't really matter. For her, the word 'impossible' didn't exist. The art world club was like a high-stakes Winner Takes All poker game and she seemed to enjoy being dealer, player and banker.

The only other rule was that appearances mattered. You couldn't expect a seat next to some of the world's top collectors in the *salon privée* of the international art world if you didn't look the part. The right address, the right wardrobe, the right private bank, turning left not right when walking onto a plane, and the right car: Helen hadn't liked the colour of the Mini she won in that raffle, so she switched it on the day the car was delivered for the mint-green model at the BMW dealership in Park Lane and paid the difference. The showroom never forgot her.

In early June, my grandmother Moira died, just a few months after her husband of over fifty years. We had been close and Philip had been my wonderful step-grandfather, after my real grandfather Captain Paul Cash MC had been killed in action in 1944. The funeral was in Sheffield, where his family had owned Roberts' Brothers department store, the Harrods of Sheffield. 'I can't believe my grandmother died so soon after her husband,' I wrote to Helen. 'They had a long and happy marriage, so maybe she just gave up on life.'

It was at the funeral in Sheffield that I finally saw Jonathan, my archaeologist uncle. He had become a recluse, living with my grandparents for more than twenty years. The last time I had been to their house, the place was a hoarder's warren, with piles of old newspapers, copies of the *Spectator* and Penguin Classics. Even the stairs were blocked with parcels of rare antiquarian books, largely unopened. To get to his bedroom, you had to tunnel through a life's debris of newspapers, books and videos.

Rather than the lithe, curly-haired academic I had known as a teenager, he now had a white beard and looked like a character from *Waiting for Godot*. He was in his late fifties. Something had changed in his inner landscape but I still felt as close to him as a brother.

The wake was at a hotel in Sheffield.

'I'll come to Upton Cressett soon,' Jonathan said.

We both knew he wouldn't.

'You're welcome any time.'

'I've got to do some more field work around Parlour Coppice,' he said. 'I'm sure there was an important Roman settlement there. Maybe a general's villa or a lost Roman hill fort.'

'Where are you going to live?' I asked.

'I'll get a flat – there's a lot of sorting out to do. I've got a lot of stuff to go through.'

'You can always store your boxes at Upton Cressett. We have an old barn. Storage is expensive.'

Once the house was sold, he moved into a four-star hotel – along with his most prized poetry first editions and some old *Wisdens*. It was not far from where my grandparents were buried. His thousands of books and archaeological notes, files, maps, field marking poles, giant tape measures, along with his archaeological photos of his work at Upton Cressett, taken on his Praktica camera back in the early 1980s, were moved into a storage unit in an industrial area of Sheffield. He was the only person with the key.

Helen and I were in Basel in late June 2010 for the Art Basel fair. But, by then, things had become strained due to the Boris factor. On the preview day when we were inside the Kunsthalle exhibition hall, Helen had stepped outside to take a call from him. This went on for two days – in the Messplatz, at dinner in the VIP lunch area and while walking around the Jean-Michel Basquiat show at Fondation Beyeler. And then, finally, when we got back to our hotel quite late.

Whatever Boris had texted her had upset Helen and she was unable to sleep; she didn't want to talk. Eventually, I couldn't take the pressure-cooker atmosphere in our room any longer, so I grabbed some clothes and went down to the bar to have a drink. I can remember watching football on a TV screen at the bar as I sank two whiskies. I could feel I was losing Helen.

When I returned to the room, Helen hugged me, crying, saying she was 'torn apart' and loved me. It was one of the few times I saw her vulnerable side.

Retired Hurt

Helen was on the committee of the Conservative Party Summer Ball in the gardens of the Royal Chelsea Hospital, so we took a table together. David Cameron gave a good speech – but this was before I had my falling out with his regime over his Government's 'Builder's Charter' that set out to wage war on the English countryside. George Osborne came over to say hello to Elizabeth Hurley and her husband Arun. I knew George a bit and his wife Frances, to whose excellent *The Bolter* we had given a *Spear's* book award.

As George talked with Helen, I remember feeling increasingly nervous. Did George know who Helen was? Had he heard anything via his Francis Urquhart-style political gossip network? He was very amusing, sharp and bright and full of anecdotes – often self-deprecating. He made it his business to know everything . . . especially anything that might harm the political ambitions of perhaps his deadliest rival.

By now the 'B' factor was heavily straining Helen's and my relationship. It never stopped surfacing. Boris's unspoken presence – even if only by text, telephone or just his blond mop appearing on the BBC news or *Newsnight* when we were in bed – was like a boil, buried for months, now surfacing. It was only a matter of time before it burst. Or was lanced.

There were moments when I could feel Helen's love and warmth drifting. She kept saying that she was 'torn'. Torn between whom or what, she never elaborated, but I sensed that, despite her steely core, she was deeply upset, and scared, at the turn of events. We all were – including Boris. Helen held wildly vacillating and conflicting views about the behaviour of her daughter's father. As much as part of her wanted Stephanie to have a real father, another part was understandably upset. Occasionally, she would lash out at those closest to her.

I remember one warm evening when I was meant to be playing tennis with my friend Bobby Read at the Holland Park Tennis Club.

I had arrived early and had parked my new car (a second-hand navy Range Rover that was not to outlast our relationship) in a side road near the club. As I waited in it, my head was slumped against the window. The next thing I knew, Bobby was tapping on the window and asking if I was OK. Twenty minutes later, we began our match on the clay court in the early-evening sun.

After two games, I walked up to the net. 'Do you mind if we stop playing? I'm just too upset. I'll explain. Can we go and have a drink instead?'

Bobby looked surprised but was happy for a rematch at the bar – no doubt it had been the shortest game of tennis he had ever played at the club. All this turbulence was making me darkly depressed; I wanted to be with Helen and for us to live between London and Shropshire once Upton Cressett was finished. But I found it increasingly difficult to fight for her as I sensed her love drifting.

We were now only months away from moving into Upton Cressett. Nikki was emailing me almost daily to make fabric and lighting decisions. By July, with the 'B' factor only getting worse, I felt I was losing control of Helen's and my relationship, and Boris was doubtless scared – not least because he was about to announce he was running for a second term as mayor – at what the exploding keg would do to his marriage and political career. My phone was ringing constantly from unknown numbers; and we had odd callers at Markham Street.

In *Just Boris*, Sonia Purnell gives an idea of how toxic the boil had become. Boris was to launch his 2012 mayoral election campaign in City Hall in late June following a State of London debate; the debate was cancelled. The excuse was given that Boris would be 'breaching rules' by using a 'statutory' event for political purposes. But this 'failed to convince', wrote Purnell. 'On the eighth floor of City Hall, however, the real story was already well known, although it would take nearly another three weeks for Boris's problem to emerge, by which time the mayor suspected he might be in serious trouble.'

Finally, Pierre had had enough and began talking, saying he knew Boris had been having an affair with Helen when he encountered the mayor in a lift late at night at the Morosani Posthotel in Davos where he was staying with Helen. When the lift doors had opened, Boris was standing there. 'He knew who I was and he suddenly got really nervous, his eyes shifting all over the place.'

The crisis in City Hall was ongoing when Helen drove up to Shropshire for an important final decorating meeting with Nikki and me in the Coach House sitting room. Just before she arrived, I knocked over one of my mother's dachshund bowls so dog meal was rolling around on the wooden kitchen floor. This may seem a small detail – and an unlikely reason to mark a shift in a relationship – but the mess annoyed Helen. It looked slovenly to have a professional meeting with my decorator leaving the scattered dog food where it lay. While I'm sure Nikki didn't care – she was used to country dogs causing havoc – I felt ashamed. That was the effect Helen now had on me.

You've Been Framed

The overgrown mess of a garden was another problem that needed tackling. Its ruinous state seemed symbolic of my relationship with Helen – as was the fate of my car, whose engine soon blew up. While I was living in the Coach House, I had no gardener – other than Darren, who did his best to keep the steep grassy moat and lawns contained with an old strimmer and a petrol push mower.

The garden's out-of-control state became so bad that I employed a self-styled 'groundsman' to cut back the huge clumps of bindweed and overgrown brambles, and dead-head what was left of my mother's once beautiful English garden. But he didn't know what he was doing. Much to my mother's horror, many of her beautiful and rambling Old English roses – some dating back thirty years – were simply dug up and thrown on a bonfire. The rest hadn't been dead-headed for several years so failed to flower. Alas, he knew nothing about the rarity of my mother's established gallicas, damasks, albas and some China roses.

My mother had been advised by Shropshire's local celebrity gardener, Percy Thrower (the Monty Don of his time), whose nursery was near Shrewsbury. I wanted to return the garden to how it had been when I was a boy – a private Arcadia of musty, deep-smelling roses, peacocks and hydrangeas. I also wanted to make its restoration part of my own journey of regeneration. I knew next to nothing about gardening or gardening history. Fortunately, Helen's mother was a keen gardener and we had made plans for a Dutch box garden that followed the designs of the sixteenth-century Dutch printmaker, engineer and engraver Hans Vredeman de Vries, who had been an inspiration for Adam Dant's murals. De Vries had been a Dutch Renaissance artist and landscape designer best known for his 1583 book on garden design.

By the spring of 2010, I had started the new planting. I put local nurseryman Nick Murphy in charge of the new yew hedge topiary, and he spent a week on his knees in the rain planting all the box hedging for a new Dutch knot garden to be under-planted with tulips. During his work, he came across the old medieval well that would have supplied the sixteenth-century house with water, originating from one of several springs around the house and moated site.

Helen was excited about the tulip garden and about helping me buy the rest of the furniture and some more paintings I needed to complete the house before moving in. By July, I was sending her the links for all the 2010 season of Halls of Shrewsbury sales. 'Halls is the Shropshire equivalent of Christie's – they are quite good and you can find a few sleepers.'

But back in London, I sensed something wasn't right; I felt we were under observation. This was confirmed in early July when Helen and I were having a breakfast croissant and coffee outside at a café on Jubilee

Green, just a hundred yards from her house. We had Stephanie with us in her pram. As we read the papers and drank our coffee, a man in a leather bomber jacket came up to us and said, 'What a lovely baby you both have. Would you mind if I take a photograph?'

He didn't wait for a reply. After he had taken the photo of Stephanie and left, I turned to Helen. 'Nobody who isn't a paparazzo would ask to take a photograph at 9 a.m.,' I said. 'I think we're being set up. How did they know we'd be here?'

'Maybe they followed us,' said Helen.

I could sense something was wrong. Was there an informer?

The other reason I was worried was that the *Daily Mirror* had started ringing up the *Spear's* offices in Hillgate Street and asking for me. A reporter had even started asking the *Spear's* editorial manager, Emily, questions about Helen. When she had reported this to me, I had taken her to a nearby coffee shop and said, 'Things are close to imploding. It's best you know absolutely nothing. The important thing is that if any reporter calls asking for me, just say I'm abroad on business.'

Helen's and my relationship ended on the morning in July that the British tabloids – leading the day before with a front-page headline in the *Sunday Mirror* – splashed photographs of her and Boris on the front pages, alleging that Boris Johnson was the father of her daughter Stephanie. At the time, the scandal seemed to close the door on Boris's Downing Street ambitions. 'Senior Tories say this scandal ends his ambitions of leading the Conservative Party or ever being prime minister,' commented the *Mirror*.

Once the story broke, Markham Street became base camp for a circus of paparazzi and TV cameras. When Helen tried to open the door, there was such a stampede that she couldn't even get out with Stephanie in her pram for a walk. For several days, her house became a prison. Photographers had started hounding her poor mother outside her house in Folkestone over the weekend.

Then the killer blow came by text. She didn't want me to return to Markham Street. Insinuating that I was somehow responsible for the leak, and couldn't be trusted, Helen let me know that my presence in her house was not wanted.

At the same time, Boris was reported as having been thrown out of his Islington house – 'like a tomcat', according to various press reports – by Marina, who had reportedly taken off her wedding ring while Boris rented a bachelor flat down the road. I retreated to the Coach House.

My marital plans with Helen were suddenly dust.

Distraught, I went to stay with Elizabeth at her farm in Gloucestershire, where Helen and I had stayed with Stephanie in much happier circumstances only a month or so before. I had been dumped or, at least, she didn't want me around. Only a week or so ago, Helen and I had placed the curtains order for the master bedroom. They were to be edged in dark plum silk velvet with tassels that could have been chosen by Madame de Pompadour. Yet now I was once again out in the cold – only this time it wasn't clear what my crime had been. Helen certainly seemed to blame me for the tabloid story getting out.

I wrote to her some weeks after the *Notting Hill*-style siege of her house by photographers and TV crews in July 2010. Once again, I told her I'd had nothing to do with 'the press stuff', reminding her that 'from the start, I wanted to kill the story dead':

> *My love, I loved you every second of our life together and would have married you in a moment (if you would have had me) were it not for various issues that were always going to have to be resolved. Once trust goes, everything else follows. All I ever wanted was to support you and protect you. I believe we can re-build that trust – because I think we both know in our hearts what the truth really is; and that – I pray in time – we will both come to our senses and*

realise that we are always going to be happier together rather than apart. I pray you will want to see me when you have thought things through.

All my love to my Dutch heart,

W xxx

I wrote to and emailed Helen for weeks and then months, trying to get her to have a drink 'so we can bring this unholy mess to a conclusion' and I 'could get my sanity back'.

I can recall lying in a crushed heap on the sofa in my cottage to watch the World Cup football final in which Holland were playing Spain. As Helen was half Dutch, I had been looking forward to watching the game with her – even though she showed little interest in football and I loathed it. As the team sang the Dutch national anthem before the match, I began crying. I had even bought some plastic Dutch flags that I had put on my car. I was forty-five now, twice divorced, with no children, and felt as close to Cyril Connolly's 'sense of total failure at forty' as I ever had.

After Helen broke off all contact with me, I wasn't sure who I could trust or who had poisoned whom. As I wrote to Helen: 'I <u>will</u> not give up on our love, Helen; and the point of this letter is to ask you, I pray, to only trust your heart and be true to what we were building, which was strong and good. You have that rare gift – to bring out the very best in people (Steph has it too) . . .'

Regardless of no response, I still could not give her up. I battled on:

I thought we had found something – after so many mistakes and years of unreality – that was real; something that could work as a real marriage; the sort of grounded marriage based on trust and openness and being totally true to each other in every way – and trusting the other in everything – that we both know in our hearts that we both want. And still want.

Yes, I added, we had 'some bad rows' but they were only because so much was unresolved. I wanted a 'proper marriage with complete trust and afternoons making love and shutting the door on the world and never really wanting to see anybody else – other than each other, and the dogs, and doing <u>everything</u> together, however tough it may get. I know that is what we really want.'

Inevitably, I tried to use the progress with the restoration over the summer of 2011 to try to get Helen back. In a final throw of the dice, in early August, I was back describing the oak panelled room where I longed to carve my wife's initials above the bed:

> *The builders are still here but we are into the final push and I still think of Upton Cressett very much as your house, my love. Our house. Our future family's house. . . . I cannot bear the thought of living here on my own without you and I have tried to keep things as I know you like them – God, I will need you when it comes to the sheet and linen buying* [Helen was particular about thread-count and only used pure linen sheets]. *The bedroom looks wonderful. Every time I walk in and see the dark-red velvet curtains and headboard – I think of you . . .*

17

Return to Sender

How reliable a letter-writer's voice may be, of course, is always a concern. Looking at the Binder Box letters today, what I left out, or twisted with the hope of winning over a woman, is as illuminating as what I actually wrote. So many are hopelessly self-indulgent attempts to win a heart or offer some thread of hope (often self-deceptive) to myself. Is the narrator of my letters really me, or a persona I created? I can't answer that. I don't know.

I usually had difficulty letting go of my Binder Box relationships – none more so than Helen. I simply refused to accept that the relationship was over. Perhaps that is one reason I wrote her so many letters; the writing was a way of trying to repossess the past, to connect with the woman I had loved.

In addition to writing some tear-stained letters, half of which remained unsent, I also fell into that other cliché of failed love and bought a dog – in my case, a working Labrador from a farm in

Montgomeryshire. I wanted her curled up under my desk as I wrote, that dear, trusting, non-judgemental black Lab.

I had seen the advertisement for Cressetta, my new puppy, in the *Shropshire Star.* I went to choose her with a new girlfriend. Some months after I had split from Helen, I started seeing an actress-turned-Chelsea-estate-agent called Kym – a good-looking blonde several years older than me who had previously dated former MP and spy writer Rupert Allason (a.k.a. Nigel West), and Charlie Berkeley, the heir to Berkeley Castle in Gloucestershire, who was about my age. Her film career was limited to appearing in *Eyes Wide Shut.*

Kym was certainly supportive and loved Upton Cressett. I started dating her in what she came to call a 'non-defined' relationship. I took her to Paris to see the blockbuster Monet show at the Grand Palais that I was reviewing. We walked in the Luxembourg Gardens – which I always visited when I was in Paris – and explored some bohemian restaurants but my mood remained sanguine. When we returned, Kym sent me a photo of myself captioned 'Monsieur Grumpy', brooding under an umbrella in the rain outside the Monet show.

It wasn't the Paris rain that was affecting my mood; nor was it that Kym hadn't been entirely straight about her age, as I discovered when I looked at her passport. The truth was I was restless and depressed.

Then, six months later, at the end of January 2011, I unexpectedly saw Helen at a party for the launch of Simon Sebag-Montefiore's history of Jerusalem. I approached her, if only to find out whether she had received any of my letters. She said only that she was happy to say hello at parties – or at least nod. At least we could *nod*! *Whatinannanameochrist*! One moment we were talking about getting married and having children and now we were discussing the public etiquette of nodding to acknowledge each other. I was clearly still accused of leaking that Boris was Stephanie's father.

I fled the party. I wrote to her about a week afterwards on a postcard from the Chesa Grischuna Hotel in Klosters, where I was staying for the World Economic Forum in Davos. I had gone hoping Helen might be there in her mink coat and knee-high sheepskin boots. But I didn't see her; I did, however, see Boris addressing a lunch of British business leaders at the Belvedere.

After the lunch, I cornered him in a corridor. 'Boris, good speech, well done. Listen, it's about Helen. I know things haven't exactly been easy for any of us with the press stories that appeared. But can I make one thing absolutely clear?'

'Go on.'

'I want you to know I had nothing to do with any of the *Mirror* stories. What on earth had I got to gain? I wanted to marry Helen and bring up your daughter as my own. It was that simple.'

'Right . . . er . . . got it. Thanks for letting me know.'

And then we walked off in different directions.

Boris looked taken aback but I understood that he'd heard me loud and clear.

Although I had sent the Davos postcard to Markham Street, I didn't know if she was still living there. I had walked past her Duke Street gallery and seen it had closed down, her name no longer on the buzzer. I had no idea where Helen was living or even working.

Then, after I had decided to cool off my relationship with Kym, a two-page article appeared in the *Mail on Sunday* on 6 February 2011, headlined: 'Boris Johnson's Amazing Love Pentagon!' The standfirst continued: 'All roads lead to Boris!' At the top of the illustration was Boris who 'seems to merrily carry on whilst others get hurt'. The article described the various other cast members in this latest Boris soap drama: Helen, his wife Marina, myself, Kym and Pierre Rolin. 'Lately all five have indulged in such a frenzy of romantic competition, jealousy and bitterness that it reads like the plot of a Victorian novel.' They weren't far off.

I immediately wrote to Helen to distance myself from this tawdry piece. I told her I was bowing out of attending the Tory Black & White fundraising party as I couldn't face seeing her there. I still couldn't deal with how I had been dumped by text and asked to leave her London house.

7 February 2011 – Upton Cressett

Although I expect nothing and hope for nothing, I will not accept or believe that what you often told me when we were together – that you were truly happy, in love and everything else – was not true at the time; I can accept that you fell out of love with me, and that you were 'torn' (as you said in your last text) . . . Why couldn't you have just ended things in person? Anyhow, I confronted B at Davos at some lunch and made it very clear I wasn't behind anything and I think he got the message.

There were moments – like when you called me in Jamaica – when I truly felt what real happiness feels like (so much better than getting married). I could have been a good father to S; and I still believe, in my heart, that I could have made you happy, more than anybody else.

I then explained how Upton Cressett was now finally 'finished . . . but it somehow always feels empty'.

I pray sometimes that I could one day write you a good letter – a letter that made you laugh or smile, or want to reply. Because I shall never forget the smile on your face when you waved at me from the beach at Jumby, or our visit in the drizzling rain and fog to Wenlock Abbey. Or just the times when we had a kitchen supper at home and I wanted to keep talking – and you said 'Let's go upstairs' – Goddamit things weren't perfect but by God you are a difficult person to replace Helen.
  Wx

In the absence of any response, I decided to walk up the King's Road in Chelsea to our former house to drop a final letter through the door. When I got there, it was evident she had moved out. Worse, when I knelt down and peered through the letterbox, what looked like months' worth of post was lying unopened on the floor, as if the previous resident had left in a hurry, without a forwarding address. I could see at least one of my postcards lying among the pile of junk mail, leaflets and bills.

For how long had I been writing into the wind?

I later discovered from notebooks seized by the police that my mobile phone had been hacked. This was the 'very likely' source of the information that led to the paparazzi ambush of Markham Street and my being 'doorstepped' at Upton Cressett in July 2010.

On the Spike

With Helen lost, we need to wind back to that crumpled figure staring up at the beamed ceiling of the Coach House during the week of the 2010 World Cup football final, unable to fathom what had happened to his life.

Looking back, I suppose the moment when the press – including TV cameras – had shown up at Helen's mother's house and Upton Cressett was the absolute low point. The former hack was not only the hunted but now the criminal.

Something else hadn't helped; the day after we had gone to the *Spectator* summer drinks party in Westminster, on the first Thursday in July, I had lunch with Helen at a wine bar in Belgravia. We had a row after the party – our first – because she had wanted to stay on in the hope that Boris would turn up. He didn't. I introduced her to his sister Rachel, who looked amazed to see her there.

By the second bottle of rosé, Helen was back to her old self, smoking, laughing and not ruling out marriage despite having once dismissed it as 'just a piece of paper'. Just as we were on this subject, an Indian fortune-teller had ambushed our outside table. 'You very lucky man with lucky face. You have very lucky chemistry together,' he said. 'Let me see your hand.'

Holding my palm, he ran his finger down a line. 'You have lucky line. You will both have good luck in the next two months. You will work hard but you will get what you are looking for.'

'Lucky in love?' I asked, half joking.

'First, I say to your beautiful lady here – there is money coming to you,' he said, looking at Helen.

Her cobalt eyes opened wide and she smiled. She was in the middle of negotiating the acquisition of an Orientalist painting by the nineteenth-century Scottish artist David Roberts for a Qatari client. Roberts was one of her very favourite painters, whose oils regularly sold for many millions.

'Now I will tell you of your future together,' he said, pausing.

I handed over a £20 note. I knew it must be a scam but it seemed a fair price to pay for some happy news.

'You will not get married or have children together. It is so written. I am sorry. But you will have good life, good health and good love.'

He skipped off into the hot afternoon sun.

Our relationship ended a week later after the tabloid headlines broke. In the weeks that followed, I fell apart as a human being. I was finished. Dead. Spiked.

My thoughts about Boris at the time? Was he fit for public office? As somebody who was flattened, Big Daddy-style, by the emotional carnage Boris created around him, I can only offer my very personal feelings on his Falstaffian character. Had it not been for the *Sunday Mirror* decorating their front cover with photos of Helen and Boris side by side, it's very possible that I might have remained with Helen and married her. We might have had our own family, along with raising Stephanie, and the public might never have known about Boris's affair.

But plans have a way of going astray when Boris's sexual adventurism is involved. When it comes to women, he is inclined to risk all. Does it even matter how a prime minister, president or mayor conducts himself, so long as he gets the job done? What about those others – wives, exes, family members and so on – caught up in all the painful mess?

When my hope of marrying Helen went up in flames overnight, it wasn't easy not to feel angry. But as the weeks and months passed, I realised I couldn't judge him. Behind Boris's mask, one sensed a complex battle between good and bad, the vote-winning angel and private devil. But the more I read about Boris's flaws and failings from a hostile press (on both left and right, and especially former colleagues of the latter) the less I took any notice. The charge sheet was to include that he was 'untrustworthy' as he was notorious at the *Telegraph* for claiming that his copy had been 'filed' whilst still being heard typing; and the fact that he failed to remove a stack of parking tickets on his clapped-out old Toyota (littered with coffee cups and junk) apparently cast doubt on his ability to run a country.

Yet my own old cars were hardly any better, nor was my behaviour always perfect during my own two failed marriages. In short, I also had a failed degree in human relations. If there was one thing that Helen couldn't stand, it was a dirty or unkempt car. It was the Dutch bourgeois in her. I'd have been amazed if Helen ever got into Boris's 1990s Toyota; and if she did, it was only more evidence of how Boris seemed to get away with more than anybody else. I also knew what it felt like to be a homeless hack on the rack whilst going through a divorce.

Oddly, many of the women in his life, including Helen, also felt unable to condemn him too harshly. The truth is that many of those whom he has let down, or betrayed, have often remained supportive. That's an unusual form of loyalty. Somehow, I never heard a negative word (well, not many) about Boris from Helen. Personally, I took the view that the opinions of smart and intelligent women (and Helen was certainly that, as is the pattern of his other wives and mistresses) were a more reliable judgement of character than jealous and politically motivated former colleagues and rivals.

As the weeks passed, and I heard nothing back, I finally wrote to Helen. 'I am sorry if I was a bit of a bore about B's calls and the way they always affected you. I only hope to God he wasn't the reason you decided to stop talking – his calls and general sense of panic about the press did get in the way of things and I hope now that everything is out in the open things will – or can – be different. I hope it will be a good thing that Steph – beautiful Steph – has a father who will hopefully now play a role in her life.'

It was time to rethink my own life. The whole point of taking over Upton Cressett from my parents, and indeed the very point of owning such a house, was to live in it with a family. This was the very reason my parents had restored the house in the 1970s – to create a family home away from London. As Vita Sackville-West, herself no stranger to romantic tumult, wrote in *The English Country House*: 'The soul of a house, the atmosphere of a house are as much part of the architecture of that house as the furnishings within it. Divorced from its life, it dies.'

With Helen walking out of my life in July 2010, I was too broken to spend much time in London during the rest of that summer. With *Spear's* now a sister title of the *New Statesman*, at least I didn't have to worry about covering monthly overheads any more.

It was nearly time to wipe the peacock shit and bat droppings off the tarpaulin in the barns, under which my parents had left a skeleton collection of family furniture, dust it all, then unpack the paintings and prints. Twice divorced, and crushed twice again in just seven months, I began moving in slowly over August and September – *sans* wife, *sans* kids and *sans* much of a clue as to how to proceed.

My relationship with Kym remained in a 'non-defined' state. The brutally abrupt end of my relationship with Helen meant that it felt more like a sudden bereavement than the end of a love affair. So Kym probably had a raw deal. I was not at my best. It was a strange relationship, of the type the French call a *'relation de commodité'*.

Finally, I settled with my Holland Road neighbour about an expensive 'right-to-light' dispute over the extension plans that had been going on for two years. But I couldn't start the works until I had also resolved my ongoing battle with the council to cut down the half-dead acacia trees. The council wasn't budging in its opinion that those stumps were still worthy of conservation status.

Then, just as my builder was muttering about blending the cocktail of Roundup and diesel that would resolve the matter of the trees' health once and for all, my neighbour Nick Archdale called me. He had lived in the top-floor flat next door for twenty-five years.

'Nick here,' he said. 'My cousin knows a bit about trees. When he was looking out of my window he said, "You should tell your neighbour that his acacia trees are not only unsightly but they're over a hundred years old and have passed their natural lifespan."'

'I know that, Nick,' I said. 'I've been telling the council they are dead for months.'

'As deputy chairman of the Council for Nature Conservation, my cousin is responsible for advising the Minister of the Environment on trees among other conservation issues.'

Ah. This was just the lucky break I needed. Within half an hour, I had composed a letter to the principal arboricultural officer with Kensington and Chelsea Council, making the point that one of the government's own top tree advisers was now of the expert view that the unsightly acacias in my garden were at the end of their natural lifespan.

This worked. Finally, the permission came through to remove them and I could progress with building works, if only I could pull the money together. My bachelor flat days might soon be over.

Dawn Commuter

So much, of course, is chance. Had it not been for my taking a dawn train from Wolverhampton to Euston one Tuesday morning in the early spring of 2011 so that I could make an early-morning City breakfast talk, my life would have taken a very different route. In the medieval world, the Wheel of Fortune was always depicted as being 'puppeteered' by a woman, often blindfolded. The capricious nature of romantic fate was seen as an ever-turning wheel rather than a 'sliding door'. Turn, wheel, turn.

'Would you like some orange juice?' were, I think, the first words I said to Anna Coutts Donald as we both stood somewhat uneasily at the breakfast buffet in the Mansion House to hear a talk by David Cameron's digital tsar, Martha Lane Fox. Anna was a striking blonde wearing a dark business suit. She was in her early thirties with big grey-blue eyes that made her look like a banker version of the sports presenter Gabby Logan. She looked like a Heathfield prefect sort of girl.

I spoke to her out of politeness as we were the only people standing by the breakfast buffet in the Mansion House. It was around 7.15 a.m. and we had both arrived a quarter of an hour earlier than any of the other guests.

But what if I had not taken the 5.24 a.m. train from Wolverhampton that morning? I had caught it by seconds. I'd had to run along the platform, and was panting when I placed my navy overcoat in the luggage rack above me as the train pulled away from Platform 2. It was still dark outside. What if I had missed that train by thirty seconds?

'Yes, some orange juice, please,' Anna said. 'I can see you're early here, too. Where have you come from?'

'Near a place called Bridgnorth,' I said.

'In Shropshire? I meant where have you come from this morning.'

'Shropshire,' I repeated. 'I'm a dawn commuter. I took the 5.24 from Wolverhampton.'

'Oh, I see. I used to drive up there. It takes for ever. It's just too far.'

'I was at Euston just after seven,' I said. 'How do you know Shropshire?'

'My ex-boyfriend used to live near Much Wenlock,' she said.

'That's very close to me. What's his name?'

It turned out that Anna had gone out with a near neighbour – at least ten years younger than me – called Ben Bishop. He was a raffish ex-army officer who knew how to enjoy a party. He was the heir to Shipton Hall, a fine Elizabethan house with 900 acres, along the Corvedale. She would have passed the turning to Upton Cressett to get there.

The Bishop family always used to sit in the row in front of us at church. Shipton was the only Elizabethan house in Shropshire featured in that architectural bible *English Homes of the Early Renaissance* by Avray Tipping, published by *Country Life* in the UK and Scribner's in New York in 1912. I had been given a copy for my forty-fifth birthday by my father. To my envy, Shipton had been included in more than eight plates, and Tipping's first sentence about it was: 'Shropshire contains no more delightful old house than Shipton.' Huh. I was amazed that Anna was being so dismissive.

'The last time I was at Shipton was with my wife for the opening hunt meet,' I said. 'Two years ago.'

'Is your wife a glamorous American? I think she appeared in *Horse & Hound*, who took photographs of the meet.'

'Yes,' I said. 'Or she was my wife. We're divorced. You mean Vanessa.'

'That's funny,' Anna said. 'I was there helping out. I wasn't riding that day. I probably served you a sausage roll!'

She did seem vaguely familiar now that I looked at her more closely. 'Do you ride?'

'I used to – quite a lot,' she said. 'But I don't have a horse now that I'm living and working in London.' She handed me her KPMG business card.

I did not see Anna again for many months. But when I did, I nearly married her.

18

Daring and Original

Approaching forty-five, I had certainly struggled with the heart – to the point of strangulation. But I was not going to give up my romantic quest for a family without a fight. So I asked Adam to employ a little artistic 'licence' in his depiction of the Four Ages up the main newel staircase. He was familiar with the Four Ages as an artistic genre so knew I was pushing it a bit with my request – I asked him to *reverse* the Wheel of Fortune.

'Adam,' I said, 'instead of having our figure of Man up the staircase running out of virility as he enters his Third Age, could you depict him rejuvenated and reborn by love?'

He obliged by reinventing the Elizabethan genre. The large mural begins with a cartouche at the bottom of the staircase, portraying the First Age of Man with a cavorting, youthful, grotesque figure of Misrule; we then see a near-naked, middle-aged man with a beard almost crawling up the oak stairs, some years past his prime. Next, a beautiful naked woman symbolises the power of sexual love, and that middle age is not too late to be redeemed by love. By the time our Man struggles to the top landing, he has been transformed into a virile strong figure. Ready for a new romantic adventure.

'English Renaissance artists used to think of their murals as being an intellectual and spiritual journey,' said Adam, as he finished the mural. 'I've tried to repeat that. So your staircase is now a journey through life.'

By June, we were ready for a visit from John Goodall, the architectural editor of *Country Life*. Although the architectural history of the house had already featured in the magazine, John had heard about Dant's decorative mural work and wanted to write a feature. He was one of the first people to arrive for lunch since the house had been restored. I was still slowly moving in.

The days before his visit were a hive of frantic activity and nervousness as the casein paint was hardly dry on the staircase. Although John was an eminent architectural scholar, whose books include *The English Castle*, it was like having the head Michelin inspector for lunch. Starched linen tablecloth and crystal glasses that hadn't been used for at least four years came out. But what was most exciting of all was that, as we sat at the elm dining table, a log fire was crackling behind us, the first time we had used the fireplace since the 1970s.

'Why didn't you use it?' asked John.

'It was completely bricked up when we arrived in 1970,' said my mother. 'We tried to light a fire once and the chimney caught fire. Jackdaw twigs probably. We thought it was dangerous. And then a builder put some ugly, huge polystyrene sheets up the chimney to keep out the draught.'

The four-page article was later to describe the murals as 'daring and original . . . a remarkable series of wall and ceiling paintings by the artist Adam Dant . . . who has been intermittently resident in the house for the past years executing three cycles of paintings.'

The article was a model of decorative-architectural academic writing, and when it was published, I began to feel as if the pain and strife (both financial and emotional) of the restoration might have been worthwhile. There was plenty more work to do, and I was still far from finding a wife, but I did feel as if the Elizabethan spirit of the house – its very genius loci – was slowly awakening, partly thanks to Adam and other local artisans.

It was satisfying to see Goodall write that Dant was 'using sixteenth-century ideas and materials as the starting point for twenty-first-century art'. John could not think of any series of painted ceiling and mural commissions on such a scale at a country house in recent memory.

The largest photograph in the article was of the cartouche panel on the upper landing of the main stair featuring a siren-like woman (the goddess Venus) pouring water from a jug into a Botticelli-style font – the Castilian spring or fountain. My only concern when I saw the fine detail of the photography for the article was Helen's reaction. Her mother was a subscriber to *Country Life* and the magazine had always lain prominently on the coffee-table of her drawing room. She could not have failed to see the article. As she read it, however, would she notice that the curvaceous figure and face of the near-naked Venus bore more than just an uncanny resemblance to her daughter?

Adam had, indeed, painted the goddess – symbolising love, sex and beauty – as a figurative likeness of Helen, *in puris naturibilis*, except for a fig leaf.

The same applied when Adam was commissioned to do a later mural sequence – his fourth – over a long wall in the bedroom (or 'Bat Room') we now call the Great Chamber. The subject was the Judgement of Paris and the elopement of the *belle dame sans merci* of the classical world – Helen of Troy. In the neo-Elizabethan style of Rex Whistler, it was a painted mural tapestry, in navy-blue tempura, mixing the story from *The Iliad* with personal autobiography and motifs – from the Cressett Cradle to my dogs – against the sixteenth-century Upton Cressett landscape. The Gatehouse became a Wooden Horse and the Hall and Norman church were reimagined as being part of the siege of Troy.

By August, the house was almost finished. Above the doorway leading up to the main stairs I had asked Adam to paint a Latin epigram that I hoped would inspire me as I walked down the stairs each morning in my dressing-gown before starting the day's work at my writing desk. I chose Virgil's *Primo Fortuna Labori* – 'may fortune smile on one's first effort' – as my house motto, as well as that of the new Upton Cressett Literary Foundation that I was hoping to start, a writing retreat for established authors who were struggling to meet their deadlines. The idea was to allow them to get away from the 'pram in the hallway', or other domestic distractions, and write for a few weeks in the quiet of the remote Shropshire countryside.

It was time to move in and move on.

Amid personal chaos and uncertainty, I had sought salvation in the calm sanctuary of restoring a small but beautiful corner of sixteenth-century England. In an era when houses have become commodities, as much a means of making a quick financial profit as a place to live, the refurbishment reminded me of how houses are not just places to live or trade up the property ladder. Their very living fabric – Tudor red brick, horsehair lime plaster, wattle and daub in Upton Cressett's case – can also be windows into ourselves.

Yes, part of my motivation was to find a wife and family; but I was also seeking refuge in something I have known all my life. The house – with its solid, fourteenth-century-aisled Great Hall and its towering oak spere-truss beams – represented, after the chaotic roller-coaster of my last twenty-five years (nine spent in LA, patron city of the dispossesed), the closest thing I have to something that I can always rely on to be there.

It wasn't just romantic ghosts that haunted me. I was also haunted by other buildings and works of art as well as several country-house poems. All, I now realise, were different incarnations of Arcadia, and both explored the idea of a country retreat as an escape from the world. In addition to Rex Whistler's mural in the dining room at Plas Newydd, the other painting was *A View of Het Steen in the Early Morning*, painted by Peter Paul Rubens in 1636, which hangs in the National Gallery. I had a framed print above my writing desk.

Four years after Rubens was widowed, the 54-year-old painter married a much younger beauty called Helene Fourment (yes, the Dutch version of Helen). In 1635, he also bought a fourteenth-century manor house in Holland, with a gatehouse and moat, near the market town of Malines. He restored the property and added a studio, where he painted his manor-house autumn landscape. The painting was a celebration of how Rubens had found happiness and love with his new wife and family after restoring Het Steen.

Similarly restored Upton Cressett was where I was meant to have lived with my family. But neither Helen, Vanessa nor Ilaria had spent a single night in the house. Whenever I opened my kitchen cupboard, I would see the set of six Delft-blue mugs that Helen's mother had given me as a house-warming present. I wasn't even sure where Helen was living any more. After I moved in, I wrote to say, 'The house is starting to look like a real home. The library is now finished; the leaded windows are in; the floorboards and panelling are waxed and gleaming; and Adam has finished what he calls the Cressett Staircase. I so wish you were here to see everything.'

I had no reply from Helen. Still, after the bed was finally carried in and I woke up for the first time in my panelled master bedroom, I felt as if my life was finally moving forward after so much darkness. As I looked out of the bedroom windows each morning to the Gatehouse facing me, I felt more and more like that male staircase figure who ended up as a regenerated man of the world transformed by life's journey. Restoring the house was restoring my own spirit of self. I wasn't going to let the Wheel crush me any more. Upton Cressett was coming alive again.

19

Better Than Blenheim?

To celebrate moving in – as well as the fortieth anniversary of my family living at Upton Cressett – I opened the house to the public over the August bank-holiday weekend of 2010 as well as putting on an open-air Shakespeare performance.

There is nothing that focuses the mind on finishing a restoration quite so successfully as opening to the public. After two years of building work, I wanted to get the house and church breathing, living and working again. That's one reason why country houses, ever since the Elizabethan era, have been used for putting on plays and concerts – they help to foster a sense of local common identity.

The idea was to encourage visitors to 'bring picnics and own seating' and pray for good weather. Because part of the old moat that surrounds Upton Cressett was levelled about two hundred years ago to make a large front lawn, the remainder made for an ideal open-air seating area. Even better, the lawn above has the natural dramatic backdrop of an Elizabethan gatehouse flanked of Spanish chestnuts (ideal for hanging spotlights in the branches) planted in 1815 to mark Wellington's victory at Waterloo.

I hired a Shakespeare touring company called Rain or Shine to put on *Much Ado About Nothing*. They played in the grounds of old castles, abbey ruins and Elizabethan houses around the country. It had been over a decade since I had put on my only play at the Edinburgh Festival – a vehicle to propel my girlfriend Louise's career – and I wasn't up to speed on box-office share arrangements. We'd settled for a 50:50 share of tickets sold.

'Hi, Adam,' I said. 'I know you've painted various theatre sets but can you knock me off an Elizabethan-style theatre poster?'

'It's possible.'

'Something similar to the original playbill that would have appeared when it was first performed in 1599.'

Within a week, his neo-Elizabethan cartouche print advertising our performance of *Much Ado* was being stuck on village notice-boards, in local libraries, pubs and butchers around the Bridgnorth and Ludlow area.

I was in charge of putting Adam's poster signs around the local roundabouts and along the A458. I am sometimes asked why I drive around with what looks like a selection of burglar's tools in the back seat of my car – crowbars and sledgehammers – among stacks of flimsy wooden signs. On the Friday before the bank-holiday weekend, I was loading up some potted geraniums from Bridgnorth market when a policeman peered inside my old black Mercedes and tapped on the driver's window.

'Can I ask what the intended *use* of these tools is, sir?' he enquired.

'For smashing poster signs into the ground, Officer,' I replied, before handing him a flier for *Much Ado* and my glossy new leaflet about the attractions of Upton Cressett.

These fliers are distributed in display boxes in local pubs, hotels and tourism centres alongside others promoting the Severn Valley Railway,

Ironbridge, the ruins of Buildwas and Wenlock abbeys and West Midland Safari Park. The flier for Upton Cressett bore the description: 'A Royalist stronghold in the Civil War, where Prince Rupert hid in the Gatehouse, the Hall and Gardens are open for guided tours with home-made cakes and tea. Attractions include a Norman church, Elizabethan gardens, costumed dancing and peacocks. Tours start at 2.30 p.m.'

On the front were a few quotes: 'An Elizabethan gem' – Simon Jenkins; 'A splendid example of the English manor house at its most evocative' – *Country Life*; 'A remarkable house of brick' – Nikolaus Pevsner.

I was back in the punter trade.

The performance took place in drizzling August rain – the rest of the weekend was perfect weather – with an audience of around a hundred, mostly bringing their own folding chairs and umbrellas. It was a good performance, but the acoustics were marred by the loud background chorus of a field of mooing cows behind the stage that the local farmer had moved to graze only a few hours before the play began. Still, most people stayed for the duration and we served guests wine, Pimm's and canapés in the large white pavilion that had been erected on the Gatehouse lawn to serve tea on our opening weekend.

The tent was a 1950s village-fête affair. It had been very kindly put up with military precision on the Friday before we opened our gates by my father's ultra-efficient, ex-army-officer, constituency office chairman, Major Prendergast (known as 'the Major') who arrived in the sort of desert khaki shorts I had last seen in *Raid on Rommel.*

The week before I opened the house was one of feverish activity, with last-minute painting, rearranging of furniture, reconfiguration of rooms and fanatical gardening. There was much beating and rolling out of dusty Persian rugs that had been in the storage barn for several years. Darren and I shared mowing duties.

One of the best moments was having Darren and Nathan carry in the portrait of Sir Francis Cressett that had been buried under tarpaulin and a heap of *Hansard* in a barn. This was ceremoniously hung in the Great Hall dining room next to my father's new portrait. Recently cleaned up and re-lined by my art conservationist uncle Mark, Sir Francis gazed down from the dining room wall with a look of baffled bemusement. The oak panelling hadn't gleamed – thanks to Darren polishing with Sheraton Beeswax polish up a ladder – so much for four hundred years. As Adam painted away on a final mural, there was still a strong waft of ammonia only twenty-four hours before the first punters were due to arrive.

'Don't worry, William,' said Adam. 'The smell will be gone when your hordes show up over the weekend.'

We had no idea how many people would appear over the three days of bank-holiday opening. My father and I had agreed to share the tours – timed according to demand. I had placed an ad in the local *Bridgnorth Journal*, and the *Shropshire Star* were sending a reporter and photographer and we were even being honoured with the presence of their society columnist, Louise Acton. Kathy was on hand to help with tea in the pavilion. We had no idea how many cakes or scones to order from our cake-maker Margaret.

I felt like a rusty provincial actor going back to the boards to revive an old role. But my 1980s house-tour script needed revising and rewriting. With my acquisition of a few Cressett heirlooms from the Thursby-Pelham sale at Christie's, it was now time to dress my restored stage set with the new props.

The fun part was deciding where they should all go. The old Cressett seals and the Royal Pardon to Thomas Cressett from Queen Mary were placed in a little glass-fronted wooden desk that I had found in a Bridgnorth bric-à-brac shop. The Cressett Cradle was placed in the Great Chamber. I was looking forward to relating how I had to bid more than £5,000 to prevent the Cressett family heirloom becoming a 'kennel' for a dandy antique dealer's cat.

As Saturday morning's 11 a.m. opening hour approached, I felt a strange combination of stage nerves and pride, the sort I imagined the stage manager of a seaside repertory theatre – Torquay or Lyme Regis – would feel in the week before his big annual touring production showed up for a week in August. I hadn't given a house tour for many years so my father and I sat down to go through the old notes and my father's 1970s house brochure with black-and-white photos.

'We can't sell these, that's for sure,' I said to my father.

'Why not? The history hasn't changed.'

'For a start, we sold them for 50p,' I said. 'I can't even remember what we used to charge for a house tour.'

One of the other things I like about house tours is that you often pick up useful new information. One of the early tours on that Saturday included an elderly gentleman who had lived in a farmer's cottage just down the lane near Meadowley.

I was standing in the entrance hall with a group of about twenty visitors and was saying how we had no idea where the secret tunnel was.

The elderly man stuck his hand up. 'I know about the tunnel here,' he said. 'Because I used to go down it as a boy.'

I stopped my tour. 'Go on.'

He was the son of a local tenant farmer, called Shrew, and said he and a friend used to go down the tunnel as a dare with a friend when they were fifteen or sixteen.

'Can you remember where the entrance was?' I asked.

By this time, the entire tour group's eyes were fixed on the elderly man.

'Yes, I think so,' he said. 'It was beneath the Gatehouse.'

'Which side of the Gatehouse?' I said. I took his hand and led him out through the main front door so that the Gatehouse was facing us. 'Can you remember? Was it over there?' I pointed to the turret to the left, closest to the church.

'Yes,' he said. 'I think that's where we went down. Under the turret.

It was all open. Only pigs and a tractor and loads of twigs.'

'What was it like down the tunnel?'

'Dark . . . We only went a short way down. But I think it was brick. And it smelt down there, I can tell you.'

The first visitors started to arrive well before the gates opened at 10.30 a.m. on Saturday, 26 August. The cars kept coming, and coming all weekend when the weather was glorious except during the open-air performance of *Much Ado*. Still, we had a memorable after-party in the pavilion and all the downstairs fires had been lit for the first time in over four years. We had over 600 visitors over the weekend, including local civic leaders, the late conductor Christopher Hogwood, local author Dr Katherine Swift, an assortment of Shropshire friends and many members of the public who had driven from miles away.

A few days later, on 1 September, I opened the *Shropshire Star* to see a full-page spread featuring photos of the house and Adam Dant's work. The headline was 'RECORD VISITOR NUMBERS FOR BRIDGNORTH HISTORIC HOME'. I couldn't have had a better birthday present.

One of the visitors was Bridgnorth's mayor, Connie Baines. She told the *Star*, 'We've known about Upton Cressett for years but so few have seen what a hidden jewel it is.'

When the last visitor left on Monday, Kathy handed me a shoebox stuffed with our takings for the weekend. It took over an hour to count all the coins and notes. We were left with more than £3,000 after I'd paid for the cakes and my helpers. It seemed a fortune. I had never seen so much loose cash, all of which had to be sorted into bags before the bank would accept my deposit.

'Had a good day, did you?' said the cashier.

'Oh, yes,' I said. 'We'll be opening next weekend as well. And the weekend after that.'

I was now realising that there was a huge appetite for spending an afternoon at a quirky historic house, especially if the tours were given by the owner. Although my principal motive in restoring the house had been to put a drawbridge up to the world, I was beginning to feel differently. Almost overnight, after closing its doors for nearly five years, Upton Cressett had become a local heritage attraction. When I had conducted tours as a boy in the school holidays, we'd be lucky to get a dozen visitors on a Thursday afternoon. Never hundreds.

That weekend, I launched the Upton Cressett series of history talks. Peter Hancock, author of *Richard III and the Murder in the Tower*, travelled from Florida to Upton Cressett to present 'new historical evidence' that substantiated the story that the young King Edward V had stayed at Upton Cressett manor in April 1483 on his way to the Tower of London.

His main source was the contemporary account of the royal journey given by Italian diplomat Dominic Mancini, found in the archives of Lille Library. After leaving Upton Cressett, Hancock said that the route taken – across the River Severn at Bridgnorth rather than Worcester – suggests that the young King and his entourage, headed by Earl Rivers, might have met his uncle, now Lord Protector, in the Midlands. Richard then ordered his two young nephews to be locked in the Tower, claiming they would be 'safe' inside its walls. But they were never seen again.

The reclusive caterpillar (i.e. me) was now ready to become more of a butterfly again. It was time to unlock the padlock on the wrought-iron gates and share the place with others, especially locals or fellow history or heritage nuts. Indeed, I was coming to agree, more and more, with my heritage hero Clough Williams-Ellis that anybody lucky enough to live in such a place had a duty to open it. Flicking through the visitors' book with a glass of wine in hand when all the punters had finally departed after our reopening, my favourite comment was: 'Better than Blenheim'.

V

20

Arcadia Exit

It wasn't long, however, before this country paradise – and the very rural dream I had tried to create – was under attack. The first skirmish came when I was driving back along our narrow lane on a glorious late-summer afternoon to find it blocked by a tractor. Its chainsaw arm was massacring one of Upton Cressett's ancient, fifteen-foot-high hawthorn hedgerows. Amputated branches littered the road.

These tunnel-like hedges had run for centuries ('hedge-row beauties numberless', as the poet William Cowper wrote) along most of our lane. The Arden of Upton Cressett was being felled – right in front of me. I jumped out of my car and asked the contractor what the *hell* he was doing cutting down the ancient hedgerow. Who was he working for?

'Countryside stewardship scheme,' he replied. 'You get good subsidies to cut down nice hedges like this. But that's coppicing today for you – you take the money where you can.'

Within just a few days many of the oldest and most beautiful parts of the old Upton Cressett hedgerows along the lane had been savagely mutilated. I was both sad and furious that the lane could be made so ugly in such a manner (a decade later it has yet to recover).

But the execution of our hamlet's hedgerow was just a teaser for the forthcoming attack on Upton Cressett that was shortly to follow. The first threat came from a local farmer called Clive Millington – he lived just a few fields away – who put in an application for two large wind turbines, around 600 metres from Upton Cressett's entrance. These would destroy the local landscape and threatened to ruin the ancient setting of the house.

For at least four hundred years, Upton Cressett's hamlet had been left alone in peace. It had not been commandeered in the Second World War; it had survived the Reformation. Under Elizabeth I, the countryside around Shropshire was 'at peace', as my gardener-writer neighbour Katherine Swift had noted in *The Morville Hours*. Katherine – who was helping me with our gardening scheme – was one of the first to express alarm when I told her that Upton Cressett and Morville were now being targeted by farmers and developers.

I had spent two years trying to heal the pain of my divorces. My kind of Arcadia was about a craving to construct something new from the old bricks, and something beautiful and ordered out of the wounds, words, broken relationships and vows that had despoiled me.

But now the house was finished and open again for tours, it was time to defend the hamlet. No more lying on the sofa blaming myself or mourning the past. No more dreaming of Old Roses, Elizabethan turf seats and garden 'dream rooms'. There is nothing more energising to a man who has lost his way in the world in his forties than a 'call to arms'. The drawbridge was now down. It was time to dust down the armour and ride out. That 'remote and beautiful place' that Betjeman had written about in 1951 was now under threat. It was soon to be called 'The Battle of Upton Cressett' by the *Daily Telegraph*.

The first sign that Upton Cressett was being targeted was a 'public consultancy' exhibition by farmer Clive Millington and his developer, Crida Community Wind, in Bridgnorth's medieval town hall. This was the black-and-white-timbered building in the high street that might have become Hitler's high command in England, had Britain been subjected to German occupation. Now it had been hired by the Ludlow-based Sharenergy company to unleash an assault of German-made turbines across the Shropshire Hills.

I had never been a member of any sort of action group. I was a politically agnostic publisher, who had never been a member of any political party. While I respected my father, I had never shown any interest in his politics or in activist campaigning. Such groups were for retired colonels. But I had to speak out – beginning with a cover article in the *New Statesman* attacking the Coalition's anti-countryside planning policies, as I felt the very identity of not only the Shropshire Hills but the English countryside was under threat. It was headlined 'A VERY BRITISH REVOLUTION'.

This was my opening salvo and I kept up a regular volley of articles attacking the Government's anti-heritage, anti-countryside planning reforms in the *New Statesman*, the *Spectator*, the *Daily Telegraph* and CPRE's *Countryside Voice*. My cause, as I wrote in the *Telegraph*, was 'the preservation of England's aesthetic soul . . . and saving England from rural vandalism'.

My neighbour Katherine Swift, another writer who felt strongly about the threat to the Shropshire Hills, rallied her garden-loving troops by sending a letter to the 'Friends of the Dower House Garden', which was reported in the *Shropshire Star*:

Dear Friends,
   The proposed turbines are 80 metres tall and will be visible from as far afield as Wolverhampton. They will loom over the Jack Mytton Way, Shropshire's best-known long-distance trail, beloved

by walkers, horse riders and cyclists. They will utterly destroy the
remote & lovely setting of Upton Cressett Hall and the ancient
church of St Michael.

When I picked up a copy of the Millington planning application in
the town hall, I felt almost sick. Relying on a 'desk-top' heritage assessment (which meant nobody had bothered visiting), it dismissed all
heritage aspects of the ancient hamlet of Upton Cressett as being of
no significance. Newly restored Upton Cressett Hall was described as
a 'dilapidated, disused and unoccupied ruin'.

A *ruin*?

Scrunching the planning application into a ball, I had to find out
who was responsible. The exhibition was being hosted by two represent-
atives of Crida Wind, Jon Halle and his older colleague, Bob Essum.

Prowling around behind them was the sleek and dapper figure of
Clive Millington.

'Are you Clive Millington?' I asked.

I knew perfectly well who he was from his photo in the paper. He
lived just a few fields away in a large Georgian farmhouse, called
Criddon Hall, that was part of the old Upton Cressett estate, which
had been broken up. He had bought it cheaply with farmland about a
decade ago.

'Why have you described Upton Cressett as a "disused and
unoccupied ruin" when you know my family have been living in our
house for forty years?'

'Er, I wasn't aware we had.'

I pointed to the reference. 'You call yourself Crida Community
Wind,' I went on. 'What's Crida? Nowhere around here is called that.'

'We are a community project.'

'Well, you certainly don't represent the community. Your backers
are an energy giant. Nobody wants your turbines ruining this part of
Shropshire.'

'We do have community support,' he said.

'We shall see,' I said.

Morville Revolution

Our first public meeting was at the Down Inn, near Chetton, on 9 August 2011, just a few weeks before I had opened the house to the public for our record-breaking weekend.

My father was not a pub man. As a family, we had never once gone out to Sunday lunch at the Down, renowned for its carvery. Its owner – who was a supporter of our rebellion – had given our action group his function room for free.

'This is not the House of Commons – this is the Down,' I said to my father, as I paced around at the bar as people started to shuffle in at around 6.30 p.m. 'This is where Darren had his wedding party,' I added. 'It's where the local farmers go for Sunday lunch. This is not the time for filibustering. Just a few well-made points. And please don't make it all about the EU.'

By 7.00 p.m. the pub was packed; at least a hundred and twenty people tried to cram into the function room. Such was the scale of the local rebellion that we had around five hundred members, with heavy demand across the county for our bumper stickers and window signs saying 'Save Our Shropshire Hills'.

My mother and Kym sat at the front. In front of me was a tense sea of local faces. Our treasurer, Tim Morris, and his partner Kathy handed out our campaign leaflets as if they were fliers for the annual Morville fête.

Nobody had seen any sort of village meeting like it in twenty-five years. It was standing room only with locals of all ages.

'Good evening, ladies and gentlemen, thank you for coming,' I began. 'It's good to see a number of farmers here, too – Roger, the Bunnings family – thank you for being here.'

Roger, a well-built man in his sixties with a weatherbeaten face, was standing at the back with some other farmers. It might have been auction day at the local cattle market but nobody was eating bacon sandwiches.

'Our beautiful countryside is under *attack*,' I said. 'Under attack by planning applications that will change the face of Shropshire as we know it. These towering industrial turbines are each over twice the height of Nelson's Column. We need to fight back.'

A few cheers.

'Village communities are now in a state of civil war. Neighbours are not speaking to each other. Many people are rightly afraid that the Shropshire Hills we love and know could be desecrated, like Wales and Scotland have tragically become. Do we want this?'

'No,' a couple of voices hailed back.

I had to speak from the heart.

'The farmers and landowners here may own the land around our Shropshire Hills, but they do *not* own our landscape. They do not own our Shropshire sky. The landscape is owned by all of us, which is why I'm standing here asking you to help us fight to save our hills. To save the very soul of Shropshire.'

This got a cheer. I could see the farmers at the back of the room swivelling around to look at each other. While there were a few 'hear, hears', they huddled together at the back and stared on impassively.

'These turbines are not hilltop windmills,' I added. 'The width of the rotor blades matches the wingspan of a modern jumbo jet. The tallest oaks in Shropshire grow to about forty metres in height so the turbines will overwhelm and disfigure the natural landscape with dire effects.'

I didn't need any notes now. I was ready to throw a few punches.

'Crida describe themselves as a "community-led" project,' I went on. 'But let me ask you here in this open meeting tonight: *which* community do they represent?'

I handed over to my father. He spoke about how we couldn't really blame the farmers as the subsidies 'made a mockery of farming as we know it'. He would do everything he could in Parliament to put an end to such 'countryside vandalism'. Then Chris Douglas of Morville Hall, our co-chair, spoke.

'This is by far the biggest issue facing our community in the fourteen years I have lived in the area, and is causing great distress and division,' he began. 'And this is the first large-scale application in South Shropshire.'

He was a veteran of presentations, having worked for many years as a senior sales executive for IBM and Hitachi in London and across the country.

'We've heard that there are up to eight new applications in the pipeline for the local Shropshire Hills area,' he said ominously. 'The council say the Shropshire countryside is the county's *greatest asset* and that its tranquil character should be retained. So, let's all remind the council of this. Please write to the chief planning officer at the Shire Hall or post an objection on the planning portal.'

At the end, there was enthusiastic clapping and an almost palpable sense of relief that we were going to put up a fight. The Douglases deserved civic medals and were known to be 'pillars' of the Morville parish community, as well as being the driving force behind the Morville spring Flower Festival. The tea tent was run by Bridget Chappuis, a former police forensic officer whom I had recruited as a tour guide and Cressett family researcher. Our photographer was Mike Wootton, who had lived in our Stable Cottage. He would rise at dawn to capture the beauty of our hamlet in all seasons.

To my great shame, I'd hardly known Chris and Tim until I invited them up to tea and we decided to get our resistance movement going. Our 'rebuttal' was orchestrated by our planning consultant, Geoff Sinclair. With his beard, camera and waterproofs, he might have been mistaken for an explorer. He drove an old Volvo estate and was a veteran of many battles against developers, especially in Wales. It was like having on board a much-decorated and battle-scarred naval commander from innumerable Second World War campaigns, who had seen too many ships sunk and friends drown to talk about his losses.

My chief contribution to our resistance operation was to throw the odd javelin in the direction of Shrewsbury's Shire Hall by way of articles for both national and local papers and magazines. *Spear's* may have been founded as a financial and business magazine, but it was now time to commit the cardinal financial crime of what hedgies call 'style drift'. I called editor Josh Spero.

'We need to be more vocal. I want to start a *Spear's* campaign,' I said.

'Oh, yes, nice idea – but on what?' he said. 'Exposing the worst tax havens? Or how about philanthropy?'

'We need to speak out to save the historic countryside.'

'Sounds more like *Country Life*!' said Josh.

'Let's call it the *Spear's* Save Our Historic Landscape campaign,' I said. 'We'll include the destruction of our architectural heritage as well. And I'm starting a petition that we'll send to Downing Street.'

Eyes on the Prize

In October, I received a letter from *Hudson's Heritage* informing me that Upton Cressett had been nominated for three categories in the Oscars of the UK heritage world. These were Best Accommodation, Best Renovation and Best Hidden Gem. They were to be held at an awards lunch on 1 December at the Marriott Grosvenor Square Hotel, the awards presented by chairman of the judges Norman Hudson OBE. The other judges were Loyd Grossman, heritage campaigner, pasta-sauce maker and chairman of the Heritage Alliance, author Lady Lucinda Lambton (author of *On the Throne: History of the Lavatory*) and Jeremy Musson, former architectural editor of *Country Life*. The awards were to recognise 'the nation's finest heritage'.

A hint that it might be a good idea to show up on time had come just the week before when I had a call on Friday afternoon – just a week before the awards – from Norman Hudson's office, saying they were making the final decisions and could Norman come for a 'quick visit' on Monday morning.

We spent the weekend dusting the furniture, repainting and polishing the sixteenth-century oak staircases, preparing for an inspection by the godfather of the UK heritage industry. For the first time all year, I ordered the heating to be turned on and all of the fires laid, ready to burn, like it was Christmas at Sandringham.

Things went well until Darren found an old tin of some Farrow & Ball 'Mouse's Back' oil-based paint to paint the front door. We had forgotten that oil-based paint takes time to dry so was still *wet* as Norman parked his BMW on the gravel by the Gatehouse. He was wearing a smart suit and could have been on his way to Cheltenham races.

Just as Norman walked towards me along the topiary gravel path and I gently kicked open the door, disaster struck – a large pebble became caught under it. Try as I might, I couldn't get the door to open without a heavy shoulder shove that would have left me and my jacket covered with paint.

'Looks like the door's jammed,' said Norman. 'Let's give it a push.'

I stuck my arm out and nearly rugby-tackled him. 'No!' I said. 'Why don't we start with a tour of the Gatehouse? I always start my tours under the archway. Follow me, Norman.'

We crunched up the gravel path to the Gatehouse arch.

'Wait here, please, while I get the key. The Gatehouse dining room is open. Why don't you have a look? There's a new painted ceiling done by Adam Dant.'

'Oh, yes,' said Norman. 'I read the article in *Country Life*. I'd like to see his work.'

I duly sent the founder of *Hudson's Historic Houses & Gardens* into the dining room, then ran like Usain Bolt around the entire house, through the kitchen door and back to the front door, which I managed to yank open from the inside. It helped that Norman, it turned out, had been to Upton Cressett before – back in the 1960s – when the manor and Gatehouse were near derelict, unoccupied and overgrown, before my parents began renovation in the early 1970s.

'I remember poking my head up the oak staircase in the Sixties when the Gatehouse had trees growing inside it. The staircase was just full of old twigs. I suppose I must have been trespassing, but nobody was living there – other than some pigs!'

That was well over forty years ago. *Tempus fugit* ...

The 2011 Hudson's Heritage Awards lunch was held, oddly, in the windowless 1970s-style Mayfair Room in the basement of the Grosvenor Square Hotel – not a glamorous venue, at least by the standards of any of the statelies up for awards.

It was a gloriously English mish-mash of old house enthusiasts united by an enjoyment of sharing their unique history with others; a travelling circus of colourful aristos, architectural writers, heritage and tourism professionals, along with stately home owners and members of the restore-a-wreck brigade. The guests smashed the cliché that the heritage movement only perpetuated and promoted the interests of the aristocratic and privileged few. It was impossible to tell duke from bed-and-breakfast owner.

Most of the winners weren't posh aristos. I took Adam Dant as my guest. The ceremony was an eccentric affair showing off the efforts of the 'unpaid curators' of much of our finest national architectural heritage. Amusing speeches and comments flowed from the likes of Lucinda Lambton and Loyd Grossman. Despite the bunker of a venue, the judging was taken very seriously.

First up was 'Best Renovation' – for which we were nominated, along with Best Accommodation. I thought we had a fair chance in 'renovation' after a four-year project that had cost me a divorce, a fortune and had nearly driven me insane, but not so much as an honourable mention.

Then came 'Best Hidden Gem'. There were some eight other nominees, including various stately homes. I felt very much like the provincial English 'indie' underdog who was up against Hollywood's Treasure Houses. But that was the whole point of the Hidden Gem category – to award a historic house that is off the beaten track.

As soon as Norman Hudson, in his judge's remarks, said that the winner was 'an Elizabethan house located down an ancient three-mile single-lane road in the middle of glorious nowhere', I knew the framed award would soon be hanging in the Upton Cressett downstairs cloakroom. We won.

In his judging remarks, Norman singled out the 'virtuoso' and original work of artist Adam Dant, who was 'keeping the country house mural tradition alive', as being a deciding factor in the judges' decision. It was an afternoon to take off as we sat drinking wine with fellow restore-a-wreck nominees and winners, judges, aristos, *nouveaux pauvres*, cord-jacketed SPAB members, trendy polo-neck academics, heritage campaigners, HHA officials, architectural historians, historic B&B owners, café owners, and Norman Hudson himself.

Back to School

Just as I was wondering how on earth I was going to pay for the upkeep of Upton Cressett, I received an invitation to attend a Historic Houses Association (HHA) seminar at Eastnor Castle in Herefordshire, entitled 'Events at Historic Houses – Opportunities and Hurdles'. This was billed as looking at ways to earn extra revenue from events in the 'house, garden and park'. It could have been called 'Make the Big House Pay'.

This was just what I was looking for. But what was clear from the outset of the seminar was that, to be a player in the highly competitive world of country-house events and 'luxury accommodation', few were brave enough to host on their own. Solo. Single. *Sans* wife. First up was Lord Dunleath, who offered a masterclass on 'The High-End Tour Market'.

'My name is Brian Dunleath,' he began. 'My wife and I live at Ballywater Park, our family home, situated on the Ards peninsula, some twenty miles east of Belfast. On a clear day, you can see the Scottish coast from our bedroom windows.'

He and his wife had decided to go after the 'de luxe grand tour' of historic houses – mainly rich Americans, Japanese or wealthy corporate or cultural groups from around the world. They were put off weddings after a neighbour and friend had detailed 'every horror you can imagine'.

'Discerning clients want to "live the dream" and that means hosting private dinners in black tie. Coming with that dream is also the expectation that everything will be clean and well maintained – shabbiness is a total turn-off.'

I underlined the word 'shabbiness'. Another word of advice – train your own staff from the nearest village or town, ideally educated college students, and pay them 'above the local wage'. As I knew only too well, the Telford agency I used often sent unqualified staff with tattoos and nose rings, something Lord Dunleath would have winced at.

Another area I was lacking was any experience of running a kitchen and producing quality menus. I couldn't cook that well, my mother certainly wasn't going to revive her duck à l'orange for my guests and Kathy, my housekeeper, was fine for a roast chicken or cottage pie but she'd never claimed to be Cordon Bleu trained. At Ballywater, meanwhile, Lady Dunleath turned out to be a 'professional food historian': 'My wife makes use of the historical menus served over a hundred years ago and her ethos is to use seasonal produce either grown on the estate or bought from specially selected local suppliers.'

My cellars were dank, muddy and empty. Brian 'selects and tastes' the wine himself from his cellar of several thousand bottles. 'The client is *not* landed with offerings from the supermarket shelf,' he added. Thinking back to my days of decanting bottles of Tanner's house claret for our Heritage Circle guests, I underlined the word 'not'.

A final word of warning was offered on the subject of haggling. Brian's strong advice was *never* to discount. 'If a client tries to quibble over price, we gently tell them that we may not be the place for them. Once you start to discount, you are truly lost.'

Next up was George Buchanan from Hodstock Priory in Nottinghamshire. His talk was called 'Heritage Weddings: A Crowded Market or an Opportunity?'

'My wife and I have turned our home into a wedding venue having seen a gap in the market for a historic home in a beautiful setting,' he began. 'While some people say it's not for the faint-hearted, it can be very successful.'

There was no way I was going to be doing weddings, not least because our lane was single track only. I began to switch off. Neither would I ever put up a 'pay-bar' in my drawing room. But then a photo of Hodstock's Tudor gatehouse flashed up on the slide screen. George began talking about the importance of being able to offer a 'bridal suite' and other 'residential accommodation' with guests wanting to stay in heritage accommodation rather than hotels.

That gave me an idea. Weddings were a non-runner. But honeymoons . . . The Gatehouse at Upton Cressett was – of course! – the perfect location for a luxury honeymoon or bridal party. What could be more romantic than sleeping in the Prince Rupert Suite where the dashing royalist commander had stayed in the Civil War? I could already see the website page, titled 'Honeymoon in History'.

Every Good Deed

It wasn't long before I got my first honeymoon booking, through Airbnb, which I had recently joined. A Canadian couple were coming over from Toronto. I had dealt directly with 'Peter', who said they specifically wanted to stay in our romantic and historic Gatehouse. I was determined the success of the booking would make it a catalyst for launching it as a first-string honeymoon retreat. All the stops would be pulled out for their stay – a bottle of champagne and a handwritten note wishing them a 'magical honeymoon'.

About a week before they arrived, disaster struck. Somehow, we had a double booking for the first three nights of the week-long stay, involving a clash with our agency.

'We don't allow cancellations,' the matron-like woman said from the bookings headquarters. 'If you cancel, you will be liable for the entire booking and the cost of moving the guests to other *suitable* accommodation.'

This was my first experience of the rural Cold War that exists between holiday let agencies and homeowners. Once the contract is signed, you felt as if the agency owned your property. They certainly policed it, and the quality of your 'welcome hamper'.

I had no option but to try to put off the honeymoon couple from Canada. I rang their contact number in Toronto, only to be told that Peter had left for his honeymoon and was currently in Europe.

My mother, Kathy and I discussed the awful dilemma I was in.

'If we cancel, they'll probably drop us,' I said. 'It's one of our first bookings.'

'I had this before,' my mother said. 'There's only one thing you can do. Invite them to stay in the house instead for the first three nights.'

'But where?'

'The Great Chamber has no en suite,' my mother said. 'Americans freak if they have to walk down a corridor in a dressing-gown. It will have to be your room. You'll be in London all week anyhow.'

'In my master bedroom?' This was the room in which I wanted to carve the initials of my wife on the panelling above my bed. Only I had no wife.

'Well, your friends Rupert and Christina had a lovely wedding night in your room.'

'That was only because the Gatehouse pipes were frozen!' I protested.

My mother was referring to the time when my old Shropshire friend Rupert Kenyon-Slaney, who lived at Hatton Grange near Shifnal, had asked if he could use the Gatehouse for the first night of his honeymoon. 'It's the most romantic place in the county,' he had kindly said.

There had been two feet of December snow on the ground and the Gatehouse heating had failed so they had spent their first night of marriage in my panelled master bedroom. The honeymooners had arrived in a Range Rover with a back-up Land Rover carrying chains just in case the bride and groom got stuck on Meadowley Bank. Having lit the Tudor fireplaces in the master bedroom and drawing room, I greeted the happy new couple with a bottle of champagne before retiring to my old digs in the Coach House.

After recalling this happy honeymoon, I grudgingly agreed to lend out my master bedroom again. The following letter was sent by email:

Dear Peter,

We occasionally invite VIP guests to sleep in the oak-panelled King's Bedroom Suite in the manor where young King Edward V slept on his way to the Tower of London in the 15th century.

We have upgraded you to the main ancient manor for three nights as you clearly enjoy exceptional and historic architecture.

Our housekeeper Kathy will move you over to the historic Gatehouse for the remaining four nights.

This 'upgrade approach' seemed to work and I headed off to London in the appointed week.

At around 6.00 p.m. on the evening that Peter and his wife were due to arrive, I received a call from my housekeeper.

'Are you sitting down?' Kathy said.

'What's the problem? Have they not shown up?'

'Peter is here,' she said, 'with his gay partner. They are having a bath before dinner. In your bathroom.'

'Did you say *partner*?'

'Yes,' said Kathy. 'They couldn't be nicer. They went up to your room an hour or so ago to settle in. They haven't emerged yet.'

'Right. Make them feel at home,' I said. 'Put pink roses in their room, light the fire in the drawing room and make some local pub recommendations.'

The following day I got an email complaining about the 'disruption' of being moved around on their honeymoon. Peter wished not to be 'disagreeable' but he wanted 'reasonable compensation', a refund of two nights as a 'satisfactory resolution'.

It was a lesson learned. I caved in and gave them a night's free stay. Every good deed – or offer of good will – in the holiday-let trade results in punishment or the threat of a bad TripAdvisor review. Our guests were given the run of a historic Elizabethan manor house, including fires lit for them and they still wanted a discount and a refund. Next time, I was holding firm.

21

The Girl Comes Around

'It feels weird to be driving along this road again,' Anna said, as we drove towards Much Wenlock on the A458 before turning off at the signpost to Upton Cressett. 'To think that I sped past your lane so many times.'

I had not heard from Anna until she sent me an email informing me she was moving jobs some six months after we had met. After Kym had spent Christmas with me at Upton Cressett, we finally split in January 2012.

On Anna's first visit to Upton Cressett, there was heavy snow on the ground. The conditions were treacherous. When we got within striking distance of the Gatehouse, we spun on the sheet ice close to the entrance to the Old Rectory Lodge, home of my neighbours Mark and Caroline Bullock. Anna's BMW had as much control over where it was going as my mother's dachshund on roller-skates. As we tried to get up the hill, we did a dramatic 360-degree turn and ended up blocking the lane at 45 degrees. Mark – who ran a Wolverhampton paint company and had a Land Rover with a snorkel – came to the rescue. He somehow managed to turn Anna's car around to face the right way and then shovelled enough grit to get us home.

Miraculously, her car wasn't damaged, despite sliding down the hill sideways before crashing into the snowdrift at the bottom. It wasn't a great introduction to Upton Cressett. But the sad truth is that Anna never warmed to the house.

Anna came from a motor-racing family. Her grandfather had been one of the three famous Aldington brothers, who had founded Frazer-Nash racing cars in the 1920s. Horsepower ran in her blood. When I walked into her parents' home, two 1000cc racing superbikes were parked in the hallway. So when Anna said she was going to be doing most of the driving on our first holiday together in France, I was delighted as it meant I could focus on the Michelin guide.

We were road-testing a white Ferrari California. When I first saw it through the Geneva showroom window, it looked as if there was just enough luggage space for a toothbrush and a pair of pyjamas. But was the car really a Gran Turismo? From the side of the road, I rang my former best man Charles Dean, who owned a classic 1970s Ferrari saloon. 'If you can get two suitcases in the boot, *and* your girlfriend and you can drive comfortably across France, it's a GT,' he said.

Did somebody say 'girlfriend'? Had I finally moved on from Helen and the ghosts of my ex-wives? I think I had. Our first holiday was a happy time. But that was always part of the problem.

As Anna later wrote to me, 'I never admitted to loving you, preferring holiday-romance status, and our trips were brilliant – Paris, Tunisia, Ferrari trip and "Wolfgang" [referring to one of the most challenging black runs in Klosters, which we ended up sliding down on our rears], and my favourite few days at St Jean.' Ah, yes, the Grand-Hôtel du Cap Ferrat where we were meant to have returned on our honeymoon.

Anna was naturally bright and had a steely strength and ambition. Her heart had a core of steel. She had quickly risen to the top of her tax-advisory profession by a combination of hard work and networking skills that allowed her to keep up with any male City types when it came to drinking Provence rosé – 'pink petrol', as she called it – over lunch.

Her determination to succeed also brought a reserve and emotional armour that I found almost impossible to pierce. But judging by the size of her red Binder Box, nobody – least of all Anna – can say I didn't try over the year or so that we went out, including two break-ups. My inability to get through her armour also caused me to second-think our relationship. I never really knew where I stood and there were times when I 'let our love down', as I put it, as a result of her refusal to lower her guard. Hitting this steel wall disoriented me, making me insecure, irrational and needy.

The first break-up, which was my fault, arose when my father was speaking at the Oxford Literary Festival about his new biography of the nineteenth-century liberal statesman John Bright, his ancestor. Kym wanted to hear my father speak so I got her a ticket. I then drove back to London with her. When Anna found out about this, an unholy row ensued. Only two months into a relationship with a woman I loved and was thinking I wanted to marry, Anna gave me my marching orders and we split up. She felt betrayed. I was devastated.

I was single and unhappy again.

So, I did what I usually did after a break-up – I reached for the cushion of my Binder Box past. Our divorce now over, I was back on good enough terms with Vanessa and managed to see her for dinner when I was in New York on *Spear's* business in the spring. But she was seeing somebody – a French photographer – and made it clear that any sort of reunion was not going to happen. While in New York, I thought about Anna constantly. I couldn't let her go. On 24 March, before a walk in Central Park, I wrote to her saying that I loved her very much and that 'one of the reasons I'm here in NY is to do some thinking about the future. I very much want us to have a future together – with lots of horses.'

That Upton Cressett didn't have proper stabling, let alone a manège or dressage arena, wasn't going to stop me. They could be built, couldn't they?

One night I had dinner with Jay McInerney. As we sank some expensive red burgundy, I explained that I was now divorced from Vanessa.

'That was quick,' Jay said. 'Don't worry, I'm on my fourth wife. It gets progressively better.'

Drinking with Jay was always risky. I had had one of the very worst hangovers in my life back in the early 1990s after going out to dinner with him in Nashville. After being put to bed in the 'Belle Meade' bed, in which his wife's ancestor who was secretary of state for war under President Taft was born, I was then caught by his Southern wife Helen sneaking out with my linen sheets under my arm at 7 a.m. heading to a local laundry. Jay has never failed to remind me that some Brit had redecorated the heirloom bed and wallpaper in a style reminiscent of Jackson Pollock.

You Can't Get Staff . . .

In the absence of a chatelaine, I needed to get the right team in place. This is a long-standing subject of potential trouble in country houses, which were designed to be run by a small army of staff and, nowadays, often have none, or at best a skeletal arrangement. At Chavenage, where *Poldark* was filmed, they hadn't hired anybody new for fifty years. Their only help was a daily cleaner called Della who had joined in 1965 at the age of fifteen.

Staff had to be good, reliable, discreet and loyal. They might have to do some house tours and I would be in charge of 'house training'. I had already had one bad experience of training when

I had spent £1,000 to send my gardener/handyman Darren on a butler training course that I had seen advertised. The idea was for him to work in the garden during the week, then change identities at the weekend.

I had been sold the butler course on the basis that the company were hiring a proper country house for the weekend and would re-enact a modern weekend house party. Tutors would train the would-be butlers – most heading for the homes of hedgies or football stars – in the art of modern country-house life, teaching them everything: how to clean a gun, arrange flowers, lay for a fish course, and decant wine and so on. Most importantly, in my case, Darren would be able to hold his own when I had paying guests or honeymooners in the Gatehouse who might want to be served dinner. By day he might have been an optically challenged gardener, but by night he would be to Upton Cressett what Carson was to *Downton Abbey*. At least, that was the plan.

A week before the course began, I got a call from Darren. He was crestfallen. 'They've postponed it,' he said. 'They didn't have enough recruits to make it worthwhile.'

This had been in the middle of the financial crisis of 2008. It transpired that the market for butlers was at an all-time low. The course was rescheduled for a month or so later. Darren arrived back looking underwhelmed.

'How did it go?'

'It wasn't in any sort of country house,' he said. 'It took place in a tiny little house that belonged to one of the tutors. We had to practise everything on a kitchen table.'

My money was largely wasted. Then Kathy left. Instead of recruiting and training up a local housekeeper or couple – as advised by Lord Dunleath at the Eastnor Castle seminar – I tried to do a *My Fair Lady* in Shropshire by hiring a young Romanian country couple who had recently stepped off an Eastern European bus at Victoria Station.

They were selling the *Big Issue* outside a Tesco on the Royal Hospital Road in Chelsea.

Trying to train them into becoming an English butler/gardener/handyman and housekeeper couple running an Elizabethan manor house – from which I was often away – was always going to be an ambitious project. But they were big-hearted and, after reading William Blacker's account of his adventures in the 1990s living in various Romanian villages in *Along the Enchanted Way*, I had a soft spot for Romanians. I wanted to give the couple a chance to prove themselves. They seemed willing and hard-working, although the two-year experience was to prove exasperating.

They were called Pedro and Luiza and they had a young son, whom we called 'Mini-Pedro', who was around five or six. 'Pedro' wasn't his real name; it was 'Petru'. But by the time I had worked this out, it was too late to change it. Mini-Pedro was sweet and loved nothing more than playing with our various dogs, especially my black Labrador. He spent most of his time while his mother was working, after school, curled up in her bed on the floor being licked by her. Hygiene was never a priority.

Romanians have a tabloid reputation for petty crime, pickpocketing and being benefit junkies. My experience of Romanians is different; I always found my Romanian couple to be honest and trustworthy. Nothing ever went missing – not even any loose change. Most of the time they were cheery, too, but they could also be infuriatingly unreliable.

Looking back, perhaps having a Romanian couple running Upton Cressett when I wasn't there was a little naïve. It wasn't their fault. While they were friendly and had many redeeming qualities, my new Romanian barman/driver/gardener Pedro could have made Manuel in *Fawlty Towers* look as professional as Stevens in *Remains of the Day*.

I got an early taste of what I and our house guests had in store when Pedro – who usually drove while chewing gum, smoking a roll-up fag and swigging from a can – came to pick me up from Wolverhampton station shortly after I had hired him.

One of his main jobs was driving our guests and me to Wolverhampton – which is just one hour and forty-five minutes by train to London. Pedro had many failings as a butler but driving – whether a garden tractor, pick-up truck or my old black Mercedes (the house 'taxi') – was something he was good at, even if he rarely had two hands on the wheel as he swilled his Red Bull and simultaneously rolled a new cigarette. And because Pedro was a good driver, I would usually switch off on the journey home from Wolverhampton, dozing to Radio 3.

On this occasion – my first wake-up call as to the socio-cultural differences between Romania and England – I was woken by a loud clucking noise. I turned around and there, sitting on the back seat of the car, was a pheasant, clearly alive, clearly clucking.

'What the hell is that pheasant doing there?' I asked.

'I found on road,' Pedro said. 'I kill and put in pot for eating.'

'Yes,' I replied, 'but couldn't you have done that earlier . . .' – I demonstrated a throttling action – '*before* you picked me up?'

Another bête noire with Pedro was his failure to understand my wish for the lawns at Upton Cressett to be 'striped' – like an Oxford college – and the grass collected. He did not understand my affection for my 1960s Atco Royale rotary mower that I had bought 'used' from a local garden-machinery dealer and which was my pride and joy. It was the old-fashioned carburettor type with a Briggs & Stratton engine. Heavy steel rollers helped to create a striped finish.

Explaining to Pedro how to create immaculately striped English lawns had proved impossible until Wimbledon, around three months after he and Luiza arrived, when I was finally able to show him from the television what a proper English lawn should look like, and that only an old Atco or Webb cylinder blade mower could create the desired effect. After being originally dismissive of my oily old Atco when he arrived, he began to look after it as if it were a classic Jaguar E-type in racing green.

The main problem was that my Romanians had little sense of historical value or professional standards. Anything old and broken was regarded as rubbish, while to me such things could be irreplaceable. One morning I placed the Elizabethan window casement with original sixteenth-century hand-spun green glass on the kitchen table to show to my architect Trevor Edwards just before we had a site meeting with English Heritage. It was the only example we had of an original Elizabethan window in the house.

On the morning of the meeting with English Heritage, I couldn't find it. 'Have you seen the window I put over there a few days ago?' I said to Luiza.

'I throw out,' she said. 'It broken.'

I ran up to the dustbins but it was too late. The council waste-disposal trucks had already carted the rare window away to a rubbish tip.

Then there was Pedro. You can take the boy out of Romania, but you can never take the Romanian countryside out of the boy. Just when he was needed, he would take 'lunch breaks' of two hours to go and buy himself more cigarettes in my car. Luiza – in her late twenties – was certainly hard-working and intelligent as well as completely honest. She even spent every Sunday morning studying in Bible class, collected in a VW people-carrier by the local chapter of the Jehovah's Witnesses. But then she would consistently let the Romanian side down – often when we had house parties, group tours or even rental-cottage property inspector visits – by showing up to work in track pants, with her unwashed hair tied up with an elastic band.

The problems we had were to do with cultural divide and a lack of what therapists like to call 'boundaries'. So when Pedro went to pick up my weekend guests from Wolverhampton station, they would walk in with horror on their faces, having been subjected to a tirade about the various merits and failings of my various girlfriends, why I needed to start a family, how he used to earn more selling the *Big Issue* and how he didn't like working in England.

He was no Carson, that was for sure. A typical conversation after Pedro dropped two house guests off at Wolverhampton station went as follows: 'He never shut up once for the whole journey. Not even when he stopped at the petrol station to buy a can of Red Bull and lit up a cigarette near the pumps. In the end, we felt we both had to give him a £20 tip just to keep him happy.'

When I tried to explain to Pedro that it is not acceptable for employees to offload about their problems or dissatisfaction with their employers to anybody who happens to be in the car, he simply shrugged and grinned with a boyish look that seemed to say: 'I don't take this job seriously. I am better than this but I am doing it because there are British idiots who will pay me more in a day than people get in a month in Romania so I am staying here until something better comes along.'

Whereas Italy and Switzerland have a proud seasonal culture of working in hospitality, Romania does not. The very idea of domestic staff is incomprehensible to most rural Romanians. As a result, it was almost impossible to get them to understand what the inspector from our holiday-let rental agency meant when they said the oven needed cleaning properly, or why it wasn't acceptable to pick guests up in a car with empty cigarette packets and a half-eaten Big Mac on the front seat.

Cleanliness was not always a strong point; a complaint was often made in our visitors' book, where holiday-let guests write their supposedly gushing comments about how delightful a stay they had enjoyed in either the Gatehouse, or another cottage property. A Mrs Bull wrote to complain on TripAdvisor that she was greeted by a Romanian who was 'a housekeeper of some sort . . . I did not find her manner to be one that encouraged me to think this was a property where we would be welcomed as guests.'

That Luiza began doing house tours – if I was in London – in her slippers and pyjamas didn't help our TripAdvisor ranking either. We soon had more 'Terrible' reports than anywhere else near Bridgnorth. Finally, I had to step in and speak to one of the heads of the rental agency to explain that I was doing my best to train the housekeeper but there were 'cultural issues'.

This last point was experienced directly by Adam Dant, one of Britain's most respected fine artists. Whenever he or his family came to stay in the Gatehouse to do some new mural painting, he noticed how the Romanians ignored them. They never made any effort to bring in wood, or to do any housekeeping for them.

Only later did it turn out that the Romanians thought poor Adam was just a house painter, like a decorator or plasterer, probably on the same wage as themselves. They had no concept of the difference between a distinguished fine artist and a handyman-style house painter.

Put simply, my Romanians didn't worry too much about dead flies on the window sills, or a burned pork chop stuck to the grill. I had spent a small fortune on renovating the Gatehouse so it was troubling to stand by the gates on more than one occasion to see fully paid-up holiday guests abandoning their romantic holiday and fleeing because the place was dirty (standards are naturally immaculate now).

The final humiliation came when I was asked to remove the agency visitors' book. 'It is not helpful . . . if guests read similar comments then, rather like lemmings, they all pick up on it. I will post a new book to you tonight. Please ensure that the old one is removed and hopefully some of the negative comments will also cease,' wrote the customer-relations manager.

England has always been a nation of social mobility, with our houses often being the stage sets of such opportunity (Thomas Cromwell was the son of a butcher, Shakespeare the son of a glove-maker). We have always been liberal and tolerant of immigrants. I have always welcomed foreigners to this country – especially those prepared to work hard.

And that is why I was delighted to give Luiza and Pedro a chance. My mother, especially, tried her hardest to make our Romanian couple part of the Upton Cressett family; and for much of the time it worked. I enjoyed the cheeky laughter of Mini-Pedro, who soon spoke excellent English after being enrolled at Morville School.

When we heard that Luiza's father – a woodsman from the Romanian countryside – was looking for work, because there wasn't any where he lived, we gave him a seasonal job, clearing and cutting down the dead trees from our medieval wood. Pedro had vanished to Romania for two months – we never were told why – which meant hiring another temporary gardener.

The true scale of the false economy of hiring my Romanian housekeeper/butler couple became most evident in the number of ruined suits I had to mourn. I lost count of the number of times I told Luiza that my suits – and other trousers – needed to be sent to the local dry cleaners in Bridgnorth. But dry cleaning was not a concept she had ever heard of. Instead, tailored suits were simply put in the washing machine and ruined.

'What is dry clean?' she said. 'I clean and then dry.'

When I asked Luiza and Pedro to put up the Christmas decorations, along with sprigs of holly, I was horrified to find that while they had stuck holly above the brass picture lights, they had also sprayed the sprigs with gold paint. As a result, several valuable oil paintings – including a seventeenth-century portrait of Prince Rupert by Sir Peter Lely, and Sir Francis Cressett – had gold spray paint splattered on the canvas and frames. It looked like a graffiti artist had been employed to do the Christmas decorating. My art conservationist uncle Mark had to be consulted as to how to remove the gold paint.

22

Poet in Residence

Following my split from Anna, during an unscheduled late-night visit to Annabel's nightclub with a friend, I met a girl smoking a cigar on the outdoor terrace. Her name was Caroline. She was in her late thirties, tall, with a mane of golden-red hair and the striking Pre-Raphaelite looks of a Burne-Jones painting. We talked poetry (she had read English at Christ Church, Oxford) and cocktails. Her father was one of the country's top doctors and specialist surgeons. She was recently divorced.

Within a few weeks, she had quit her job – working for a public-health think-tank – and half of her London storage arrived at Upton Cressett. It included dozens of boxes of books, including a large collection of modern poetry. She was super-bright (an Oxford first), eccentric, wild, unpredictable, fun, glamorous, generous and had a true bohemian poetic spirit.

She threw herself into our battle to save the Shropshire Hills. Our resistance group had a fight on its hands to win over the council's planning committee. Caroline wrote speeches for me, swotted up on Upton Cressett parish history in the local library (where she would often disappear) and was on hand when we erected a large village fête-style tent on the Moat Lawn. Within moments of it going up, she was opening a bottle of champagne.

'It's meant to be a tea tent, not a champagne bar,' I said.

'It will be ideal for wine and champagne tastings,' she said, waving a glass. 'I can organise them. Isn't there an English vineyard in Morville?'

She loved croquet, fine wine, cigars and writing poetry in the middle of the night. I would often find her writing downstairs at 3 a.m. It was romantic stuff. There was so much to love about Caroline, from her poetic intellect to her lack of interest in money or the material world. It was like having a young Vita Sackville-West – only perhaps more artistically manic – padding around the house in striped pyjamas. I would get dawn poetry left on the kitchen table with a note saying, 'Scrawled yesterday first thing.' One poem was called 'Upton Cressett' where 'we shall share the beauty with all who come'.

She seemed to believe in me, worrying that I had lost my way in the world but that Upton Cressett offered a chance of redemption. She understood what I meant when I quoted John Donne's line about 'my heart' being of 'self-murder, red'.

'Return to the place your manor girls love . . .' her poem began:

> Cash is our king, but not in the way he imagines.
> You have wedded fame and fortune but
> Here
> Your apples will grow

This was written at the end of May when I was urgently trying to get my London flat finished so it could be sold to solve my precarious financial position. The works had gone way over budget.

Caroline also enjoyed playing chatelaine and hostess. During the Much Wenlock Poetry Festival, we had Gillian Clarke, the National Poet of Wales, to stay in the Gatehouse. She arrived with her husband, whose politics, it's fair to say, were not Thatcherite. I will never forget the look of pure horror on his face when Caroline and I showed them into their first-floor bedroom and I said, 'This is where Margaret and Denis Thatcher spent the night. I hope you find it comfortable.'

'Oh, yes, thank you,' said Gillian.

Her husband was clearly appalled at the prospect of having to sleep in the bed the Iron Lady had once occupied with her husband. A similar horror story once happened at Chavenage when Labour deputy leader Margaret Beckett MP booked the house to host a special dinner and invited several leading Labour politicians, including home secretary David Blunkett. As her guests had drinks in the Great Hall, a number of staff and family members arrived back from the local Beaufort hunt and walked through the throng wearing pro-hunting badges that said, 'Bollocks to Blair'.

Caroline had a darkly poetic nature but she was just too free-spirited and spontaneous. There was something of a Hampstead Sylvia Plath about her. I thought she might be too much to handle as a chatelaine when she accompanied me to the Hay Festival in Herefordshire. *Spear's* was sponsoring the fringe philosophy festival, *How the Light Gets In*. On our second day, Caroline said she wanted to go off and buy some poetry books, so we arranged to meet for lunch at the Black Lion Inn. It was reputed that Oliver Cromwell had slept there while his troops sacked Hay Castle, a royalist stronghold, so as I waited I read up on the history.

By 1.30 p.m., I was getting concerned so tried her phone. No response. By 1.45 p.m., I was starting to fret.

A few minutes later, she walked in and sat down at my table, helping herself to a glass of wine. 'I've just bought a house,' she said.

'Sorry? What?'

'I've just made an offer and it's been accepted – it's walking distance from here. I'll show you after lunch.'

'But you've never been to Hay before. You never mentioned anything about house hunting.'

'Well, I saw this for-sale sign,' she said. 'I knocked on the door and made an offer. They have accepted my offer. We will exchange in a few weeks.'

'I see,' I said. 'Didn't you try any negotiating?'

'I like it here. Life's too short to haggle,' she said. 'Hay is stimulating. It suits me. I don't want to live in London any more. And I'll be close to you.'

I never knew whether or not she went through with the purchase as the relationship ended after three intense months. When I went to London for *Spear's* meetings and left Caroline alone at home, smoking her cigars and writing poetry, I became increasingly worried. Would the house go up in flames? She would rely on Pedro to drive her around, but they soon fell out, so she bought a car.

I then got a call from a local farmer. 'William, a red-headed girl's been driving down the lane at high speed – smoking a cigar. Can you please tell her to slow down?'

By June, I couldn't take her manic but loving nature any more. She was a great organiser ('Knowledge is power, with organisation a close second') but took her need for filing too far when she announced she was reorganising my father's thirty years' worth of political papers for his memoirs. He started getting very edgy when Caroline began talking at lunch about 'bonfires' and 'archiving' in the same sentence. He told me he 'did not want a single box of files moved' and that he was 'quite angry'.

Then Caroline found God. Everything was suddenly falling into place, because He was being let in. By the middle of May, it was clear that things weren't going to work out between us. She also accepted that we needed to spend time apart. 'We communicate in different ways and I think you have some things to reconcile, too,' she wrote.

She was right – I hadn't got over Anna. Although I had moved into Upton Cressett, there was still some final decorating and other works going on and, as usual, I associated restoration work with trying to rebuild my own relationships. I wrote to Anna of the 'familiar sound of sawing, hammering and general builders' mayhem at Upton Cressett as I now embark on the final phase of restoration here.'

I described the new hand-blocked wallpaper in the Gatehouse; the new navy velvet Rubelli half-tester bed in the Great Chamber; and some new leaded windows, which I described as a form of 'Elizabethan laser eye surgery so the house can once again see as it was meant to see in the sixteenth century, through hand-spun, light-green diamond-patterned glass'.

> *If only, I sometimes think, I could apply the same zeal for restoration on myself and to repair the ruin I have so often made of things – rather than simply restoring my house. You were the rock upon which that rebuilding of my life was going to take place – and I loved you for it. I do believe that anything ruined or broken can be restored – often better and more beautifully than in the original. Not just houses but hearts as well.*

After I ended it with Caroline, Anna finally agreed to give me another chance. Although I loved her, it hurt that she still wasn't keen on coming to Shropshire for weekends.

With her reservations about Upton Cressett, I started devising improbable scenarios so that I could see as much of her as possible. I even started looking for a house or cottage to rent near her parents' home just outside the Hampshire village of Owslebury. I then decided to buy some black-market tickets to the dressage team finals of the London Olympics in Greenwich, featuring some of her heroes. In my

Binder Box marked 'A', I can see a photograph of myself and Anna waving plastic flags and both of us looking so happy.

In September, with my flat ready to be sold, Anna and I decided to go 'official' with a birthday drinks party in the newly refurbished flat to celebrate my forty-sixth birthday. There was a mixture of media and literary friends. It felt like a pre-engagement party. Anna's parents were there, as were mine. They all met for the first time. Life seemed to be coming together.

'Welcome to Racetrack Lodge,' I began. 'Anna says there are so many lorries and cars roaring by outside that it feels like sleeping in the pit area of a Grand Prix track. It won't come as a surprise to anybody who knows her that the gin-marinated smoked salmon was chosen by Anna. I'd like to thank her for making me so happy, especially the last few months. To Anna and the *future*!'

23

Shire Rebels

Next came another assault on Upton Cressett – an industrial pig farm 600 metres away. My fears for the industrialisation of Upton Cressett were already being realised with a number of similar rebellions across the country. According to Simon Jenkins, chairman of the National Trust, it was the most serious threat to our British countryside since the uncontrolled ribbon development of the 1920s and 1930s.

When Anna first visited in January, almost the first thing she would have seen was a sign on the gates saying 'No Pig Farm Here'. It wasn't the ideal welcome. Even before making her a gin and tonic, I asked her to write a letter objecting to the industrial pig farm, backed by a supermarket, that was threatened on our doorstep. After driving for three hours from London, Anna was faced with the prospect of being greeted by the wafting smell of pig waste spread across the fields surrounding Upton Cressett. Not to mention the horse flies. And horses hated the smell.

(*above*) It's a 'Yes'. Taken by the Boscobel Royal Oak in October 2001 moments after Ilaria first slipped on her engagement ring.

(*right*) Dejected in Bavaria. In the German town of Lindau where I went on honeymoon with my best man in October 2002.

Cutting the cake with Ilaria in February 2003. Bruno Rotti lights the sparklers.

Wedding day with Vanessa in June 2008. Taken after our service at St Mary Undercroft in the Palace of Westminster.

Cutting the cake for the second time with Vanessa. *(Tim Griffiths)*

Upton Cressett: Time Present and Time Past. Vanessa is writing under a tree by the church and Ilaria is under an oak tree in the hills. Laura is waving from the wall.

With Helen before the Conservative Party
Summer Ball in July 2010. *(Alan Davidson)*

On our holiday in Antigua, May 2010.

(above) Celebrating with Anna in Greenwich at the
2012 London Olympics.

(centre right) With Turkish novelist Selin Tamtekin
at a summer party. She didn't like the countryside.

(bottom right) 'Monsieur Grumpy' in Paris. Taken
by Kym Erlich as I struggled to get over Helen.

Upton Cressett under scaffolding as we began works. *(Mike Wootton)*

Craftsmen at work. Some members of my building team including the Seedhouse blacksmith family, brickie Gary Higgins and ground works man Brett Evans.

The discovery of Elizabethan wall paintings put a stop to the works. *(Mike Wootton)*

The drawing room under dust sheets during restoration. *(Mike Wootton)*

Adam Dant working on the mural frieze in the Great Hall dining room. *(Mike Wootton)*

The painted ceiling of the Great Hall dining room after Dant spent three months on his back with a paintbrush. The portrait is of Sir Francis Cressett.

Cartouche on the upper landing with Helen as Venus. *(Country Life)*

Adam Dant painting the Great Stair. *(Mike Wootton)*

(*above*) With Laura in Italy in 2013 having ordered the ring but not yet proposed.

(*right*) Cutting the cake with Laura at our wedding on 28 February 2014.
(*Tim Griffiths*)

With some 'tea-and-tour' punters in the Bosworth field tent. (*Andrew Fox*)

At my fiftieth birthday with *(left to right)* Sophia Money-Coutts, Philip Kerr, Nicholas Coleridge and India Clarke.

Elizabeth and Henry Dent-Brocklehurst at my fiftieth.

The Shropshire Hills saved. Our resistance group celebrates.

With local MP Philip Dunne and Chris Douglas in Morville Village Hall.

(left) With 'cousin' Rosanne Cash in Atlanta.

(above) Binder Box files and letters from the LA years.

(left) Laura with some of her hats. *(Alex Bramall)*

(above) Our white peacock York.

The pig farm at Upton Cressett would require weekly deliveries of pigs in large lorries. After a series of accidents, including a large grain lorry jack-knifing at the steepest bend on Meadowley Bank, the council had classed the single-track lane as 'Unsuitable for HGVs'. There had also been several accidents and farmer John Cantrill – whose father Roger had submitted the pig farm application – had narrowly escaped death after overturning in a farm vehicle at the steepest bend of the notorious hill, where professional cyclists trained.

During the restoration works, delivery drivers often rang to say they were turning back after trying to scale Meadowley. The most treacherous bend is now known as 'Boyce's Corner' after John Challis, star of *Only Fools and Horses*, overturned his Land Rover (with wife Carol inside) while trying to negotiate the icy hill before a snowy Sunday lunch with us (John is a fellow restore-a-wreck romantic after restoring Wigmore Abbey near Ludlow). They had to be towed out of a steep ditch by John Cantrill with a tractor.

Soon after their pig farm application had been submitted, my father and I went to see Roger and John Cantrill to express our neighbourly concerns.

'Roger,' my father said, as we sat in their kitchen, 'we've known your family for over forty years, since you used to play for Bridgnorth Rugby Club. But we have some grave concerns, not the least the impact the pigs will have on William's heritage and holiday-let business.'

'Farmers have to make a living,' he said.

'We don't think our visitors are going to enjoy the smell of the pig waste being spread just yards from the lawn where we serve our teas . . .'

I turned towards John Cantrill, who now largely ran the farm. 'The lane is unfit for big industrial vehicles,' I said. 'It's just not safe. It's falling apart. Somebody could have been killed when you had your accident.'

I could sense the atmosphere becoming strained.

'The problem, William, is that you may have lived around here a while,' interjected Roger, 'but you're still just a townie.'

A *townie*.

In the end, reason prevailed, and the pig farm application was withdrawn. It wasn't long after our meeting that Roger got cancer and sadly died. His funeral at St Gregory's Church in Morville was packed as he was a highly respected member of the local community where he had lived all his life. He was a splendid farmer of the old school. He could not have imagined how local agricultural land prices had rocketed in the final decade of his life to over £10,000 an acre. His Upper House farm estate and pretty Georgian house were worth millions.

But perhaps Roger was right. Although I'd never thought of myself as a townie, I suppose that was how many other locals viewed me. As a young boy, I had been brought up in Islington and Stockwell. I was not only a townie but I had made little effort to get to know the real community; I had never attended a Morville parish council meeting. To my shame, I hardly knew most of the people in our hamlet. I had never attended the annual Christmas concert at Morville Hall hosted by Chris and Sara Douglas.

That was to change. For well over two years, our resistance group attended weekly meetings, drank tea, munched biscuits and quietly – but resolutely – organised our very English rebellion. Our *Art of War* was a planning battle manual called *Not in Our Back Yard* by Anthony Jay, co-creator and writer of the BBC series *Yes, Prime Minister*. He become our Sun Tzu. His main philosophy was that, while it might seem like an unwinnable battle ahead, bureaucrats were all 'immensely vulnerable'.

Jay's key advice was 'eternal vigilance' and 'criticise the proposal, never the personalities'. And if you lose, you lose fighting but accept it. At least you will have given the council and the developer, or landowner, a bloody nose and ended up with a 'far more healthy, neighbourly and unified community'.

This last point touched a nerve over the three years of our fight. What I came to realise, as countryside campaigner Christopher Booker had noted in his preface to Jay's guerrilla war manual, is that fighting such planning battles as a local team makes people come together in a common cause. It is not until you are faced with some catastrophic threat to your little slice of English Arcadia that you realise how lucky you are to live in such a place, and why it is special.

As part of my campaign lobbying, I managed to get a meeting at the House of Commons with planning minister the Rt Hon Greg Clark, who was in charge of the Government's National Planning Policy Framework reforms. I had met Greg at a fringe meeting at the Manchester Tory Party conference sponsored by Taylor Wimpey homes. He remembered me from our Cambridge days.

'The draft reforms hardly mention the word "heritage", Greg,' I said, as we drank tea with a senior member of his department sitting in. 'The presumption in favour of conservation has been removed. So has most of Planning Policy Statement Five, which covers the historic environment.'

'There will be safeguards for protecting heritage,' Greg said.

'If an important Grade I medieval building like Great Coxwell Barn is no longer protected, what's the point in having statutory protections?'

'I'd be very happy for you to set this all out in a report,' the planning minister said. 'You can submit it to my department and it will be read, along with any recommendations you may have.'

My report ended up being eighty pages long and was based on three months of travelling around the country looking at historic sites, buildings and landscapes that were under threat. These included Naseby battlefield (the most important of the English Civil War); the Grade I Elizabethan mansion and gardens of Lyveden New Bield (featured in the Gunpowder Plot); Grade I Kimbolton Castle, home of King Henry VIII's first wife, Catherine of Aragon; the Somerset village of East Coker, immortalised by T. S. Eliot in *The Four Quartets*; and Upton Cressett.

The first draft of the new planning reforms had greatly diluted heritage and landscape protection. Indeed, it looked as if almost a century's worth of hard fighting from such heritage and countryside defenders as Lord Curzon, Patrick Abercrombie (founder of the Council for the Protection of Rural England in 1926), Clough Williams-Ellis, J. B. Priestley, John Betjeman, Olive Cook, and more recent champions like Roy Strong, Marcus Binney, Max Hastings and Simon Jenkins would be undone.

The reference to Great Coxwell Barn – a Grade I thirteenth-century wheat grange standing majestically alone on the edge of a village in the Oxfordshire landscape – was one of the first places I visited. It was easy to see why the setting of the barn was described by William Morris as 'the finest architecture' and 'unapproachable in its dignity'. With the new planning reforms only in draft form, an 'executive housing development' had been greenlit by a planning inspector that would harm its noble setting. The truth was that the threat to the historic landscape of England was as great as that to the country house in the post-war era. This battle wasn't just about Upton Cressett any more.

I realised how bad things were becoming nationally when I was sitting inside the former manor house of Sir Thomas Malory in Winwick with my planning-adviser friend Adrian Snook. With quiet determination, and the persistence of a self-trained planning lawyer, he helped people ('fighting for the cause') escape from the threat of developers. These were often European energy giants.

The historic village of Winwick is set in unspoilt countryside around six miles east of Rugby and has a population of around forty. The tiny village has no pub or shops and just a small church, whose celebrated bell tower has been the only notable feature of the skyline for the last eight hundred years. It was a picture-postcard village for the idea of England that David Cameron was so keen to champion in 2008 as 'national treasures to be cherished and protected for everyone's benefit'.

No longer. As I drove into Winwick village, the first thatched cottage I saw had a Union flag flying above its black-painted door. In the window was a large sign that read: 'No Desecration Here'. The centre of life remains its village hall and its annual church fête, held in the manor's gardens. The owner of the Grade II* manor was John Temple, a former chairman and senior partner of a Milton Keynes-based law firm, who was formerly with legal powerhouse Slaughter and May in London. He collected art, maintains an Elizabethan knot garden (co-designed by his wife), and his company biography listed his interests as 'art, architecture, and walking'.

John Temple was the sort of Englishman who did *The Times* crossword, went to the Royal Academy summer exhibition and always voted Tory. As he stood in the afternoon sun collecting £2 each (proceeds towards the church) from fête visitors to enter through the triumphal arch of the manor opening on to the original entrance court – the time-worn stone spandrels of the arch still bear heraldry of the sixteenth-century family owners after Malory – he looked every inch your quintessential English solicitor just retired.

But, despite retirement, he was now spending most of his time poring over planning appeals and planning law. German energy giant EON wanted to build a cluster of seven gargantuan wind turbines on a ridge of unspoilt countryside directly behind the manor. The proposed turbines were the equivalent of putting twenty-five double-decker buses on top of each other.

As we sat in his manor drawing room after the fête, drinking wine with Adrian Snook, Temple made clear that the planning reforms were riling him. 'We do not want our landscape wrecked,' he said.

The planning reforms – with a new 'presumption' in favour of development – were causing an outbreak of civil war in the shires, with farmers and developers being pitted against villagers and many councillors. Whether it was housing, green-belt ribbon development, caravan parks, HS2, pig farms, bypasses, turbines, solar parks or gravel pits, once-harmonious rural villages were being ripped apart as people tried to defend themselves against an unwanted plague of planning applications that threatened to change the face of the English countryside and our historic market towns and cathedral cities.

Of course, the country needed new housing and infrastructure, but there was a sense that the battle was being taken to the very edge of the village green. The Town & Country Planning Act of 1954 (which separated town and country) was being ripped up.

'The countryside has not seen anything like it since the enclosure system defiled rural life,' said Adrian, after we left Winwick Manor. We retired to a local pub for a pint of beer.

'What's your advice to save Upton Cressett?' I said. 'If they can stick seven giant turbines in the back garden of Malory's old fifteenth-century manor, they can do the same at Upton Cressett.'

'What grade listing is Upton Cressett?'

'We're Grade II*,' I said. 'The church is only Grade II.'

'Were your listing to be upgraded, it could be a game-changer,' Adrian said.

'I think our listing goes back to the 1950s when there were pigs living in the house.'

'The whole listing system is in need of reform,' Adrian said. 'Many buildings were designated without sufficient architectural knowledge by unqualified surveyors just cycling around with a camera and a clipboard.'

As we ordered another pint, Adrian then outlined a 'double pincer' strategy to save Upton Cressett. The campaign had to be both local and national.

'Upton Cressett is such a historic site,' he said. 'Have you got any other ancient monuments?'

'My uncle is – or was – an archaeologist who used to bang on about there being a lost Roman fort or settlement in the surrounding fields.

He discovered a farmer with a hoard of Romano-British artefacts and coins found near the house. I don't think anything came of it. There's also a medieval village but I don't think that's designated either.'

'Can you speak to the farmer? A lost Roman settlement could be a clincher.'

'We have troubled relations,' I said.

'Photographs?'

'There were some – jewellery, pottery, axe heads. Heaven knows where they are.'

'Get on to your uncle,' Adrian said. 'Your only real chance of saving Upton Cressett is to have your Roman settlement designated by English Heritage as a Scheduled Ancient Monument and get the main house and church upgraded to Grade I. The Gatehouse as well. That is pretty much your *only* chance of winning. Have any royals been to stay or visit?'

'Not lately,' I said. 'One of the princes in the Tower, reputedly, back in 1483 and Prince Rupert in the Civil War.'

'Excellent. Any historical connections with a house will always help with designation,' he said. 'The more royals, the better.'

My Uncle Jonathan had hardly left his Sheffield hotel room in a year. I hadn't seen him since my grandmother's funeral. He had no car. His Upton Cressett archaeological papers were still in the Sheffield storage unit, although he had been muttering about the cost.

'One final tip,' said Adrian. 'If you do get anywhere, don't reveal your cards too soon. It's like a murder trial. You need to wait until the *very* last moment to produce your new evidence. Anything Grade I, or a new Scheduled Ancient Monument designation, is a potential killer punch.'

Mon Oncle

My Uncle Jonathan hadn't been to Upton Cressett for over a decade and had become an academic recluse and book-hoarder who belonged in a Harold Pinter play. When we were once tramping around a hill fort in Somerset, I asked him why he became an archaeologist. He had been taught about the Dark Ages and battles of Romano-British history from when he was about eight, but it wasn't until he went on a cruise around the Aegean and the Greek Islands with my grandparents (who loved a cruise) in the early 1970s, aged sixteen, that he had decided digging up the past was his calling: 'We were in Crete and we were going around the Palace of Knossos – the oldest Bronze Age city in Europe – and I somehow split away from the tour party. I saw this ladder heading into a pit and climbed down it. At the bottom, I found a bearded man excavating with a trowel.'

The man turned out to be the head of the British School in Athens and was leading the dig on the Palace of Knossos that had been started by Sir Arthur Evans in 1900. He explained to my sixteen-year-old uncle that he was examining a chalk Bronze Age burial site and showed him what he had found.

'This just fired my imagination,' recalled Jonathan. 'I knew from the moment I got back on the ship that that was what I wanted to do with my life. To be an archaeologist. I was down in that chalk pit so long the cruise tour guide had to send a search party to find me.'

My uncle was an intellectually gifted historian who could have become a leading archaeologist in his field (he had been attached to Sheffield and Liverpool universities), but he was a troubled soul whose fragile health subsumed his promising academic career. He had never married.

After my grandparents' deaths, he blew his small inheritance on moving into a four-star hotel in Sheffield – the closest hotel he could find to their graves. He stayed for nearly two years. Much of the rest of his inheritance was spent amassing a vast collection of academic books on British history, classical history and archaeology, along with signed first-edition copies of W. H. Auden, T. S. Eliot and Sylvia Plath.

His collection must have numbered at least four thousand hardback books. Most of the books ordered had not been taken out of their brown parcel paper or Jiffy bags. Signed books were also collected with zeal; one morning ten signed Hatchard's copies of *An Adventure*, Artemis Cooper's biography of Patrick Leigh Fermor, arrived by Royal Mail; another day half a dozen signed copies of *All Hell Broke Loose: The World at War 1939–45* by Max Hastings. Why so many copies?

His photos of the Pugh Hoard and his archaeological field notes on the Roman fort could only be somewhere in the Sheffield storage unit, along with my grandparents' entire house contents and papers – down to their telephone directories, Georgian silver, cruise-liner suitcases, Second World War mess kit and unused kitchen rolls.

An initial attempt to access the storage unit failed when Jonathan refused to hand over the key; he thought his entire archive and vast library of history books were being sold off. Eventually, my father arranged for a giant removal lorry to transport the contents to a barn at Upton Cressett. It took a team of two men an entire day to offload the contents of hundreds of sealed and taped cardboard boxes. None was marked. The chances of my uncle making it to Upton Cressett were zero.

'Jonathan,' I said, into the phone, 'I need your help to save Upton Cressett. We need to get proof of that Roman site you always thought was there.'

'Everything is in my files. You also need to speak with Roger White at Birmingham University,' he said. 'I shared my notes with him.'

When I contacted Dr White, he sent me a copy of his seminal paper, 'Upton Cressett; An Archaeological Assessment'. At the top of the paper he states: 'The author is indebted to Jonathan Roberts for bringing the site to his attention.'

Grade I buildings made up only a tiny fraction of the estimated half-million buildings in England that are listed and appear on the

National Heritage List. When I told my father that I was applying for a listing review upgrade, he initially thought I was mad. Others said the same thing: 'Don't do it – you'll never again be able to make any alterations.'

'But the current listing says Upton Cressett is an *unoccupied* wreck,' I said.

The church of St Michael had only been listed in 1954 and was described as 'deconsecrated and suffering from neglect'. By the late 1950s, when Pevsner came to inspect it, it was in a pitiable state, with broken tombs and gravestones hidden under overgrown brambles. Many of the best features had been removed in 1959, including the Cressett Brass, the Norman font and some seventeenth-century 'Dürer' glass that John Betjeman had liked and noted in *Shropshire: A Shell Guide*. The twelfth-century medieval fresco of golden angels in foliage – whitewashed over in the Dissolution of the Monasteries – was not discovered until 1968, after Pevsner had visited.

As I read through the Shropshire Archaelogical Society report from 1975, my attention was drawn to a strange line at the bottom of the second page under 'Church': 'The Norman Font was acquired by Gordonstoun School in the 1960s but was returned.'

Gordonstoun? When I asked my father what this was about, he said he had been told the story of the font's Scottish journey by Ivor Bulmer-Thomas, a journalist and former MP who was the first chairman of the Redundant Churches Fund, which had taken on St Michael's. The font moved to Gordonstoun School, in Moray, while Prince Charles was at the school, starting in May 1962. According to Bulmer-Thomas, who knew the Duke of Edinburgh, it was 'requested' that the font be moved to Gordonstoun in the Sixties. Why Gordonstoun? One idea was put forward that the heir to the Crown should, while being educated in Scotland, be surrounded by objects of 'ancient *English* beauty'. Bulmer-Thomas also told my father that he had 'a hell of a business' getting the font returned to Upton Cressett in 1969 when it was invested as one of the fund's first churches.

The Prince of Wales is president of the Churches Conservation Trust – as the Redundant Churches Fund later became known. In 2013, he wrote a foreword to Matthew Byrne's *Beautiful Churches: Saved by the Churches Conservation Trust*. In it, he said that 'On every occasion, I marvel at the beauty and history each contains. These churches are a defining feature of the English landscape and of the towns and villages which they serve.'

In the section on 'Earliest Churches', just five Saxon and Norman churches are included. One is the church of St Michael, Upton Cressett; a photograph shows the ancient Norman tub-font that journeyed to Moray for the duration of his education. So that was a third royal connection.

The Case for the Defence

Next stop was the SPAB headquarters at 37 Spital Square, not far from Liverpool Street station. I had been a SPAB member for some years. A phone call established that they had a library going back to its earliest campaigns to protect old buildings and, yes, they had a file on Upton Cressett.

I was handed a thick file of letters and cuttings, then led into a library reading room. The correspondence cast a fascinating new light on the twentieth-century history of the house – a period for which we had only sketchy details, mostly through local farmers and their descendants, as well as elderly house-tour visitors with hazy memories of the Hall after the war.

I soon found a key letter, dated 16 July 1953, sent by Lord Euston, chairman of the SPAB, which began to explain how and why the society had become so interested in trying to save Upton Cressett in the 1950s and '60s. Indeed, without the SPAB president's personal interest, the house might not have survived. When he eventually succeeded as the Duke of Grafton, he later became patron of the Historic Houses Association.

The letter was written by Lord Euston to Sir Herbert Smith Bt, the son of the famous Kidderminster carpet baron – known as 'Piggy' Smith, due to his stocky build and bulldog manners – who had bought the 1,000-acre Upton Cressett estate cheaply in around 1938. He had died in 1943 without doing any restoration. It seemed that he never had much interest in living there.

Dear Sir Herbert,

I was travelling in Shropshire a fortnight ago with Mr Lees Milne of the National Trust and we visited and were very much impressed with the importance and the interest of the Gate House and the . . . house adjoining it, also with the church. Altogether they form one of the most interesting groups of buildings I have ever seen.

I wonder whether there is any prospect of your re-conditioning the Gate House and whether this Society can help you at all in advising on repair. We should be very pleased to make a report for you on the condition of the building. I feel that Upton Cressett is of national importance and this Society is most anxious to help you over it.

I hope you will forgive my bothering you about this but I should be very interested to hear whether you have any plans for the building.

Lord Euston received no reply, so he wrote again. But Smith remained unresponsive. When he did reply, he was evasive to the point of rudeness. He did not live at Upton Cressett and had only inherited the Hall and estate from his father, who had been chairman of the Carpet Trade Rationing Committee in the First World War. He bought the

Upton Cressett estate after a dramatic fire in 1937 had destroyed Witley Court, the former grand Worcestershire house he had bought from the Dudley family in 1920 when the second earl had mounting debts.

But it seems that Witley also became too much for Smith. It was long locally rumoured that the fire had not been an accident and that Smith couldn't afford the upkeep of the lavishly appointed stately home, which had been a royal residence between 1843 and 1846. After the fire, a garden urn had been found in the grounds stuffed with unopened bills. When the Hon Alexandra Foley, direct descendant of Lord Foley, came to stay with us at Upton Cressett for a weekend, she told me, 'It was always said that Smith started the fire by lighting a curtain as an insurance claim.'

Despite repeated efforts by Lord Euston to persuade Smith's son to spend money on repairing the Hall and Gatehouse, he refused, and continued to do so until his death in July 1961. He had no heir, so Upton Cressett continued to decay. Further neglect resulted in the Hall ending up in the late 1960s on the SPAB's endangered-property register, by which time the SPAB were directing their letters to Colonel Henry Marsh OBE (known as 'Peter'), who lived in Monkhopton. The Lord Euston SPAB letters show he had decided to take up Upton Cressett as an architectural cause.

The SPAB file was of great help in putting together my case for Upton Cressett's architectural defence. I began to compile a comprehensive dossier for English Heritage that chronicled the opinions of many of Britain's leading architectural historians, or architectural conservation societies, about Upton Cressett over the last century

Not long after my research at the SPAB, I made a new royal discovery to add to the English Heritage application. I was reading through the Thursby-Pelham and Cressett papers that my father had been handed in a small cardboard box by Deirdre Bird as we left her house in Sussex shortly before the Christie's sale in 2008. One letter sent to James

Thursby-Pelham, who had moved the Cressett family collection of paintings and furniture into 55 Cadogan Gardens, stood out.

It was dated 27 May 1904, written in neat black ink on smart grey embossed paper from Cound Rectory, Shrewsbury. It was from the Reverend Augustus Thursby-Pelham to his nephew James at the Manor House, Kineton, in Warwickshire. The rector wrote that the Gatehouse was 'built to commemorate' the visit of a young royal prince 'who came over on a visit from Ludlow Castle'. This was critical new family evidence that the elder prince in the Tower, the twelve-year-old King Edward V, had indeed stayed at Upton Cressett in 1483.

'The situation is now critical,' I wrote to English Heritage, as the developer had stated in their planning application that my family house was supposedly an 'unoccupied and dilapidated ruin'. Their initial application had gone in a week before. It was now live.

I noted that English Heritage had recently upgraded the lost Tudor garden of Lyveden New Bield's grounds to Grade I status after a German Luftwaffe photograph revealed a historically important garden labyrinth. Since the 1951 listing, when Upton Cressett was derelict, important new information had likewise emerged.

Finally, to support the designation application for the Roman settlement, I needed to find evidence of the Pugh Hoard. To set about the task of trying to locate the Parlour Coppice file, I airlifted in my friend Mowbray Jackson for a few days of what I described as a 'file-hunting holiday'. Mowbray was blessed with natural charm. He belonged in the pages of Waugh's *The Sword of Honour* trilogy. He would have thrived as a cricket-playing officer in the Royal Halberdiers with his first drink religiously mixed for him at 5.45 p.m. in the officers' mess. He threw himself into the task and soon rooted out my grandfather's entire mess kit, along with a ceremonial sword.

We sifted through a ten-foot-high jungle of Jonathan's suitcases, boxes, archaeological marking equipment, golf clubs, video tapes, boxes of old Christmas cards, a decade's worth of *Private Eye* and the

Cricketer, endless antiquarian book catalogues, bin bags filled with school uniforms from the 1960s, boxes of shoe polish, skis, fencing equipment, an unopened box containing a Hilditch & Key shirt, an unopened box containing a Bvlgari silk tie I had sent him one Christmas, and parcels containing enough books to fill a college library. As we threw unopened tins of Fortnum & Mason ginger biscuits and Turkish Delight – years past the expiry date – on to a bonfire, I felt as if we were sorting through the possessions of a dead loved one.

Mowbray went back to London. After another two days, I found a cardboard box that contained tubes of Ordnance Survey maps for Upton Cressett, along with some faded photocopied papers of the Shropshire Archaelogical Society and sheaves of neat handwritten notes on A4 paper. There was a small plastic bag with a label marked 'Parlour Coppice' and field notes relating to various finds Jonathan had made from the ploughed soil ('Field 6874 N/W of Parlour Coppice, Seven Valley Ware, 9mm width'). Another note said 'Lower Golden Furlong Field, 28/12/94, v. windy/rain'. Then there was a brown envelope with 'Do Not Bend' on it. Inside was confirmation of the Pugh Hoard. The details matched later 'surface-collected' photos taken by Professor Roger White on the kitchen table in the Pugh farmhouse. I felt like Heinrich Schliemann on first seeing the gold funeral mask of Agamemnon in 1876.

I sent a copy of all the archaeological work done by Professor Roger White relating to the medieval village and the Romano-British settlement; and finally, I included Jonathan's evidence of the Pugh Hoard that he had first seen when he returned to our kitchen, panting with excitement, after running back through the muddy ploughed fields in the rain. After he had written to me confirming what he had seen in the 1980s, I wrote:

> *The Pugh Hoard included brooches, axe heads, large amounts of pottery and coins. Derek Pugh, the farmer behind Upton Cressett, has over 1,000 pieces collected from the Upton Cressett site – many*

of which are displayed in the kitchen at his farm next to the Hall
and which form part of a valuable archaeological collection.

Dear Dave

Restoring Upton Cressett and reopening the house had made me realise how lucky we are in Britain to be able to step inside our history.
We can walk around the very ruins where the story of England took
place. This was a heritage worth fighting to save before it was too late.
John Ruskin and William Morris were right – our stones of history, our
ancient monuments, architecture and landscape can be redemptive
and need to be defended. They are part of our aesthetic soul and exist
to become sources of delight and to teach us who we are.

Protesting the lack of heritage and landscape safeguarding in the
draft planning reforms, I sent a letter to David Cameron at Downing
Street signed by eighty luminaries from the world of heritage, arts,
finance, business and politics, headed by Loyd Grossman, chairman
of the Heritage Alliance. The letter also appeared as a news story in
the *Daily Telegraph*.

David Cameron replied with a typed two-page letter on 10 Downing
Street stationery that arrived at *Spear's* offices on 5 May 2012. He said
that the Government had made it 'very clear' in the new National
Planning Policy Framework (NPPF) that protections for the 'historic
environment' would remain 'robust'. 'We have listened carefully to all
those who commented on the consultation . . . and we believe it has
been strengthened by their responses.'

I then watched on television as Greg Clark announced the final
changes to the planning system. When he singled out 'heritage' for
special protection in the new NPPF, I punched my fist in the air.
All the campaigning had seemingly paid off. Although there was no
return to the former 'presumption in favour of conservation', the new

planning framework included the critical reinstatement of 'special consideration' being given to preserving the 'setting' of buildings of significance. In the preface of the National Planning Policy Framework, published on 27 March 2012, Clark wrote: 'Our historic environment – buildings, landscapes, towns and villages – can better be cherished if their spirit of place thrives, rather than withers.' It was a victory of sorts.

At the end of October 2012, I received a bulky letter franked with English Heritage's logo. Inside were five different letters. The first, from a senior designating officer, applied to the main manor house:

Dear William Cash,

Upton Cressett Hall, Upton Cressett Hall, Upton Cressett, Bridgnorth – List Entry Amended
   I am pleased to inform you that having considered our recommendation, the Secretary of State for Culture, Media and Sport has decided to amend the entry for Upton Cressett Hall on the List of Buildings of Special Architectural or Historic Interest. The building is listed at Grade I.
   I attach a copy of our advice report, which gives the principal reasons for this decision.

I glanced through the extensive report, which had removed the errors of the 1951 entry and gave a richly detailed account of the history of the house. As I excitedly read through the new designation listing, I picked up on certain lines: 'Edward V stayed at Upton Cressett in April 1483 on his fateful journey from Ludlow to the Tower of London'; 'It is recorded that a troop of royal horse was garrisoned there for part of the Civil War'; 'Sir Francis Cressett was a significant member of the Royal Court'; and, finally, 'Throughout the house are extensive early-twenty-first-century schemes of painted decoration by the artist

Adam Dant, which incorporate the Upton Cressett sea monster motif and other Tudor-inspired designs.'

I was delighted that Adam's series of murals had been acknowledged as breathing Elizabethan life and colour back into the house and that it had helped with the case for the defence.

The second letter was in regard to the Gatehouse. This was also now designated Grade 1.

The next letter I opened concerned the Church of St Michael – previously only Grade II. This had now been designated Grade I. I could hardly believe what I was reading.

The fourth letter related to the medieval settlement at Upton Cressett. This was now officially an Ancient Scheduled Monument.

It didn't stop there. The last letter was, in many ways, the most emotional to read: 'Roman Settlement, 390m north-east of New House Farm, Upton Cressett . . .' This was my Uncle Jonathan's beloved Romano-British Parlour Coppice site we used to tramp around in the 1980s; it was now officially on the National Heritage List. It was a fantastic result. Under 'Reasons for Designation', the report singled out 'the recovery over many years of substantial quantities of Roman artefacts within the plough soil horizon. The finds included an extensive assemblage of early Roman pottery . . . Pottery and coins from the site have shown that it was occupied from the first century AD, with evidence for activity continuing into perhaps the fourth century.'

I had to sit down at my kitchen table to read the rest of the English Heritage advisory report in full. The upgraded designations would surely be the killer blow to the developer's plans to industrialise the Shropshire Hills around Upton Cressett.

First, I rang Jonathan. As usual, there was no reply on his mobile. He never picked up.

'William here. I have some incredible news. You did it! Your hunch about the Roman site proved to be right. It is now officially a

Scheduled Ancient Monument. Same with the medieval village. Look online tomorrow on the Heritage List.'

Driving back along the Kidderminster to Bridgnorth road after the designation had been made public, I stopped off in the farm shop at Quatt to pick up some sausages and chops for a solo dinner. On the counter, I saw that the Upton Cressett Gatehouse was decorating the front page of the *Bridgnorth Journal.* The headline was 'Grade I Listing for Tudor Hall' with a photo of me at my desk.

That Anna wasn't there with me to savour the victory almost didn't bother me. As I sat alone with my grilled chop and glass of wine, I read:

> An historic gatehouse and hall near Bridgnorth has become one of the most protected sites in Shropshire following a year-long project run by English Heritage. The 12th-century Norman church has also been upgraded. The Gatehouse at Upton Cressett is one of the jewels of Shropshire heritage.

24

Not So Des Res

There had been plenty of good news that would hopefully see off the developers wanting to destroy Upton Cressett – but I also had new financial pressures. Racetrack Lodge's building costs had spiralled and the flat had been on the market since June but was showing little sign of selling. After seventy viewings, there had not been one offer.

The bank was becoming edgy and wanted me to keep lowering the price. My neighbour wanted his 'right-to-light' settlement fee and various lawyers were writing strongly worded letters. The flat had to be sold but I couldn't afford a fire sale.

I moved estate agent. 'If we drop the price again, the flat will be "burned",' said my new agent, Geoff Wilford. 'You may need to be realistic about expectations. Your new front door is on one of the busiest roads in west London. As an agency, we *like* Holland Road . . . but we are one of the few local agencies that does due to the traffic volume. I also think you need to get rid of the incense-burning candles in the basement bedroom. That's a sure giveaway of a smell you're trying to hide.'

Then I came up with the bright idea of contacting my friend Eleanor Mills at the *Sunday Times*. She wrote a regular 'Beyond the Brochure' property column in which she reviewed a 'Property of the Week'. We arranged a date and time and, on the day, before Eleanor arrived, I bought a few bags of logs to welcome her with a burning log fire – like in a London club. One of the best features of the flat were two original fireplaces that worked. Sometimes. It wasn't until I got home that I realised the logs were damp. Still, I had some firelighters and, with some liberal squirting of barbecue lighting fuel, I'd have the fires crackling away nicely.

The logs wouldn't light. They would only smoke. By the time Eleanor arrived, I had had to put them out.

The 'viewing' seemed to go fine; we chatted and gossiped amicably. I had pointed out Simon Cowell's house across the street and the electric gate had managed to open on command. The traffic hadn't been great but at least I had triple glazing to block out the noise. She left, saying she would let me know when the piece was running.

A couple of weeks later, Geoff called to say he had a wealthy Lebanese client who was building a high-end London property portfolio. He had seen Century Lodge, the flat's new official address, and was interested. He also wanted to buy the adjacent basement flat and knock them together. Did I know the basement-owner and could I persuade him? 'Yes,' I said. 'I'll speak to him.'

'The offer is some way from what we wanted but he's a cash buyer,' my agent said. 'He also wants to buy your master bed, all the furniture, art, and anything in the flat you will sell him. He is thinking of renting the flat to start with.'

'My *art*?'

'Don't you have a Howard Hodgkin above the bed?'

'You can tell your client that a property piece on the flat, with colour photographs, is appearing on Sunday and is likely to flush out more interest.'

The Lebanese buyer had come along just before I had taken Anna to the annual Hallowe'en party of my good friend David Ross, co-founder of Carphone Warehouse, at his Elizabethan house of Nevill Holt in Northamptonshire. Made up in greasy war paint for a 'Zombie Apocalypse', we knocked back Espresso Martinis as I discussed the offer with a London 'buying agent' friend at the party who knew my flat.

'Take *any* offer,' he advised. 'The market is sliding since the new stamp duties and nobody wants to buy on Holland Road.'

On the weekend the article was appearing, I had managed to get Anna to stay at Upton Cressett. By 8 a.m. on the Sunday morning, I was down at the local Spar convenience store in Bridgnorth where we bought our newspapers. When I opened the property section of the *Sunday Times*, however, I began to feel the sweat run as I read the 'Beyond the Brochure' headline: 'MISSING THE "X" FACTOR'.

That was one of the more flattering parts of the review. Kingsley Amis liked to say that a bad review might ruin his breakfast but not his lunch. Back at the house, I felt sick. Breakfast was not an option, lunch unimaginable. The buyer was going to pull out – that was almost certain. The bank was going to ask for a revaluation.

I walked into the bedroom with the paper. I felt as if I was holding a death warrant. 'It's a hatchet job, I'm afraid, Anna. I'm finished,' I said. 'The bank is going to see this and will not revise the loan. They will force a sale. And, after reading this, I wouldn't blame them.'

'What does it say?' said Anna. 'It can't be all bad.'

I began reading out excerpts. Each felt like a stroke of the Mills lash: 'I was instructed to meet him "outside Simon Cowell's house" in Holland Park . . . I'm not sure why William wanted me to meet him there, as Century Lodge is on Addison Crescent — hardly adjacent.

It's a couple of busy roads away, on a traffic island in the middle of the Shepherd's Bush–Kensington contraflow.'

'That's true,' said Anna.

'I know, but it's not helpful to say it's on a motorway.'

I read on: 'The master bedroom has a whizz-bang stereo that pipes in music from hidden ceiling speakers — on my visit, Billy Joel's "Uptown Girl" — but it's on the small side (only 11ft wide) and the narrow en suite has no window . . . Downstairs, there's a further small bedroom and bathroom – with the unmistakable smell of damp . . .'

'*Damp?*' repeated Anna. 'Oh dear. What happened to the incense candles?'

'My agent said they were a giveaway.'

'Well, the downstairs does smell musty – she's right about that as well.'

The article continued: 'Dingy subterranean living is not what I'd expect for Holland Park prices . . . Cash is at a loss to explain why his "brilliant bachelor pad" has been on the market for nearly six months . . . Frankly, it has one nice room, a study, an OK main suite and a stinky one downstairs . . . Maybe Cowell will buy the flat to house his butler. Sorry, William, but anyone else should pass.'

Which was exactly what I was expecting my agent's Lebanese client to do.

The following afternoon, Geoff called. 'I've got some good and bad news,' he said.

'Go on.'

'He still wants to buy the flat – but he's lowering his offer by twenty-five thousand. He feels it's been tainted by the review. The flat is also going to need total new damp-proofing in the basement area.'

'That makes it quite a costly review – but I guess we have little choice. Nobody else will touch it now.'

'That's not the only thing,' added Geoff.

'What?'

'He wants all your contents – the bed, the kitchen table, the art, even the stereo in the bedroom.'

I called Anna and told her of the revised deal.

In the end, I agreed to the price drop and to hand over about half of the furniture – including my bed, stereo and ancient Italian olive trees – but not the art (the Hodgkin was only a print). We exchanged in November. I had never been so relieved in my life.

And, of course, Eleanor had been right. The flat was overpriced and the basement bedroom felt like a dank prison cell. I couldn't wait to spend more time at Upton Cressett where I had tried to make a real home. But could I persuade Anna to spend Christmas with me?

When Anna had said to me at our first meeting at the Mansion House that she used to ride, she was being modest. In her bedroom at her family home, she still had her British junior eventing team blazer hanging up. Not long after we started going out, she decided to buy a new horse. It proved no easy task, and when she finally bought Fred, an expensive seventeen-hand colt, his fate and mine became inexorably entangled.

When Fred first arrived from Ireland – bought 'unseen' – Anna called me in tears. 'His leg has swollen below his right knee and he's lame,' she said. 'He's such a lovely horse but I can't enter him in anything. He's going to cost me a fortune and he's only good for horsemeat.'

It was a strange form of third-party emotional osmosis. After finally meeting Fred at his eventing livery yard in Oxfordshire, I, too, became attached to the beautiful grey. I had persuaded Anna not to give him away; I felt somehow that if Anna could turn things around with Fred, she could do so with me as well.

Anna admitted to me that she often found it easier to have close emotional relationships with her horses than with men. In December, we went to the Horse of the Year Show at Olympia with her mother. As we walked around, I saw her eyeing a stand that sold Butet saddles from France. It was as if she had walked into a Maserati dealership.

'Aren't you going to need a new saddle for Fred?' I said.

'But Butet is like buying Hermès,' she said. 'They cost the earth.'

'What makes these French saddles so special?' I asked the woman on the stand.

'A saddle for yourself or your wife?' the Butet woman asked. She looked like a former professional showjumper.

I turned red. 'I don't ride,' I said. 'But my girlfriend has a new horse. A seventeen-hand grey.'

'These have a classic forward balance point for the rider,' the saleswoman said. The most desirable saddle hides were strong but 'thin-cut' luxurious Italian and French leathers that were 'cured' through a traditional and lengthy process. Out of the corner of my eye, I could see Anna examining one particular saddle like a fifteen- year-old after watching *National Velvet*. She had told me that growing up, as a young competitive English junior team showjumper, she had had to work as a waitress and babysitter to pay for crucial bits of tack. She could only ever dream of an expensive French saddle.

The next day, I bought the saddle from the Butet dealer. I would give it to Anna at Christmas. I was optimistic that the new saddle – with a giant red bow tied around it – would be a winning present.

A few days later, Anna called me. 'About Christmas plans,' she said. 'I've got my brother, sister and her family coming, and I really don't think you want to be with us all, and a screaming young baby.'

'Oh,' I said. 'That's a shame, I was hoping we could spend Christmas with your family – and see Fred.'

'You can see me after,' she said. 'I'm sorry.'

There was no point in continuing the conversation. Anna made it clear that she was spending Christmas with her parents and family and I wasn't invited. I spent the day with my parents in Shropshire.

I ended up giving her the saddle after I'd driven down to see her in Hampshire a few days after Christmas. It looked beautiful. Our relationship limped on with a final holiday – a skiing trip in Switzerland at the end of January that included a few days at the World Economic Forum in Davos where *Spear's* was an official magazine.

When I first rang Madame Guler at the Chesa Grischuna in Klosters to get a room, she said they were full. I had been introduced to her back in the late 1990s when I was seeing my fleeting fiancée Louise, whose family always went to Klosters. During Davos, guests included Tony Blair, Bono, Naomi Campbell and the Dutch prime minister.

When I rang up a second time, Madame Guler said, 'Sorry, but we are still completely full, Mr Cash. However, if you don't mind a very basic room, I can put you into a twin maid's room in the staff quarters at the back.'

I took it.

It looked as if it hadn't been redecorated since the 1950s. The change in status from a suite at the Grand Hotel in Cap Ferrat to an attic room in the staff quarters was a metaphor for Anna's and my sliding relationship. We didn't even have a double bed.

Then Anna got 'flu, so she couldn't ski, drink or eat. She just sat shivering in our attic room while I ate alone. She was pretty miserable.

When we got back to her house in Fulham, I carried our suitcases in from the taxi. Standing with the front door open in sleeting rain, I said, 'Check the cab.'

Half an hour later, with Anna asleep and feverish upstairs, I realised we'd left my laptop in the taxi. It had half a novel on it and endless notes. If that wasn't bad enough, I had to finish my piece on Davos, which had been, mercifully, saved overnight on my Gmail, but I now had no computer. I found Anna's tablet in her handbag and stayed up until I'd filed. I slept on the sofa downstairs.

The next morning, she was still feverish and we had a bit of a row. 'I think you should sleep elsewhere tonight,' she croaked.

So, having no flat, I moved into a hotel in Cadogan Gardens, near Peter Jones in Chelsea. It was very close to 55 Cadogan Gardens, the former Thursby-Pelham home where, for so much of the twentieth century, the original collection of Upton Cressett furniture and family paintings had been relocated.

The hotel was comfortable but strange. There was a choice of two very different sorts of room: there were the flowery, chintzy traditional rooms that had been decorated with Colefax & Fowler fabrics and wallpapers in the 1980s; and then there were the 'boudoir' rooms, with huge antique brass beds, 'distressed' bare oak floors and dark-red silk and black tasselled curtains. These had the atmosphere of an expensive Paris '*maison*'.

I opted for a boudoir room.

After I'd broken up with Anna again, I continued to write to her, sometimes just a postcard. In one letter, I wrote in Freudian terms about giving Fred a second chance 'to prove himself'. Clearly, I was hoping she might throw me a lifeline as well. 'I'm just so happy that you are hopefully going to be keeping him on. He's a lovely-looking horse, with a big heart, and I'm glad you are not sending him off to the knacker's yard. It shows you believe in him . . .'

Is it possible to love more than one person at once? I certainly had little difficulty. Is the 'truest' love even the 'right' one? Can love have an afterlife?

My Binder Box letters provide some of the answers, but not all. I was conflicted. I thought I had been in sight of marriage with Anna. But she continued to put up a wall. The truth was her negativity towards our relationship – and Shropshire – had led me to consider jumping ship for a while. I felt I was being pushed away. So low did I feel that I had been in contact with various exes and was even thinking about trying to contact Helen (not that I knew where she was living). I loved Anna but how much emotional torture could I take? I wrote:

Breaking up has oddly been as hard to deal with on some levels as the ending of either of my marriages; of course it wasn't a 'holiday romance'. I am exhausted by life and love. I feel like an old Mercedes with too many miles behind it, whose engine no longer has the heart it used to. If I were a horse, I should probably taken into a corner of the stable and shot.

25

St Valentine's Day Massacre

The end came during dinner on Valentine's Day 2013 before we even got to the first course. The wreckage was beyond salvage.

The dinner was at the Enterprise, an upmarket gastro-pub on Walton Street in Chelsea. I arrived early and had reserved a window table. Recovered from her 'flu, Anna looked radiant in a fur hat. The fact that she had agreed to see me for dinner on 14 February meant she might want to give our doomed relationship another chance. I had written to her several times since my eviction. Maybe the letters had worked.

We began drinking a bottle of champagne. The restaurant was full, we had a table set with a large pink rose and I'm sure that most other diners would have thought we were a lucky couple. We laughed like before. I apologised for blaming her for the laptop loss and thanked her for tracking it down.

'I've been thinking hard about things, Anna,' I said. 'How would you feel if I started to look for a cottage to rent near your parents?

Just for six months? It really hurt me that you didn't invite me for Christmas, you know.'

'What about Upton Cressett?'

'I'm sorry you don't like Shropshire. But I'm prepared to make some changes if you are as well.'

'Would you ever sell the place?' she said, bringing up the unmentionable. 'It's too far for me. I work in London. I have a horse in Oxfordshire. I have to be in the office by nine o'clock on a Monday. You can work in the country but I can't. To be honest, I don't think we have a future, William. Our holiday romance is now *over*.'

A coldness had entered her tone.

'What do you mean, over?'

She was now getting up from the table. We hadn't even ordered yet.

As she stood up she reached into her handbag and pulled out a green envelope. Inside was a card with two sides of her convent-school writing.

'Happy Valentine's.'

'Just sit down a second, please,' I said. I opened the card.

'Tonight saddens me greatly,' she said. 'When we first had dinner, I really did think I'd met a wonderful guy. Tall, dark, intelligent, entertaining, older, wiser . . . fascinating worldly insights. You appeared to be very romantic, thoughtful and caring.'

I could hear a small revolver being loaded. The bullet was coming.

'I know men don't change, and although I thought you might, I was wrong . . . Did you honestly think I wouldn't find out? No wonder you've had two failed marriages and multiple relationship breakdowns. Well, add another to the list.'

'What are you talking about?'

'I remained guarded because I didn't trust you and it seems I was correct. Only last week, after the ghastly return journey from Davos, when I was so ill, you were trying to woo another girl . . .'

I looked up. 'Who?' I said putting the card down. I could feel sweat running down my back.

She pulled out a wad of stapled-together emails with pink fluorescent highlighter pen marking up lines. They had the Google logo at the top of each page.

'Take a look at these,' she said. 'You made the mistake of not logging your Gmail out of my tablet when you wrote your Davos article on my kitchen table. So I've been trawling through your correspondence.'

I glanced at the various email chains. Most looked like friendly emails to old friends – often married – or work communications to women in my professional banking and legal network.

'I use my Gmail for *Spear's* work,' I protested. 'I get pitched the whole time by female journalists, PRs, bankers and lawyers. Taking them out is my job, just as you do with clients.'

'And you've been in contact with various exes again. You just can't fucking let go, can you? You know I hate you talking about your exes. It makes me feel second best, which is why *I* never fully "let go".'

'I'll be honest with you, Anna,' I said. 'I always loved you. But all your negativity, about me, my friends, even *selling* Upton Cressett . . . it became too much.'

At this point, she placed the stapled wad of paper on my plate, grabbed her coat and walked out. I might as well have been served with divorce papers. I deserved it but Anna's coolness – especially about the impossibility of living at Upton Cressett – had driven me to despair.

I sat at the table on my own for around half an hour. I kept an eye on the window. But she wasn't coming back. Valentine's was cancelled. My Binder Box letters had come back to haunt me.

I finished the bottle of champagne and stood outside on the pavement. It was a cold and clear night. There were no taxis. As I looked up to the St Valentine moon and the bright stars above me, glimmering like a galaxy of tea-lights, I felt oddly liberated. I raised the velvet collar on my navy coat and began to walk towards Sloane Square.

* * *

'An awayday return to Folkestone, please,' I said at the ticket counter.

'When are you returning?' the man said.

'I honestly don't know,' I said. 'I have no luggage.'

'We don't do a same-day return any more,' he said. 'A standard return is valid for a month.'

'That will do,' I said.

I had no idea where Helen was living. It was possible she was with her mother in Folkestone. We hadn't had any contact for around two years. The last postcard I had written her had received no response. I remembered the card as my blue-black ink had been smudged by the tears that ran down my face as I got to the final line. So, I was going to Folkestone, but I hadn't arranged to see Wilhelmina. The chances were she'd tell me Helen had a new boyfriend or was engaged. But it was worth a try.

When I was seeing Helen three years before, we would go for after-noon walks along the famous Leas promenade with her baby daughter Stephanie in a buggy. We'd stop in cafés and have a hot chocolate or sit on a bench by the Leas Cliff bandstand.

I never made it to Folkestone beach that morning, but I saw the newly listed arches and viaduct of Folkestone harbour. The harbour was tatty, run-down and badly in need of regeneration. The pubs had old men with leathery tattoos staring into their glasses and watching last night's European football. There were the usual loan shop and currency exchange kiosks, fish and chip and kebab takeaways and pawnbrokers. Everything was closing down or expiring from lack of hope.

But that is exactly what I liked about the new English Heritage listing designation for the thirteen viaduct arches of Folkestone harbour and its historic swing bridge. In awarding Grade II listing to the arches, the nation's heritage guardian invested the 'striking viaduct' with historic dignity. It had been listed due to the 'sombre significance' of its role during the First World War.

As I stood on the harbour quay, with seagulls swooping above, and looked out towards the old docks where hundreds of thousands of soldiers had embarked on their steamships for Flanders, so many crossing the Channel for the last time, it was almost impossible not to believe in the 'Spirit of Place'. The soldiers would have marched down from the 'rest camps' on the Leas and their last steps on English soil would have been along the street – now known as the Road of Remembrance – to the old docking harbour; some would have come direct from the harbour railway station.

By midday, I was hungry and nervous. I felt as if I was heading towards my emotional Western Front. What if Helen was there? As I began slowly walking back up the Road of Remembrance towards the clifftop promenade and Helen's family home, I thought of our correspondence. I had always liked and admired Helen's mother Wilhelmina but she had made it clear to me in various letters that she didn't want to become embroiled in my relationship with Helen or act as my go-between.

Before reaching the turning to Helen's house, I passed a florist. If I was going to knock unannounced on the door, I needed a gift or, at least, a gesture. A beautiful bouquet would do fine.

At around 1 p.m., when I thought Wilhelmina was likely to be in, I headed towards Jointon Road clutching an enormous bunch of yellow and white roses. I recognised the house. Or I thought I did. I had no idea which number it was. All the driveways looked the same. But then I recognised the car. I heard a dog barking. Wilhemina was at home.

She opened the door.

'William,' she said. 'What are you doing here? Helen is not here.'

'I'm not here to see Helen, I have no idea where she's living. My letters went unanswered. I was just hoping to see you. There are a few things I wanted to talk about.'

'Come in,' she said. 'It's good to see you.'

I handed her the flowers and she led me into the drawing room.

'Are you hungry? I was just making some lunch. Would you like some tea, or a glass of wine?'

'If a bottle is open. Thank you.'

As she cooked some lunch, we chatted almost as if nothing had happened between Helen and me. We spoke about Stephanie, and how she was getting on at nursery. We talked about Upton Cressett and how I'd finally moved in. It was all friendly. I never once asked if Helen had a boyfriend or where she was living.

'I saw the photos and story in *Country Life*,' she said.

The issue featuring the Dant murals was lying on her coffee-table in the drawing room.

'I'm lucky to have found Adam,' I said.

'He is a genius,' Wilhelmina said. 'We did all so enjoy spending Easter with him.'

No mention of the Venus nude cartouche resemblance.

Finally, I decided to get to the point. 'The reason I wanted to see you is that I haven't heard from Helen in a very long time. I wrote to her a couple of times at Markham Street but had no reply.'

'She moved out not long after the press arrived.'

'That would explain why I never heard from her.'

'She's no longer in London.'

'I'm here because I'd like you, please, to have a word with her,' I said. 'You know I loved her. I think you could see we were very happy together. Maybe we can still be. I'd hate to spend the rest of my life not knowing. One moment we were very close and then . . . when the Boris story appeared and the paparazzi showed up here on your doorstep, it was suddenly all over. I just want you to know I had nothing to do with any of it.'

'I always said any press would be bad for your relationship with Helen,' Wilhelmina said. 'I know you loved her. But she always makes up her own mind.'

'That's why I wanted to get the super-injunction. You were there when I said I'd pay for it. But the lawyers said it wasn't worth the money as a judge was likely to rule that the identity of the father was in the public interest.'

'Yes, it would have been a waste of money.'

'Helen may have told you that we ran into each other at a book-launch party. It was very distressing. What I didn't know then, but do now, is that my phone was regularly hacked when I was with Helen – I imagine hers was as well. And probably Boris's.'

'So, the information in the paper came from your phone?'

'Yes. Or hers. You can tell her that. I was called twice by Scotland Yard after various raids to say my name and number appeared on the hackers' phone lists. I know Helen and Boris thought I somehow was to blame for the story leaking but I think you know that's not true. That was the very opposite of what I wanted. I wanted to marry her.'

'You certainly had nothing to gain.'

'I loved Helen very much and I'd hate never to see her again, or for her to think I betrayed her. Could you have a word with her and see if she'll have lunch with me?'

'William,' she said, 'I cannot and will not speak for Helen. She is now a thirty-eight-year-old woman. But I can try.'

'Do you think she will ever want to ever get married?'

'I cannot and will not speak for my daughter,' she said again. 'As I told you before, I have been through much in my lifetime. For better or worse, Helen will make her own decisions.'

About a week later, I received a text from Helen; she agreed to meet me for lunch.

I didn't want to go anywhere we were likely to see anybody we knew, so I chose Rules in Covent Garden, London's oldest restaurant. The restaurant's walls had seen and heard everything before. I had no idea if Boris had ever taken Helen there but I was determined to avoid all mention of him.

I got to Rules early and ordered a bottle of champagne. I made sure we had a discreet corner table. I knew Helen had probably made up her mind as to how things would progress before she even walked into the restaurant.

In case it went well, I had bought her a bottle of Guerlain's L'Heure Bleue (gift-wrapped that morning at Peter Jones), which I had in my overcoat pocket. 'For Guerlain loyalists' was how the *parfum* was described. From the moment I inhaled the tester bottle's heavily musky floral scent, I was transported back to my grandmother's mink world of the 1950s – the world of Sybil Colefax, Nancy Mitford and oyster dinners at Prunier in St James's Street.

Helen arrived on time, wearing her mink coat. She drank a glass of champagne and looked as beautiful as I had remembered. There was very little awkwardness. Within twenty minutes, we were laughing and talking as if the last two years had never happened. She had lost none of her disarming candour and wit. Although I mentioned the phone hacking, she wasn't interested in such banal details. She looked happy to see me and she was doing what Helen did best – living in the moment. The past was past. We talked about Upton Cressett, Folkestone, my meeting with her mother, her daughter Stephanie, her dachshunds, Pierre, and her Fissler cooking pans. Anything but Boris.

She was now living in a rented manor house in Kent – with the same nanny – so she wasn't too far from her mother. By the time we launched into the second bottle, I was relieved to hear no mention of any boyfriend. Neither had the 'B' word surfaced.

'You were right about the cooking pans,' I said. 'I swear by them. You never told me the best thing about them is that they have special handles that don't get hot. You'll have to come up to Upton Cressett and try them out. And you can see Adam's murals.'

'I heard from my mother that they're wonderful. Maybe I should do another show with him.'

'I'm meant to be seeing him at an opening tonight – we could drop by if you like.'

'You were right about number sixteen being lucky as well,' I added. 'Did you ever get that postcard I sent you from Monaco?'

'No.'

'Well, I was there to test-drive a new supercar before the Monaco Grand Prix. I never got to drive the car but I did end up in the casino and I put some money on sixteen and the neighbours, as you always used to. And I won!'

She laughed. 'Well, there are no casinos in my village in Kent.'

As the waiter cleared away the remains of our steak and kidney pudding, Helen said, 'I'm going outside for a cigarette. Will you keep me company?'

It was cold and we were coatless as we stood on the Maiden Lane pavement outside the Rules canopy. Helen asked me to light her cigarette. Then I kissed her. It seemed as natural as when I had first kissed her in the parking bay off Sloane Avenue just over three years before.

When we got back to our table, I gave her the L'Heure Bleue. She opened and dabbed a little on her wrist and her neck. She smelt divine.

'The bottle and label haven't changed since the 1950s,' I said. 'The Queen Mother used to wear it, and the Queen apparently.'

We left Rules at around 3.15 p.m. Instead of hailing a taxi, I led her across the street to the Church of Corpus Christi, which had been founded in 1873 as a 'sanctuary specifically devoted to the Adoration of the Blessed Sacrament'. It was sometimes known as the Actors' Church.

I lit a candle and knelt in prayer away from the few tourists with rucksacks. Then we had a drink at a hotel bar and went to Adam Dant's exhibition launch in St James's. When I walked in with Helen, Adam looked pretty startled.

'Hello, Adam,' said Helen. 'I've been hearing about your wonderful murals at Upton Cressett. I'm hoping to see them soon.'

After the Dant show, Helen returned to Kent on the train. The next day, I got a text inviting me down to see her, Stephanie and her village manor house – 'Come down and stay the weekend.' The weekend with Helen! I could hardly believe it. I suddenly thought all my prayers were being answered at once.

Happy days, indeed, and, yes, it was a happy lunch.

I went to Kent early on a Saturday morning. At the station, I picked up a present for Stephanie (I had something for Helen in my suitcase) and sat on the train to Ashford trying to read the paper but mostly staring out of the window. After so many romantic derailments, I thought I was now heading through a tunnel marked 'Happiness' with Helen.

It had been a long voyage. For some time – and not just since moving into my hotel – my life had been as unstable as a spinning top.

Helen was at the station to collect me. The personal numberplate was the same but she had changed the car. It was now a smart navy Mercedes convertible. Everything went well. We had lunch in front of a cosy fire in a pub not far from her home. Stephanie was as enchanting, bright and pretty as I had expected; I had absolutely no problem with the idea of helping to raise her or becoming her stepfather.

In the afternoon, we drove to Broadstairs on the south-eastern Kent coast and visited the old lifeboat station, which sold beach toys, walked around Viking Bay, had a knickerbocker glory in one of the half-empty ice-cream parlours and took Stephanie to an amusement arcade. I saw where Charles II had landed on the beach after returning from exile to claim the Crown. I felt as if my life was finally on track. I saw my weekend invitation as a form of divine Restoration. There was a sense of the last pieces of a jigsaw fitting into place.

We then returned to Helen's house for dinner. It was not a grand and sprawling manor with a long drive but rather a small village manor house right on the edge of a green with a large garden leading down to a small stream. I could see why Helen liked the idyllic Kent village setting with the water below. After Stephanie went to bed, and Helen began cooking dinner, I unpacked the gift I had brought for Helen and carried it downstairs.

'I got you this some time ago,' I said, placing the rectangular object on her kitchen table. 'I was waiting for the right moment to give it to you. I notice you've got quite a bit of empty wall space so hopefully you can find a spot for it.'

It was a framed drawing of an English village church by one of her favourite artists, the Scottish painter David Roberts, RA. I can recall reading in bed once while Helen – on the other side – tried to negotiate the sale of a Roberts Orientalist painting in a private collection for several million dollars.

'It's part of a pair of Roberts drawings I bought at auction,' I said. 'The other hangs at Upton Cressett, so you can see it when you come up. They belong together.'

'Any idea what church it is?'

'No. But it's the sort of English village church I'd like to get married in – one day.'

Helen loved it.

After we'd sat down to dinner, and I'd opened a bottle of wine, I asked if she had been wearing the Guerlain scent I had given her at Rules. I noticed she wasn't that evening.

'I'm afraid something awful happened, William, which I'm very sorry about,' she said. 'I obviously didn't put the stopper back on properly after opening it at lunch. When I travelled back to Kent on the train, the bottle must have knocked over in my bag. By the time I reached my station, it was almost empty.'

'Don't worry,' I said. 'I'll get you another.'

'It made me very upset.'

The idea of her L'Heure Bleue spilling was a blow. Replacing it wasn't the issue. It just felt like a bad omen, like losing – or cutting off – an engagement ring.

Dinner continued. The Guerlain incident was soon forgotten as I started tentatively to map out what sort of life I could see us having together. There came a point when I had to bring up Boris. If I was going to have a future with Helen, I would also be bringing up his daughter.

'Stephanie is such a lovely child,' I said. 'If things move forward like I hope they do, I just want you to know that I will be the best possible stepfather to her. I also have absolutely no axe to grind with Boris. The important thing is that he knows Stephanie is going to have a secure life with a loving mother and family.'

I hadn't dared raise the question of where we might live. The way Helen was talking about her 'home' in Kent and being close to her mother in Folkestone, I was getting the impression that she was very happy bringing Stephanie up in Kent. I wasn't sure she would jump at the prospect of moving her entire life to Shropshire. I hadn't properly thought through all this when I had been dreaming out of the window on the train down thinking of how my life was about to change.

'Shropshire has some good schools,' I volunteered. 'I went to Moor Park, near Ludlow, aged seven. I was very happy there. It's all co-ed now.'

'Steph is doing well at her school here.'

'Have you discussed schools with Boris?' I said. 'I remember when you came back from that summit meeting with him at Brown's, you said he was happy about the idea of Stephanie growing up in Shropshire. And you liked the idea of Stephanie having a brother or sister, or both, so that she grew up as part of a larger family.'

'I've built a new life for Steph in Kent,' Helen said.

And then came the unexpected body blow. 'I'm glad you're here, William,' she said. 'I loved Rules and seeing you again. But I have to tell you something important. I want to be honest with you.'

'Go on,' I said.

'I'm not sure I want to get married any time soon . . . I'm perfectly happy, just me and Steph.'

I hadn't seen this coming. Then I remembered what she had said two years ago: 'Marriage is just a piece of paper.'

'But two years ago, you were keen to start a new family. You said you wanted Steph to have a brother or sister. That made me very happy. You know how much all I've ever wanted is to have a family. I thought you did as well.'

'Let's not discuss it now,' Helen said. 'Before we take things forward, we've got to talk this through.'

And so dinner continued. I quickly changed the subject. But I was beginning to panic. I loved Helen but this had come completely out of *le bleu*.

The next morning, I got up early and needed to go for a walk. I was rattled. Was my love for Helen based on a dream? Was I deluded? Could I honestly be happy bringing up Boris and Helen's daughter as my only child? Unmarried and without the prospect of my own family? Perhaps not even living at Upton Cressett?

I walked for several miles around the Kent countryside brooding. I headed towards Ickham. It was a blustery day, cold but with broken clouds of sombre grey that hovered impatiently in the sky. I passed thatched cottages, watermills and even an old toll house. I just needed to walk. As much as I felt so happy to see Helen, I was now worried.

Later, we read the papers, cooked breakfast, then headed off for another day of local sightseeing. I avoided the subject of marriage, Boris, Shropshire or children. We had a nice lunch, Steph dozing in her pushchair. No doubt everyone in the pub thought we were just another local Kent couple taking our little daughter out for Sunday lunch. If only they knew.

It began to rain – cold March rain – as we headed into Folkestone. We had Sunday tea with Helen's mother and stepfather Kerry. I enjoyed their company but I was not my usual self. I ate my slice of cake, drank the Darjeeling tea, then started to think how much I was looking forward to staring out through the carriage window, rain streaming down it, as I headed towards Wolverhampton station.

'I've got to get home,' I said. 'I have to go back to London and change at Euston.'

I can remember exactly how I felt as Helen dropped me off at the station. When I kissed her on the lips I sensed it was for the last time.

Can you record or gauge levels of human love? Like V8 or V12 horsepower on a car engine? I had loved Helen as much as either of my wives, maybe more. She had made me as happy as any woman had ever done. But in what I thought would be my final victory lap, the engine had blown. 'DNF – Did Not Finish'. When Helen said she didn't want to get married and was happy with 'Just me and Steph', it was as if a sleeping spaniel had suddenly raised its head from under a card table and knocked my Het Steen manor jigsaw puzzle off in one awful blow. The carefully assembled pieces – almost finished after three years – were now scattered in a mess all over the carpet.

It was a strange and conflicting time. Life-changing decisions needed to be made, so much so that I had called my old therapist, Leona Raphael, and asked to see her for several sessions at her office in Roehampton. I was being pulled apart by opposing romantic currents. I felt she was the only person I could speak to.

I had also received a set of handwritten postcards from Anna ('I finally write ...!'), who was now remorseful about walking out of dinner ('I was very rude about Shropshire'), and grateful that I had stepped in at the eleventh hour to stop her equine vet putting down Fred because of his leg. She had recently been at a business event at the Mansion House and it had shaken her: 'The last couple of months have been tough . . . When we met two years at the Mansion House, I was a different person . . . less worldly, forthright, less easy-going, focusing on wrong values, but you've changed all that. When I was there two weeks ago, I felt terribly sad and, frankly, left terribly sad. I just couldn't tell you I've tried to deal with my feelings for you by silence and hoping time will heal these. Perhaps that is what you felt with Helen?'

But I had finally to let both Helen and Anna go, not least as my journey had taken a surprising new turn – an unexpected sighting of an Arcadian vista that I thought had closed.

A few days after I'd returned home, I wrote to Helen on an Upton Cressett postcard:

> *Just a short note to say thank you for the weekend at* Le Manoir *in Kent. It was so lovely to see you and I am looking forward to hopefully seeing you here at UC in the near future. It's such a beautiful day here – not a house for living alone in in the winter.*

The card was never sent. My Binder Box still contains the original. A few weeks later, I wrote again apologising about 'being useless' at calling Helen; I wasn't able to bear the thought of starting a new life with her and not having my own family as well.

> *Another side to me thinks that if you were truly happy and secure in love you may very well change your mind but I could never bear the idea of losing you again because we were arguing over this issue. Elizabeth thinks you would come around if I made you truly happy – but you are right. You can't really love somebody and then start laying down conditions.*

I ended by asking her to think about meeting up for lunch in London 'once I've got the book finished and I'm less gloomy about life'.

But there was to be no second Rules lunch. The card was *The Picnic* by the twentieth-century American artist George Bellows, painted shortly before he died suddenly, aged just forty-two. I had planned to see his new Royal Academy show with Helen. I went alone and knew when I posted the card that that truly was the end of the affair.

There was another reason why the first postcard was never sent and why the second took weeks to be posted – I was happily in love again.

Her name was Laura.

26

Venice in the Rain

In Rex Whistler's Venetian-inspired love-letter to Caroline Paget in the dining room at Plas Newydd, Rex depicts himself in several guises. In one section, as I have mentioned, he is dressed as a gardener with a broom, sweeping away the rose petals scattered along an Italian colonnade. He also paints himself as a Venetian gondolier, plunging his pole into the water as he ferries his boat across the choppy fairytale lagoon.

It was time to plunge in my gondolier's pole – with a trip to Venice. With Laura. Yes, *that* Laura, who I was long resigned to thinking had been a mirage. Ever since the sight of her black taxi tail-lights disappearing off into the February rain, I had been haunted by the song from the 1944 film noir *Laura* directed by Otto Preminger: 'And you see Laura on a train that is passing through . . . That was Laura but she's only a dream.'

But what if it wasn't only a dream? What if the way I had felt on our first meeting had never changed, and she really was the one?

If revisiting my Binder Boxes of over twenty-five years has taught me anything it is that people do not usually know the truth about why they make the ultimate and most important choices that they do; or why, or *when*, they act as they do.

While an inner voice had told me that Laura had just been a dream, the reality was that I had never been able to forget her, or that first dinner where I had sat next to her at that long since closed-down Italian restaurant on Elizabeth Street in Belgravia.

I may not have contacted Laura for a long while after that night in February 2010, after I slammed the taxi door behind me, but I had rarely stopped thinking of her.

When architectural historian Jeremy Musson was launching his book *English Country House Interiors* at Sotheby's, I arranged for *Spear's* to sponsor the drinks. I also sent an invitation to Laura.

She couldn't come to the party, but she had seen the *Country Life* article of Adam Dant's new murals at Upton Cressett and wrote that she had been wanting 'to get in touch . . . Annoyingly I have plans on Monday which I would usually cancel but I have done it too many times. Would love a catch up and update on Upton Cressett progress. Lxx'

Just two little crosses can bring an eternity of hope. The dinner date Laura proposed was the same date that I was meant to be co-hosting a business dinner. When I cancelled, Wendy Coumantaros (now back to intercepting my invitations at *Spear's*) said to me, 'William, you *never* cancel, and you are not ill. It must be something important.'

It was. We had dinner at one of my favourite restaurants in London, the Noor Jahan off the Old Brompton Road, with Laura's close friend Emma Wigan, who had worked for me at *Spear's*. At around 10.00 p.m., Emma went home. Over the following hour, alone with Laura, I felt that I would never need a large Binder Box marked 'L'.

When we had first split there had never been a Laura Binder Box, other than a few postcards. To this day, my Binder Box marked 'L' has few letters, just the occasional note or card inscribed: 'To my dearest Laura, my muse and milliner extraordinaire'.

Yes, milliner. One of the first things I had learned about Laura at our first dinner for two years was that she was no longer an interior designer. After attending the London College of Fashion, she was now a milliner, with a small studio on the Lower Pimlico Road. At dinner, she had shown me some of her designs – they were exquisite. Every couture hat (with blocks made in Luton) was hand-stitched and bespoke. Laura was a true artist; and what's more she wasn't tortured by her craft. It was simply an extension of herself, and her natural style and spirit.

The breakthrough came when she agreed to a long weekend in Venice – our first holiday together. The trip was nearly derailed before we left, due to heavy fog at London airports. I was so concerned that I resorted to a drastic – or desperate – plan to save it.

When I picked Laura up on the Lower Pimlico Road, she was wearing one of her own silk berets and looked divinely beautiful.

'The Dorchester,' I said to the taxi driver.

'The *Dorchester*?' said Laura, incredulously. 'I thought we were going to Heathrow.'

'The flights have been grounded until tomorrow due to fog so I thought we'd start the holiday today anyhow. I'm a London hotel critic tonight.'

We checked in and were led to a smart junior suite with more white marble in the bathroom than a Carrara quarry in the Apuan Alps.

'It's very hot in here,' said Laura, struggling with a window. 'I can hardly breathe.'

I finally managed to get the window open about six inches. 'I guess they don't want anybody throwing themselves out,' I said. 'I'll see if they can get somebody to fix it while we're at dinner.'

We walked to the Guinea restaurant, off Berkeley Square, where I ordered two giant T-bone steaks washed down with a bottle of wine and a large plate of cheese.

'Delicious,' said Laura. 'But I've never seen such a large steak. Will you finish mine?'

When we got back to the room, the window had not been fixed. It felt like a Dubai sauna. Nobody from Maintenance was around to sort the issue until the morning. Worse, I couldn't see how to turn the heating off.

At around 2.00 a.m., I woke up with a stabbing cramp-like pain in my chest. The room was stifling and I crawled to the bathroom to get a glass of water. I felt as if I was having a heart-attack. 'Laura,' I croaked. 'I'm not feeling at all well. I have terrible pains in my chest and I'm getting palpitations. Can you call the hotel doctor?'

'William,' Laura said. 'You have to hold it together. Take some deep breaths. This is not the place to die. My mother doesn't even know I'm here! I don't want to call her and say I'm at the Dorchester with a dead man in the bed.'

'"Death in the Dorchester" would make a good headline,' I muttered.

I heard Laura reach for the phone.

'We have an emergency in our room. My . . . my . . . friend here . . .'

Laura didn't know what to call me. Boyfriend? Partner? Lover? Nothing was established yet. Very few people knew we had even started seeing each other again, and Laura had made it very clear she didn't want to go official. This time I certainly wouldn't make the mistake of rushing in.

'. . . My friend here thinks they might be dying,' she said, in her distinct 1950s cut-glass voice. 'Is there a doctor on call?'

I had forgotten about her voice and how I had fallen in love with it. At this point, however, I was pounding on my chest and gasping.

'There's no doctor available until the morning,' Laura said. 'They're bringing some paracetamol. Shall I call an ambulance?'

'No,' I said. 'I've been wanting to take you on holiday for three years – I'm not cancelling now.'

I knew that calling an ambulance would be the end of our trip. Our rescheduled flights were the next morning. They would probably keep me under observation for at least a day. I took a few pills and slowly began to feel a little better. 'I had a similar experience when I was previously married to my Italian wife,' I said, as I lay on the bed and inhaled deeply. 'I ate half a wheel of Camembert when I had a hangover. I had to be taken to hospital by ambulance and was there for two days. Turned out to be heartburn.'

'*Heartburn?*'

'I think the 16oz T-bone steak, plus half of yours, may have been too much. Plus the wine and cheese.'

'Are you *quite* sure you're OK to travel?' Laura said.

'If I die, let it be in Venice.'

By the time our water taxi chugged up to the landing stage of the Gritti Palace Hotel, I had made a full recovery. There had been a good omen for the trip before we arrived – my father had given me his 1965 copy of *The Companion Guide to Venice* by historian Hugh Honour. 'He's still the best tour guide to the city,' he'd said. 'We never left our hotel without it.'

Reading the introduction on the plane, I had enjoyed Honour's laconic style of offering advice when it came to Venetian local customs and eating out. He cautioned that while sitting in the bars around San Marco's piazza, we would be offered Prosecco, which was what Venetians usually drank. He added, 'After the second bottle, the local Prosecco begins to taste like champagne.'

I turned to the hotels and restaurants section as I wanted to see if any restaurants my father had marked were still going nearly forty-five years on. As I opened the section, an old handwritten hotel bill fell out, with a list of sightseeing venues scrawled in brown ink on tissue-thin airmail paper in my mother's handwriting. There was also a menu card from a restaurant called Musicanti (a 'seventeenth-century tavern with songs and entertainment of the period').

My parents had stayed in Room 209 at the Metropole. I noted my father had underlined and placed a question mark by the entry for the Gritti Palace Hotel on the Grand Canal. It looked as if he might have made some enquiries but had had to settle for something not quite so grand or expensive.

'Look at this bill from the early 1970s,' I said to Laura. 'This is where my parents must have stayed. We must go and have a drink there.'

'My parents went to Venice for their honeymoon,' said Laura. 'I've only been once before. I was eighteen and it was for a ball in a palazzo on the Grand Canal given by a friend of my parents. I hardly saw anything of the city so I can't wait.'

We stayed in a corner suite at the Gritti Palace, which had just been refurbished by American designer Chuck Chewning, and Rubelli of Venice, the textile firm that had supplied the navy velvet for the Great Chamber half-tester bed at Upton Cressett. Special attention had been given to the refurbishment of the hotel's three most famous suites – Hemingway, Maugham and Ruskin. Each had been newly decorated as bedroom shrines to each author. In the 1960s, there were only six 'de luxe' hotels in Venice, of which Honour wrote that the Gritti was 'probably the most sybaritically comfortable and has the added charm of association with the most distinguished list of visitors in the city, or perhaps any hotel in Europe'.

I had long wanted to visit the Gritti as that was where Ruskin had written much of *The Stones of Venice*, in rented 'boarding rooms' overlooking the Grand Canal. This book had been my aesthetic bible when I was an impressionable undergraduate. Yet Ruskin's former rooms deserved to carry a romantic health warning. His infamous first honeymoon night at the Gritti on 10 April 1848 with his virginal young bride Effie Grey was so disastrous that the episode was turned into a film by Emma Thompson. Ruskin had recoiled from the marital bed, shocked by the sight of his wife's naked body, assuming it would be as slender and smooth as a classical marble statue. She later got an annulment and married the Pre-Raphaelite artist John Everett Millais.

Thankfully, we found the refurbished hotel to be delightful. On our first morning, while walking through a little piazza near the hotel called Campo Santa Maria di Giglio, Laura stopped outside an old Venetian textile shop called Maria Bevilacqua with a carved stone lion in the window. We entered an Aladdin's cave of Venetian fabrics: dark-crimson armchairs fit for a doge; rolls of richly coloured damask velvets standing upright; there were lampasses (striped fabrics), brocades and tapestries on wooden hangers. In a corner was an old Venetian manual loom to show off the 300-year family history as one of Venice's oldest weavers. The shop was bursting with colourful cushions, trimmings, key-tassels and tiebacks.

Then Laura spotted some dark-red velvet cushions with huge tassels and embroidered gold sea-dragons. 'These would look good in the drawing room,' she said, as she ran her hand across one. 'Or maybe the Knole sofa in the entrance hall.'

That was the first hint of hope I had that Laura was thinking of the future. She was right and every time I plump them up on the sofa, I think of that first trip to Venice. In another shop down a small alley we bought a set of Bugatti cutlery – with polished amber handles – and some fine Venetian, hand-stitched, linen damask tablecloths and mats.

We also bought a pair of water jugs with red Murano glass sea-dragons inside them, which we thought would complement Adam Dant's sea-dragon murals in the dining room. Other Murano glasses had hand-blown stems in the shapes of different fishes.

'Let me show you other fishy glass I have for you,' the glass-shop owner said, as he wrapped the water jugs in tissue paper. 'You can have the *fishy* dinner parties for your friends.'

Back at the hotel, glass of wine in hand, we sat on our balcony where we had the use of a large brass telescope on a tripod, making the room feel like a ship captain's cabin as we could look out to see the armada of boats passing our window. The wintry afternoon light cast the canal in dancing, glistening colours and shadows. Across the lagoon, we could see Palladio's noble church of San Giorgio Maggiore, built between 1566 and 1610, making it almost exactly contemporary with Upton Cressett's Elizabethan gatehouse. But no two buildings could have been more different. San Giorgio was a white Baroque basilica of classical marble, the other an Early English Renaissance turreted hunting lodge made from Shropshire red clay bricks. Both were beautiful in their own way.

'Doesn't that church look like a wedding cake made from Italian vanilla ice-cream?' I said, swinging the telescope towards Laura.

'Beautiful,' she said. 'Can we go there?'

'Tomorrow,' I said. 'Do you know what Ruskin said about it?'

'Of course not.'

I picked up my abbreviated *Stones of Venice*. '"It is impossible to conceive a design more gross, more barbarous, more childish in conception, more contemptible under every point of rational regard . . .'''

'That sounds like crap,' she said. 'I can't wait to go there.'

On our second evening, just after we thought a rainstorm had stopped, we walked towards the Metropole Hotel from the Gritti through San Marco square towards the Riva degli Schiavoni promenade, which looks out towards the lagoon and the island of San Giorgio.

It was now dark. The street drains were overflowing and a river of water ran along the promenade. The stone steps leading down to the gondolas and water taxis were invisible in the Venetian gloom. Not far from where we could see the sign of the hotel, it began to rain heavily again.

'There's the Metropole,' I said. 'Let's run for it.'

'I'm in heels!' said Laura.

But it was too late. I didn't hear her words as I headed off at full sprint, *sans* umbrella.

The next thing I knew, Laura was yelling, 'Watch out, William!'

I hadn't seen that the water level of the canal was now indistinguishable from the promenade. Just by the hotel, I nearly plunged right into the Grand Canal; what I'd thought was pavement was actually a ten-foot drop into the water. I skidded to a stop inches from being swept out into the lagoon.

Soaked and shaken, we made it into the Metropole, which was like a quirky Venetian museum. In 1900, Marcel Proust had stayed there, and Thomas Mann while writing *Death in Venice*. The hotel had a collection of antique paper fans, lace, mother-of-pearl and silk, some festooned with ostrich feathers that Laura loved. There were also old crucifixes and nutcrackers, corridors lined with shells, ancient Chinese vases, nineteenth-century visiting card cases, belle-époque evening bags and the Beggiato collection of eclectic corkscrews.

We soon found a cosy corner of the Oriental Bar, which was dark, louche and exotic, decorated with antique mirrors on the walls and ceilings. I ordered two Macallans.

'You don't normally drink Scotch,' said Laura.

'Tonight we have to,' I said. 'Have you ever seen *Don't Look Now*? A wonderful horror film in which Julie Christie plays a married English beauty called Laura on a trip to Venice.'

'No, I haven't.'

For just a second I felt my age. The famous sex scene between Christie and Donald Sutherland in Nic Roeg's 1973 classic film noir had been shot in Venice (at the Bauer Grunwald hotel) more than a decade before Laura was born. Nic had been one of the last to leave at my thirtieth birthday dinner in LA. He had been sixty-eight then but still enjoyed staying up.

'When you see the Venice hotel bedroom scene, you'll know why I ordered Macallan.'

In the film, Sutherland pours himself a large post-coital glass of the eighteen-year-old malt from a bottle beside the bed. It was slipped into the script by writer Allan Scott, who also happened to be chairman of Macallan.

The barman placed our glasses in front of us. I looked at Laura. 'Isn't it strange that over forty years ago my parents would have sat in this very bar having a drink before dinner?' I said.

We were dining in a restaurant around the corner that Laura had discovered when she had got lost near the Arsenale on a millinery-fabric expedition earlier that day. 'I don't know where we're having dinner tonight but I've found this little trattoria, which looks heavenly,' she said.

It was called Al Corvo and was owned by chef patron Cesare Benelli and, once again, Laura was right. It was one of Venice's best little restaurants. It was not flash or fancy and there were no costumed singers. A review by the late R. W. Apple Jr of the *New York Times* was framed in the entrance.

'If Johnny Apple liked the place, then this is a great find,' I said, as we were handed the menus. He was a legend among reporters and food writers. We had sat next to each other in the press tent covering President Richard Nixon's funeral in Yorba Linda, California, in 1994. I knew instantly who he was because of his bulk.

As I looked around the restaurant, I then saw the eighty-something figure of John Julius Norwich, son of Duff Cooper (1st Viscount Norwich), sitting two tables away. I knew him as I had interviewed him for my book on Graham Greene. I didn't bother him but whispered *sotto voce* across the table to Laura, 'If John Julius is here then you really have found the best restaurant in Venice.'

'Why?'

'He's Venice's foremost historian. His mother was Lady Diana

Cooper. He helped set up the Venice in Peril fund. He's regarded as a living saint in the heritage world.'

'I've read some of her letters,' Laura said, smiling across the table. 'They are very amusing. Wasn't she known as Pug?'

'You could always ask her son, whom she used to call Monster.'

As I glanced towards John Julius, we both began laughing.

'You know my family are great pug lovers,' Laura added. 'I have a little black pug in Norfolk but my mother's adopted it.'

'I'd like to meet Olive,' I said. 'You have no idea how happy I am tonight with you, Laura. Thank you for coming to Venice.'

'We nearly didn't make it,' she said, 'but I'm glad I'm here. And I'm glad you didn't get swept out to the stormy lagoon.'

John, You're Dumped

Our visit to Venice was very much off-season, when the city is almost at her very best, with cold grey skies and sleety rain enabling the umbrella-carrying visitor – and Gritti guests are given smart personal umbrellas – to enjoy the near-empty piazzas, churches, canals and bars in almost solitary pleasure. Like the melancholy and sorrowful-eyed paintings of the Venetian masters that we saw in the Academia, the rain somehow adds an extra sensory and emotional gloss to the stone architecture of the city – helping to bring out Venice's richer and darker colours.

That visit to the Academia was another comic moment. Laura was wearing a bohemian-looking, dark-plum, silk velvet beret that she had made for herself. It covered her ears.

'Two tickets,' I said at the ticket counter.

'Would that be one adult and a student?'

'I don't think so.'

'We have student price to age twenty-one.'

'Two adults, please.'

I was learning that it was a misconception to imagine that being with a beautiful younger girlfriend made you feel young. The opposite was true. Incidents like that one made me feel old. When we went skiing, I looked at her pass on the lift; Laura (she was wearing a bobble hat with rabbit ears) had been given a child's pass. The ticket officer had obviously thought I was her father.

The afternoon early darkness, the rainswept promenades, closed hotels and bars, and the lack of queues for the vaporettos suited us. I do not know why those in love, or falling in love, are attracted to places of sadness and decay, but Venice delivers. As Henry James wrote, it is the only city on earth where 'the deposed, the defeated, the disenchanted, or even only the bored, have seemed to find there something that no other place can give.'

The happiness Laura brought me was like the lifting of some old curse, or the sense of 'invisible darkness' that had subsumed me ever since my first divorce. It seemed to dissolve as I held Laura's hand while we walked along the flooded near-empty streets and alleyways of the city. We enjoyed some clichés, like drinking hot chocolate from little silver jugs at Florian's in St Mark's Square and eating a very mediocre risotto at Harry's Bar (even off-season there was a 'tourist' menu and another for Venetians). And we visited the Rubelli Palazzo on the Grand Canal to see its textile museum, a gondola repair shop and, after many wrong turns, finally managed to find Vittore Carpaccio's famous painting sequence of St George and the Dragon at the Scuola di San Giorgio degli Schiavoni (highlighted with ticks in my father's guidebook).

I had been to Venice before – most recently as a critic at the Venice Biennale – but never had I felt so happy. It is the sort of place where you can measure your relationship quickly – it's either right or wrong. The city has something of a fortune-teller's spirit about it. If you can enjoy the Venetian temperament and the city's decaying beauty in cold and rainy March, the chances are you can enjoy being together anywhere.

If you can't enjoy the simple beauties of life in Venice together – off-season – then what can you enjoy?

Being with Laura was its own reward. We had visited the church of San Giorgio Maggiore, as I had promised, arriving by vaporetto in the rain. We had sat on an old pew in the back of a side chapel as a Benedictine service was celebrated. The small chapel was full of incense as the clanking thurible was hoisted and shaken by an elderly monk. I had prayed before the Blessed Sacrament that God would bless our time in Venice and the love I felt for Laura. Palladio's wedding cake of a church, of course, was a sublime Baroque miracle.

'I love it,' Laura had said, as we looked up inside the church's magnificent nave.

It took a day or so of travelling in Ruskin's footsteps to realise that Laura was teaching me another important lesson – that true beauty and love need no justification. She believed in me, and this made me – after my spirit had long felt stripped out – believe again in myself, and in what love was. Although she was Catholic, we hardly ever discussed religion, or politics. Her philosophy was simply that artists just needed to be true to themselves, and that was the best one – or God – could hope for. Laura had an acute eye for beauty, whether it was a Venetian fabric she picked out, an Oriental fan, or the look of wonder on the faces in Vittore Carpaccio's paintings. She opened my eyes to Venice in a way that I had never expected. Previously, I had been walking around in a blindfold.

Being with Laura felt like I had been handed some rare and precious gift. Instead of my mind being awhirl with competing and often contradictory thoughts, I began to have less faith or interest in the rational and material. I felt a new hidden power – or flame within – in just doing what I felt was 'right'. Without questioning or self-doubt. I knew it felt right to be with Laura.

As I was falling for her, I began to lose my affection for Ruskin, my old critic hero. With Upton Cressett now pretty much finished – albeit for a few Venetian tasselled cushions – I came to see that restoration was not about the ascetic devotion to the 'rule' of William Morris or John Ruskin; it was more about being true to the spirit of place and using what resources one had to create honest art, architecture or craftsmanship.

As Adam Dant had taught me through his art, it was about taking the past and reinventing it in a way that was original and new, not just a copy. Such lessons could apply to the heart as well. It was about accepting the imperfections of one's own history and, above all, perhaps being more forgiving and celebrating the mystery of beauty and love. It was time to look at the world differently.

It was Venice itself, rather than any guidebook, that gave me eyes. For it was during those precious few days in the city with Laura that I first felt, and realised for the first time, that my instinct on first meeting her – that I wanted to marry her – had not been a delusional dream.

I felt liberated, happy, whole again, redeemed by a new love and a great beauty, and the beauty of a city in the incessant rain, which washed the past away. It helped, as well, in washing away the darker stains of memory. Our buildings, churches and lives teach us who we are. Beauty teaches its own truths.

On our last day, we chose not to go out at all after noon and ordered a pasta lunch with a bottle of wine in our large room overlooking the canal. As we stood looking at the gondolas and vaporetti passing us below, Laura said, 'I am not sure life can ever get any better or more beautiful than this.' She later told me that, on that last day, she sensed her life was about to change in irreversible ways.

For a few wet, glossy and beautiful days in March, the Gritti became our Pleasure Temple. The new Gritti was not really new at all; if anything, it was a historic return to the values of the peculiarly Venetian sybaritic pleasure for which the city has always been known, and best indulged without guilt. I did not make the mistake of thinking the Gritti – or Venice for that matter – was a place where I would get any honest work done. I was also thankful that we had not been given Ruskin's former 'boarding rooms'. I was in Venice purely for reasons of love and nothing less than the restoration of my heart. People talk of saving Venice. But in so many ways, it was Venice that helped save me.

Not long after we got back from Venice, Margaret Thatcher died in a suite at the Ritz Hotel in London. Following her death in April, my father attended her state funeral at St Paul's and brought back a copy of the Order of Service.

'Don't you think you should frame it?' I said.

'It should really hang in the Gatehouse bedroom where she stayed,' my father replied.

That gave me an idea. Certainly Lady Thatcher's stay was a notable event in the 800-year history of the house, so when I saw Sir Mark Thatcher at a party not long after his mother's funeral, I asked him if he would have any objection to us naming the bedroom she slept in the 'Thatcher Suite' to mark her visit. Mark said he was happy for us to do so as my father and she had become close friends after she had left Downing Street. Upton Cressett thus became the first guest accommodation in the world officially to commemorate a bedroom where the former prime minister had actually slept.

The Thatcher Suite in the Gatehouse was opened in May 2013 with the *Shropshire Star* running a photo story of how the room – previously known as the 'Prince Rupert Bedroom' – now included a framed copy of the Order of Service and various biographies of Margaret Thatcher as well as a book of her quotations. There is also a framed photograph of my parents standing outside the Gatehouse with Lady Thatcher and Sir Denis.

The owners of historic properties – in Britain and America – have never been shy about using their visitors' books as a form of marketing. The Cromwell Room at Chavenage has long been turned into a money-spinner, with many sex scenes and death-bed scenes, as well as

Viyella catalogues, being filmed there. It's good business to boast that previous guests include royalty, prime ministers and writers. In our leaflet, I call it 'Sleeping with History'.

Yet some figures are more controversial than others. The only problem with naming a bedroom after Margaret Thatcher is that many people are appalled by the prospect of sleeping in a bed she once occupied. I always say that the bedroom is named in her honour as a historic British figure, not simply a political one.

Because of Lady Thatcher's Marmite reputation, guests in the Gatehouse have a choice of staying in the same bed that the former prime minister slept in or they can opt to stay on the floor above in the Prince Rupert Suite (our honeymoon suite). We occasionally market the suite as the Elizabeth Hurley Suite as she has stayed several times. The suite's sumptuous four-poster bed-linen fabric by Melissa White is based on a fifteenth-century wall painting of a hunting scene in a forest. A kind quote from Elizabeth in our brochure calls it 'the most romantic escape in England'.

Which led me to a question that began to vex me: If Boris Johnson ever became prime minister, we could also have a 'Boris Bedroom' at Upton Cressett. But which bedroom had he slept in? Alas, when I asked my mother, she wasn't entirely sure. Some detective work was required. When I repeated that we weren't sure where the bedroom was during a house tour, a 'punter' interrupted: 'It may have been more than one!'

27

Toilets and Tears

As much as I was enjoying opening Upton Cressett to the public, I found my patience with punters occasionally running short. The house needed a family and wasn't suited to being run by a forty-five-year-old publisher who was in London much of the week.

I suppose it was my fault. The problems began when I had an assortment of different-coloured Upton Cressett staff polo shirts made up by a local clothing firm. When I sent the pink shirt to Laura at her millinery studio in London, I received a brusque response: 'It's hideous,' she said on the phone. 'It makes me look like a boat hand. I'm not walking about looking like a yachtie.'

'I've been getting complaints on TripAdvisor,' I said. 'Standards have to be improved. We need some sort of uniform.'

'Anything but pink,' said Laura. 'But don't think I'll ever be seen dead in one. They look like you've had them made for your crew. And you don't even own a boat.'

But a house uniform was becoming a necessity. The complaints had started when Luiza had led a Wednesday afternoon tour group wearing what one disgruntled TripAdvisor punter described as 'her pyjamas and slippers and dressing gown with her hair in strange pins . . . she looked like an East European gypsy.'

But the final sartorial straw came when Pedro emerged one afternoon to help in the tea pavilion wearing a white T-shirt – emblazoned with the words 'Heidi Wear' on the front in thick lipstick-red textured print. It was not the sort of staff uniform that I expected for serving tea to a group of wealthy 'culture tour' Americans.

'Pedro' I said, '*what* are you wearing?'

'Mr William, it was with the old clothes that your mother said were for the bonfire. I hope you not mind.'

I had never worn the T-shirt. Pedro had obviously found it in our storage barn when my mother had decided the hot August weather was the ideal chance to start clearing out my old LA trunks and suitcases, covered with 'LAX' shipping labels and nearly fifteen years of bat and peacock shit.

A large American man wearing a button-down shirt and tie, with a crumpled linen jacket, waddled towards the table where the cakes and scones were standing. 'You really have the best Victoria sponge cake,' he said. 'I'd like to try one of your scones, if I may.'

'Please go ahead,' I said. 'They were made this morning. Would your wife like to try one as well?'

'Well, that would be nice. You can't seem to get a good English scone in Boston.'

As Pedro turned around and carried the scones to him, I saw, to my horror, that the back of his T-shirt bore 'Call 1-800-PRO-VICE' printed on the back. There was also what seemed to be child's handwriting in a black felt pen. This *certainly* wasn't a new line of Upton Cressett-approved clothing. At first, I couldn't work out what the 'Call 1-800-Pro-Vice' T-shirt was about. Then I remembered: the T-shirt had been given to me personally back in the late 1990s by the famous Hollywood madam, Heidi Fleiss, whose list of clients in her little black book was said to include the likes of Charlie Sheen, and many of the Hollywood A-list establishment.

I was given the T-shirt by Heidi Fleiss as a goodie-bag gift when I managed to obtain an exclusive interview with her after she got out of jail, having served just twenty months following a conviction for tax evasion and money-laundering. To try to reinvent herself, she opened a sportswear boutique in Santa Monica. I visited her in her shop and had written the interview when I was working for the *Telegraph* as their US Special Correspondent.

The black felt-tip writing was a dedication to me in Heidi's own hand. Inscribed 'To William, love Heidi' with a felt-tip pen, it was the type of signed shirt that was auctioned at charity dinners and framed to hang in a downstairs loo – not to be worn by my Romanian gardener/butler/handyman to serve Victoria sponge to American tour guests.

Still, none of the American tour group complained.

'I never heard of this Heidi,' Pedro said later. 'What is Heidi? German film star?'

I told him that Heidi was a 'very naughty woman' who had been to jail, and that he could keep the signed T-shirt. 'But please don't wear it when we have any guests or punters around. You can wear it for mowing and gardening but not in the house,' I added. 'It doesn't send out the right message for Upton Cressett.'

It wasn't only Pedro and Luiza who had been letting the house's sartorial standards slide. The exceptionally hot and balmy August weather had also drawn some raised eyebrows from house punters when they had asked who the semi-naked man was sunbathing or pottering around the new gatehouse garden during house tours.

'Oh, that's my father, Bill Cash,' I would say.

'You mean Bill Cash, the *MP*?'

In his seventies, he prefers to dispense with any clothing on his upper torso when the sun is out and walks around the garden, even on open days, wearing only a pair of tennis shorts, sunglasses and a Moroccan-style, red velvet cap with tassels. He also favours occasional topless mowing on the garden tractor.

Enough was enough. I called Stitches of Bridgnorth – a corporate-wear company – to order an entirely new Upton Cressett house uniform.

P. G. Wodehouse himself could have scripted the bizarre afternoon. The August tea-and-tour pantomime started from the moment I opened the front door at around 2 p.m. I was expecting a group tour of around thirty local Women's Institute members, who had booked some months ago. As I opened the door, I saw not one group of thirty but more like sixty people, a mixture of blazers, summer dresses and walking sticks, resembling the sort of queue one would expect on a cruise-ship deck when it docks for a shopping trip in Tenerife.

It turned out that there was a second tour group – apparently a local Women's Guild – only I wasn't aware of the booking.

But what the hell, I thought, as I saw the group standing around the freshly mown Gatehouse lawn, boasting smart stripes, in front of the main house. They were all happily chattering away. I would do my best to give them all an enjoyable time, even if I was running the show more or less on my own. All the help I had was Luiza, and Pedro, if he could be found.

I'll just have to do two separate tours, I thought. One of the groups can sit in the garden and enjoy their cake and tea for an hour or so and then they can switch over.

The only problem was that Luiza was nowhere to be seen. The kitchen was empty. Her cottage was empty. There was no way I could conduct a tour of more than thirty people. I bolted the kitchen door that leads out on to the back garden where the teas are served (visitors have a way of snooping around any rooms whose doors are left unlocked), then ran outside to find Pedro. I found him in the shed tinkering with the Atco mower, puffing a cigarette.

'Mower not working,' he said. 'I fix carburettor.'

'We have an emergency,' I said. 'When's Luiza back?'

'Gone shopping to Bridgnorth with your mum.'

'Get your new house T-shirt on,' I said. 'We need to be serving the first teas in ten minutes!'

I walked over the Gatehouse lawn to where the two groups were hovering. Collecting any admission fees would have to wait; this was not the moment. 'Welcome to Upton Cressett on this glorious summer's day,' I said. 'We seem to have two tour groups. Which of you would like to have tea first?'

The WI group elected to do so.

'Can I suggest you take a short walk down to the church? Then can we all meet under the arch of the Gatehouse at two-thirty?'

I hurried back inside to check we had enough home-made cake for sixty.

The very moment I walked through the front door into the entrance hall, I was confronted by a tall Worcester Woman with white hair and glasses. She had marched into the house behind me – although the Hall was very clearly not 'open' yet. 'Are you staff?' she said, looking through her spectacles at my Upton Cressett logo T-shirt. 'Where's the toilet?'

Her manner was direct. Not the sort of woman who takes no for an answer.

I know very little about Women's Guilds but I have a feeling they can occasionally make even the WI seem pale by comparison. 'I'm not staff,' I replied. 'If you want, you can use the private loo under the stairs.' I pointed her in the direction of the downstairs loo and headed off towards the kitchen.

About ten minutes later, the first round of tea was almost ready to be served – thanks to Pedro and his six-year-old son setting up the tables and chairs outside in the garden while I boiled kettles, located teabags and sliced up the cakes in the kitchen. Once tea was prepared, I walked back to the Gatehouse lawn and started encouraging the leaders to round up their respective groups.

The atmosphere remained jovial. Just as this all began, I saw Worcester Woman emerge from the front door . . . and forcefully pull it shut behind her. With a loud clunk. The front door has a deadbolt security lock that means it cannot be opened from the outside when locked. 'Oh dear,' I said. 'We're now locked out.'

'Haven't you got a spare key?' the woman asked.

'The key is inside the house,' I said. 'The kitchen door is locked as are all the other doors.'

'The tours are now being delayed as we are now locked out of the house,' I announced to the gathering on the lawn.

The former mood was faltering – there was clear anxiety etched on many of the elderly faces now. Whether it was the prospect of not getting a cup of tea or a tour I couldn't say but, as I delivered the news, I felt like a pilot having to calm down an impatient group of passengers stuck on the tarmac.

I walked around the main house seeing if there was any obvious way in – such as an open window.

I found Pedro. 'We have sixty guests out there all baying for tea, tours and toilets, with no way into the Hall.'

'I break window,' said Pedro. He picked up half an old brick and waved it at me.

I scowled at him. I had recently replaced almost all the old Victorian windows on the north front elevations of the house with new leaded ones. They were glazed with hand-spun glass (the palest of medieval greens) that had been made in Poland. I wasn't in any sort of mood to start smashing windows.

We reached the steps leading down to the old dairy. At least this door's windows were not leaded lights so I told Pedro to smash the pane. While he was trying to remove the shards of glass, he cut himself so blood started pouring from his thumb. He managed to get the door open from the inside, but that was as far as we got – the door leading up the stairs to the kitchen was locked from the inside. So that idea failed.

At this point, with no way in, I returned to the groups on the Gatehouse lawn. I explained that Upton Cressett was built as a fortified domestic manor in the fifteenth century and was specifically designed to be difficult to break into.

At this point, I was feeling bad; I had little option but to call off both tours and send all sixty people home. Then Pedro tapped me on the shoulder. 'Mr William, I think Mini-Pedro can climb through window.' He pointed to a small open window on the first floor.

'Get a ladder,' I said.

Ten minutes later, with Mini-Pedro's mission successful, the front door was finally open again.

Around this time, Luiza arrived back and we were able to start the tours and get the tea flowing.

After this unfortunate start, both tours went well, with the two groups seeming to enjoy themselves. I even managed to make an adventure of us all being 'locked out'; I explained that the ability to squeeze through a small leaded-light window had a special resonance for the Hall during the Civil War. Back in 1648, I explained, Francis Cressett, royal spy and steward to Charles I, led the escape attempt to rescue the King from Carisbrooke Castle in the Isle of Wight.

This light tour banter seemed to go down well and, by about 4.15 p.m., after dozens of cakes had been consumed, with buckets of Earl Grey tea, I thought it was time to say goodbye and collect a cheque.

The Women's Guild group was led by a reed-thin woman with dark hair in her late fifties or thereabouts. But the real trouble didn't start until her colleague joined us. When she marched up to me, I sensed trouble. She had the air of somebody who'd done her share of student protests in the 1970s and would still take to the barricades to prevent a bypass.

'I hope your group enjoyed their visit,' I said to the leader.

The women's faces were without expression.

'I'm ready to settle up now if that's convenient,' I went on. 'You haven't already paid any sort of deposit, have you?'

'No, we haven't,' she replied. 'Is a cheque all right?'

Before the conversation went any further, Ms Knotty Hair stepped forward, glaring at me, seemingly looking for a fight. She wore an expression of self-righteous haughtiness and indignation, laced with a secret love of confrontation. She was almost licking her lips with anticipation as we stood under the Gatehouse arch.

'You owe one of our members an apology,' she snapped at me. 'And because of your lack of toilet facilities, we want a discount.'

'Sorry?' I said.

'Yes. We'd like a discount. On account of poor toilet facilities.'

I smiled back. She didn't miss a trick, clearly accustomed to sticking her nose into things that were not her business.

'She didn't mean to lock the door behind her. You should carry a key in your pocket.'

There was always one. I had been giving tours of Upton Cressett since I was a teenager and had learned that there was always one who loved to find fault and would be the first to write some rude comment in our visitors' book. These were the sort of people who enjoyed the power that came with being a 'Senior Badge' reviewer for TripAdvisor or would complain that the oak spiral staircase was too steep and needed rubber treading. Their complaints usually followed their second helping of lemon drizzle cake and Earl Grey.

Many of the arch-moaners had axes to grind. It was not really about the lack of toilets or signposting. It was about something else, some long-forgotten disappointment that made them lash out in anger at the world. Why so many seemed to be middle-aged, middle-class ladies

I had no idea. The Women's Guild and the WI do many wonderful things – keeping the art of knitting alive, or championing belly dancing – but some of their members seem to pride themselves on dishing it out.

Ms Knotty Hair was exactly why certain national institutions had such a mixed press. A recent issue of *Women's World* opened with the observation that 'Grown men flinch at the prospect of talking to WI members en masse.'

I had no such fear and I certainly wasn't going to be intimidated by this particular visitor. 'I don't expect people to be rude to me in my own house,' I replied calmly. 'I nearly had to cancel the entire afternoon. I had my gardener smash a window pane and he has injured himself as a result. I said she could use the loo, as I did all your group all afternoon, but still got no thanks. And now you want a group *discount*?'

My mind flashed back to Brian Dunleath's words at the Historic Houses boot camp – never haggle; once you do, you've lost.

'Our members must have access to public toilets,' she continued. 'It's a basic requirement. Your toilet facilities are lacking so it is only right that we ask for a discount.'

'You know what?' I said. 'I'm not enjoying being spoken to in such an offensive way by you and your friend here. We don't run the tours here just as a business; we do it because we enjoy sharing the heritage. I don't expect to be treated like a lavatory attendant. I expect some basic thanks. Now, can we settle up, please?'

Ms Knotty Hair stepped in again. 'I'm not sure we feel the day has been satisfactory.'

That was it. I was not prepared to be insulted any longer. 'I've had enough,' I said. 'Why don't you all just kindly leave right now? You can keep your money. In thirty years of giving tours, your group is the rudest I have ever encountered.'

At this point, the WI members, who were standing behind and who had behaved impeccably throughout, had pricked up their ears and could hardly believe what they were witnessing – an order to leave the premises. I should add that the WI party had behaved very patiently throughout. They were not to blame at all.

'You and your group are no longer welcome,' I said to the Women's Guild leader and her deputy. 'Please leave the grounds.'

After looking at me aghast, the Women's Guild made a sudden run for the car park. Middle-aged and elderly women clattered up the stone garden steps with bewilderment, astonishment and a certain glassy-eyed excitement on their faces. With free cake and tea and a free tour, and banishment by the owner, most looked as if they had not had so much afternoon entertainment for years.

Once they had gone, I turned to the very friendly and polite leader of the local WI group. 'I want to apologise for the little commotion just then,' I said. 'You have been a model tour group and are very welcome to stay in the grounds and gardens until five o'clock. I hope you have had a nice visit.'

I left them to drift around the grounds. It was around 4.30 p.m. and I had been guiding and talking for over two hours. I poured myself a cup of tea and reflected that, just because a few pounds have passed hands, guests don't have the right to abuse the house owner's hospitality.

In the local Women's Guild case, some members of such groups delight in their reputation as formidable, no-nonsense women. The Townswomen's Guild have roots in the Suffragette movement, which I admire. But some, when backed up by sisterly numbers, don't know the difference between being robust and plain rude.

After the story of the Women's Guild ejection from Upton Cressett became headlines in the local papers, and a feature story in the *Daily Telegraph* and *Daily Mail*, I received a surprising number of letters of support from fellow historic house owners. Many had their own – often far worse – stories of rude tour-guest behaviour.

My favourite anecdote came from Chavenage in Gloucestershire, Elizabethan home of the Lowndes-Williams family. During a tour of the *Poldark* house with some Texans, the family member acting as their guide was interrupted by the leader: 'Can you stop yakking on about all this English history? We've haven't come all this way to hear all this house history stuff.'

The Texans abandoned the tour halfway to return speedily to their London hotel without even having their tea and cake. 'It was quite staggering,' the family member said. 'And unlike most Americans we have who are normally very polite.'

A few days after my tea and tears ordeal, I had a visit from the Shropshire Arts Society, a local painting and watercolour group, which has been around since 1948. During the afternoon, there was a storm. Looking out of the kitchen window, I could see a group of around a dozen people huddled under a tree beside the moat, stoically trying to defend themselves from the rain by using their deck chairs as umbrellas. They were too polite to ask to come inside, but the moment I saw them getting drenched, I invited them in and gave them cake and tea in the dining room.

A few hours later, they knocked on the front door and presented me with a thank-you card, featuring a watercolour of Stiperstones Ridge, a local beauty spot, painted by a member. 'Thank you so much for allowing us to paint around Upton Cressett,' the card said. 'All our members have really enjoyed the day, despite the rain.'

In truth, this was the tone of most of the letters we receive at Upton Cressett, ever since we began opening our doors in the late 1970s. We have kept shoeboxes of thank-you cards from every society and civic group imaginable. A typical example, dating back to the early 1980s, was from the National Trust's Midland Centre volunteer group: 'It was a delight to see the Hall so beautifully restored and the members who had seen it in its ruinous state were particularly impressed and happy that it had been saved.'

A Heart Restored

Since Venice, Laura and I had enjoyed several magical months together. We had spent a weekend in Paris in the spring, where I had returned to the Catacombs (the usual exercise in emotional exorcism), and taken her to the Luxembourg Gardens, where we had sat drinking hot chocolate in a café on one of the metal chairs that doubtless hadn't changed since Richard Aldington had sat in the gardens before writing his 1930 bitter-sweet and nostalgic love poem, 'A Dream in the Luxembourg'. I had first read it as an impressionable and romantically naïve eighteen-year-old.

As we sat in the café in the heart of Paris, surrounded by manicured lawns, statues, gravel parterres and flowerbeds in their April bloom, I glanced towards Laura. She was gazing towards the children in the little sailing boats that dipped and bobbed like ducks in the park's pond. A large jet fountain was spraying its water in a frothy cascade. She looked so beautiful and serene, wearing sunglasses I had bought her in Venice, and I was so happy to feel that I was living my life in the present tense, rather than among the bones of the past.

I also reflected privately on something else I had discovered about Paris's most famous public gardens, dating back to 1612; although they are relatively small – some twenty-three hectares – once you are inside, the tree-lined lawns, puppet stand, rose gardens and pear orchards seem to stretch across Paris in an almost limitless and Eden-like way. More importantly, each of the public gates opens upon a different quarter of the capital, all leading out to entirely different parishes with different characters, different histories, each almost a different country.

And so it is with our lives, relationships and marriages. We walk in our own garden, wood, or forest, or whatever Bluebeard's Castle we have made of our lives, 'where the evening sun floods in as the woman I love dresses for dinner . . .'

When we choose a marriage or relationship, we do not know what the future will hold. We like to think that our actions have consequences, that we have our hand firmly on the rudder of our voyage, or at least hold the puppet strings of destiny. But so much happiness and misery are because of random chance, timing and luck. We are more like the little toy boats on the Luxembourg's pond, whose direction is as arbitrary as the April wind. Now I wanted to make the right decision. The last time I had been in the gardens I had been with Vanessa, and I could still remember the impending sense of a gate slamming shut. As Laura and I headed towards lunch, I made sure to leave by a different entrance.

With Laura, I truly felt that I had finally found 'the woman I love' as I wrote in that letter after my thirtieth birthday of 1996, a woman who had long walked the subconscious corridors of my mind in my dreams and scrawled letters of the heart. 'When I was twenty-six I wasn't ready to get married,' she told me later. 'But three years can change everything.'

And, yes, the red-velvet embroidered cushions that we had brought back from our trip to Venice did look wonderful at Upton Cressett. Laura had immaculate taste. She also told me that she 'hated surprises', so I took her to meet jeweller Stephen Webster to co-design her ring. So, she knew a proposal was coming, although not when. I asked her father Charles (a Government whip) for his permission over lunch in Westminster in late June before Parliament broke up for the summer recess. Since the ring took two months to make, I had to wait until the end of August to propose when we had a house party of friends staying for the bank-holiday weekend. When I asked Laura if she thought her father would be worried about our age difference (which was seventeen years and nine months) she laughed and said, 'I'm sure he'll be delighted – you're twenty years younger than my last serious boyfriend.'

We were having a summer concert in the church on the Saturday of the bank-holiday weekend in August, so I planned to get Laura to St

Michael's before the concert. It was a beautiful late-summer afternoon; the sky was a pale inky blue and there were few clouds. Pedro and I had been busy with the tractor mower and the Atco. The lawns had glorious Wimbledon stripes.

'Would you come down to the church with me?' I asked Laura, at around 5.00 p.m. 'I need to check the lights are working.'

It was an odd request, considering the church had no electricity, but Laura joined me as we set off across the lawn, where a few white peacock feathers were strewn. We walked past the Bosworth tea tent, down the wobbly stone steps and on to the church yard lawn.

Earlier that afternoon, I had lined the Norman stone font with a bed of thistles, Laura's favourite flower, and hidden her pink sapphire engagement ring, with diamond thistles down each side, in a box at the bottom of the leaded font. Before covering the box with thistles, I placed my hand on the cool lead and the carved fluted arches of the ancient stone. I said a quick prayer and headed back to the house.

'Where are the lights?' said Laura, as we stepped inside the little Norman church. 'I can't see any switches.'

'That's not the reason I brought you down here.'

I began walking towards the ancient Norman font.

'The font is lined with flowers,' I said. 'Somebody must have dressed it for tonight's concert.'

Laura looked at the font more closely. 'How pretty – Scottish thistles,' she said. 'My favourite!'

'Why don't you look inside the font?' I said. 'Try a lucky dip.'

It didn't take her long to find the black jewellery box.

Within a few moments Laura was wearing her beautiful ring and smiling radiantly. We were engaged.

I had found my own form of sacred love. I was beginning to remember what hope felt like. The winds of my romantic fortune were finally blowing in the right direction.

28

A Very English Victory

After three years of fighting, farmer Clive Millington's planning application decision date was upon us. If we lost, the Shropshire Hills would become industrialised and more developers would target the landscape.

The day before the vote, the South Shropshire planning committee made a site visit, its members arriving in a minibus. It was one of those magical Shropshire summer days that P. G. Wodehouse must have had in mind when he described the countryside and lanes around Bridgnorth – which he explored as a boy – as the 'Paradise of England'. With the new gardens looking immaculate, and the lawns freshly mown, Upton Cressett stood to attention, ready for inspection.

After the councillors had refreshed themselves with lemon barley squash, I showed them around the ancient hamlet of Upton Cressett. My hope was that by experiencing some of the beauty of the place they might have a better understanding of why English Heritage were recommending they refused the application.

I had recently found a 1937 touring volume on the county by the 'Midlands Correspondent' of a pre-war newspaper in a second-hand bookshop in Much Wenlock:

> *There is another part of Shropshire which is quite different from all the rest – that part of the Severn Valley – where you feel that beauty has gone as far as beauty can. That is our Shropshire, whose chief characteristic is that it has no characteristic because it has them all. Shropshire is neither North, South, East or West England – but just England.*

I was going to quote from this at the Shire Hall meeting but it wasn't necessary. Just as I was about to start writing my speech, I received an email from Grahame French, the council's chief planning officer, saying the developer had withdrawn the application.

Our David versus Goliath battle to save the Shropshire Hills had ended with a damp squib of an email.

The killer blow – as Adrian Snook had predicted so many months ago – came from Bill Klemperer, English Heritage's chief inspector of ancient monuments for the West Midlands. His report said that significant harm would be done to the 'setting' of the new Grade I assets at Upton Cressett. Perhaps the planning system was working after all.

The voice of the Shropshire Hills had been heard. With our five hundred supporters, our local resistance operation had been armed only with a passion for the English countryside, a sense of right and wrong and a good supply of digestive biscuits. It was a very English victory.

It was only by fighting to save our hills and landscape that I managed to descend from my turreted existence. For years, I had pulled up the drawbridge and nursed my marital wounds. But I was a different man now. Which was why, on hearing the news that the application was withdrawn, I wasted no time in sending out invitations to a party at Upton Cressett for our supporters.

For perhaps for the first time in my life, I felt I wasn't a 'townie' outsider any more. Three years before, I would have known hardly a single face on that lawn. Now many were friends, not just to wave at in the local supermarket, but friends for whom I opened my best wine at Sunday lunch. Indeed, that was what the last three years had been about – fighting for the very aesthetic soul of England.

I drained my Pimm's before I addressed the guests. 'When we first gathered together at the Down Inn, some three years ago, I said we needed to fight back. We were not just fighting to save one hamlet but our whole skyline, and the beauty of our Shropshire Hills, and our buildings, which give us all so much pleasure. A landscape that belongs to all of us. Thank you again.'

It was a warm summer's evening and, as jazz music drifted into the evening sky, I reflected that it wasn't just our guerrilla campaign, or our supporters, that had won the Battle of Upton Cressett, which had mirrored my battles of the heart. In some elemental way, the time-scarred ancient buildings of Upton Cressett – and the Norman church – had stepped up to the fight and defended themselves.

The story of England is really the story of our buildings, villages, towns and landscapes. Our Gatehouse was built in 1580 for a time of Elizabethan peace, not war, not for defence against cannon balls but as a pleasure tower for guests to enjoy watching the hunt in Upton Cressett's surrounding deer park.

But then, over four hundred years later, the manor had had to return to its fortified fourteenth-century moated and defensive origins. And it was the raw power of its ancient timbered oak beams – the old ribs and heart of the medieval house – along with the Norman church, with its zigzag chancel arch and almost magically charged carved twelfth-century stone font, that had had the last word.

Over nearly a thousand years, Upton Cressett's ancient stones, oak crown beams, diapered bricks and wattled walls had seen off many assaults, from the church wreckers of the Reformation to the crooked antiques dealers of the twentieth century. If the weathered bricks and leaded windows could survive such threats, Upton Cressett could defend itself from a farmer with a fancy Range Rover.

When the 900th anniversary of the church of St Gregory the Great in Morville was later celebrated, the programme of community events began with evensong, celebrated by the Reverend Simon Cawdell. As I looked around the packed Morville village church, its pews filled with our supporters, I noticed that Clive Millington was not present.

29

Pug Mug

One thing about marrying into Laura's family – I had to get used to pugs being part of my life.

At the time, Laura's mother, Viv, had two snuffling black pugs – one was ancient and half-blind – that went everywhere with her. The first time I went to stay at the family home in Norfolk, I noticed by the bed *A Pug's Guide to Etiquette* by Norfolk author Gemma Correll. In the downstairs loo there was a volume entitled *How to Think Like a Pug*.

So, I did the obvious thing expected of me when Laura and I became engaged – I said I would buy her a pug as an engagement present. Until I met my wife, and her family, I had not been aware of the special magic of the pug breed. It was clear from my first weekend staying with Laura's parents in Norfolk that snorting, mischievous pugs were an essential part of family life.

As I lay in bed in the guest bedroom, I began reading up on what to expect. 'This manual is an essential item for any pug aspiring to be a sophisticated, civilised citizen.'

Pugs play by their own set of rules. When you want them to sit, they stand; when you want them to stay, they go. Traditional schools of canine thought put these pug peccadillos down to a stubborn refusal to be trained that's inherent in the breed. They are wrong, Correll informed me. This behaviour relates to an 'ancient set of rules, passed down from pug generation to pug generation'.

I was beginning to get the message. Laura said she wanted a black pug bitch, as opposed to fawn. At the time of my pug promise, I'd had no idea how tricky it can be to find black ones. Not only are they in high demand and rare, but they are also expensive – around a thousand pounds was the going rate.

But once you commit to a promise of a pug puppy, there is no way out, so we started our search. We rang Kennel Club-accredited pug breeders; we trawled the local papers. We even endured a two-month 'phantom pregnancy' from one pug breeder. Finally, after about three months of looking, we followed a lead through Paddy Magan, a former flatmate of Laura's who worked in private aviation.

'I think I've found you your pug,' Paddy told me over the phone. 'I was talking with a former air stewardess who has a litter of five-week-old black pugs with a girl available. It's first come, first served.'

'Where are they?'

'Dartford – in Kent.'

I looked at the map. I knew from my days of seeing Helen that it was one hell of a drive to Kent from Shropshire – probably four hours. The next day, Laura and I headed off to a housing estate near Dartford where we found the female pug living in a children's play pen with about five other dogs.

They were another family of pug fanatics and were clearly upset to see her go. As she did not have all the correct Kennel Club registration papers, I offered £800 on the spot. This was accepted. I paid half as the deposit, with a view to collecting the puppy in January when she would be around six weeks old. We decided to call her Damson – her coat was near-black, but not jet. There are ancient damson trees here at Upton Cressett, so we liked the connection.

Damson soon settled into life at Upton Cressett, bonding with my Labrador and spending most of her waking life lying on a dog bed in front of the stove in Laura's millinery studio as she made her hats. Since the floods, storms and rain in Shropshire were incessant during February, she hardly ever went outside, and had no idea of the garden or surrounding fields or woods around the house.

Around two weeks before our wedding in London, Laura went away for her hen weekend in Essex, leaving me in charge of the dogs. The main event for the bride-to-be was an all-girls limo trip to a nightclub near Dagenham, so I wasn't expecting Laura back until late afternoon on Sunday.

On the Sunday morning, I went into my study to do some work. The two dogs were happily curled up on their shared bed in the kitchen. What happened next unravelled into one of the more traumatic experiences of my life. About an hour later, when I went into the kitchen to make a coffee, I saw that the kitchen door was wide open. There was no sign of the dogs. It looked as if the door had blown open in the howling rain and wind.

I immediately donned wellington boots – I was still in my pyjamas and dressing-gown – and started walking around the grounds and lane, calling for them. To no avail. I ran inside, changed into practical clothing for pug hunting in a storm and started tramping around the local fields. Still no sign of either dog.

I was now seriously worried. There was so much rain that the normally grassy dry moat was half full of water. Damson could have drowned.

To lose Laura's beloved pug just a few days before our wedding would have been catastrophic – possibly seeing the end of my marital hopes. I was sure she'd call the wedding off saying I wasn't fit to be a dog owner, let alone a husband.

Around lunchtime, now in a state of panic, I rang BBC Radio Shropshire, and managed to get some time on air, alerting everyone to what was now an emergency situation. I asked for anyone in the Bridgnorth area who had an hour free to assist with a search-and-rescue operation in the fields and countryside around Upton Cressett. I also sent a Mayday out to supporters of our Save the Shropshire Hills campaign. Then I posted a hastily written news blog on the house website; it invited the public to join the search party and gave details of a handsome reward. After posting it, I rang my near neighbour Lucy Birley, who lived near Monkhopton, not far away. She was a serious dog lover. Lucy was the wife of Robin Birley, owner of 5 Hertford Street club in Mayfair, and they were both good family friends. Lucy and I shared Martin Reidy as our builder.

'Hi, Lucy,' I said. 'Laura's pug puppy, Damson, has gone missing – I've been searching for hours. Could you bring the lurchers?'

'I'll be right over,' she said.

The lurchers were hunting dogs with a refined sense of smell. Perhaps they could sniff out the little pug if they picked up her scent from her bed.

At around 1.30 p.m., my Labrador, Cressett, returned alone, soaking wet and covered with thick Shropshire mud. There was no sign of the little pug.

I was getting increasingly desperate, not least as Laura had rung to say she was taking an afternoon train and would be home by around 7.00 p.m.

Various members of the public had now started showing up at the house offering to help with the search, until three parties were trudging around the fields. We found nothing.

Lucy and I scoured the fields for another hour or so with her lurchers. Lucy wondered whether a hawk might have swooped down and grabbed the little pug for breakfast, or if she had drowned from being washed away in one of the brooks at the bottom of the surrounding fields.

By around 3.30 p.m., I decided that the cause was lost and decided to put plan 'B' into action. I went into the kitchen, took off my boots and typed 'black pug bitch puppy' into the Google search engine. It had taken nearly four months to find a pug, but such was my love for Laura that I wasn't going to give up until I found a replacement.

My prayers were answered within twenty minutes. I found a black puppy with a pug breeder called Mandy, who lived in Birmingham.

Soon, I was driving at speed in the pouring rain towards the Birmingham suburb of King's Heath, which I had never heard of. All I could see was that it was close to the Moseley area on the Alcester road. The only thing a quick Google search told me about the place was that UB40 had played their first gig there in a pub in 1979.

The address I had been given was off Stanley Road. I was using my phone sat-nav and blindly following directions. Suddenly, I found myself heading into a pretty rough-looking estate, which ended in a neighbourhood cul-de-sac. There was no way out. As I got out of the car, I could see a large tattooed man in a hooded tracksuit standing in front of the gates to Mandy's house. Oh, God. He probably had a knife, I thought.

So this was how I was going to meet my end – before I'd even married Laura – as the victim of a 'pug mugging' for the thousand pounds in crisp fifties I had in my pocket. I reasoned that, of course, there was no little black pug for sale; it was just an Internet scam to steal the cash from a pug mug like me.

As I walked up to the gate, I was terrified. But once I saw the sight of a large plastic pug in the front room window, I thought Mandy might be for real. Luckily, the potential mugger turned out just to be a friendly Birmingham neighbour. So much for my stereotyping.

I knocked on Mandy's door. There was terrific barking and the noise of a chain being removed on the door.

'Hello,' I said. 'I've come for the pug puppy.'

Clearly, they weren't going to sell any of their beloved litter to just anybody. I needed to convince them that I was of the pug faith. There was certainly going to be no mention of this one being a replacement for a fourteen-week-old puppy I had just managed to lose.

The moment I saw the pug, I said I would buy it – no haggling, no questions about its parentage. No, thank you, I would not like a cup of tea with a Wagon Wheel.

Mandy looked at me a little suspiciously. 'If you just wait here, I'll get all her Kennel Club registration papers, her medical records, and you can look at the family history. She's got all the paperwork, don't worry . . . She's been wormed and vaccinated, and she's been weaned. She can eat her own puppy food now.'

'You said she's nine weeks?'

'That's right. Look at her mother here. Isn't she a beauty?'

'I'm sorry to sound rude,' I said, interrupting. 'But I'm in rather a hurry. Could you send me the paperwork? It's a surprise present for my fiancée, you see. Her family are pug lovers. We live in the countryside, near Bridgnorth. She will be going to a very good home.'

I pulled out the wodge of cash in an envelope. 'You said a thousand pounds on the phone,' I added. 'Here it is. Can I write down my address for all the Kennel Club pedigree forms? I'm afraid I need to hurry back.'

I was now getting curious looks from Mandy. Nobody had ever conducted a pug sale at such speed. There was no pug small-talk. This was just a cold cash transaction.

'Final question,' I said. 'What's the difference in size between a fourteen-week pug puppy and this little one at nine weeks? Do they grow fast?'

'She will fatten up fast in a few weeks. Give her puppy food only.'

Once I had the pug in a cardboard box, I started heading for the door.

'Thank you very much,' I said. 'I'll send photos. Look forward to getting the registration papers.'

Once back in the car, I saw that it was around 5.00 p.m. It was almost dark. I needed to drive like Lewis Hamilton to get home before Laura.

I made it back in just over an hour. Still there was no sign of Damson, so now I faced my moment of pug reckoning. Would I just place the new pug in Damson's old basket and pray that Laura didn't notice the swap? Or did I tell her up-front about the new pug?

I decided to opt for the former and play it by ear. The new pug did look very like Damson although she was smaller and had slightly different markings. Hopefully, Laura wouldn't notice. I imagined that she'd be very tired after the hen weekend and would probably want to go straight to bed for a rest. There was certainly nothing in the *Pug's Guide to Etiquette* to cover my pug predicament.

Twenty minutes or so later, I could see Laura walking down the brick path to the kitchen door. I decided to say nothing. Pretend all was normal. If I was busted, the marriage would be off.

'How was the hen do?' I asked nonchalantly.

'Great fun,' she said. 'I'm shattered. It was rather a late one.'

She knelt down to pick up her pug. 'William, what have you done to her?' she blurted out. 'She's lost so much weight! And what's this white marking on her chest? Have you . . . have you killed my pug? This is not my pug!' She burst into tears.

At this point I had to come clean and tell her the whole unfortunate saga about poor Damson.

It took Laura some time to recover and I was banished to a guest bedroom for at least a night. But her new pug was adorable and sweet. We decided to call her Thimble.

'Don't mention *anything* about Damson in your wedding speech,' said Laura, a few days later. 'My family are all pug lovers. It would go down very badly. You could get lynched. If they hear about it, the wedding could well be *off.*'

To prevent another escape, no expense was spared in building an Alcatraz-style yew hedge courtyard that would operate as Thimble's private garden prison. Alas, we never found Damson.

Almost a week later, on a fine February morning at 11 a.m., we were married at the Church of Our Most Holy Redeemer in Chelsea. Laura was twenty-nine.

Laura wore her hair in a glamorous 1950s-style beehive and arrived early on Upper Cheyne Row with her father, Charles. My best man – number three – was my old friend Gus Hochchild, whom I had known since we were at the same Oxford tutorial in the mid-1980s. One of my ushers, Mowbray Jackson – by then a veteran in the role – had to send their wedding car around the block twice before the service could start.

My father's wedding present to us was not some dinner service or a set of leaded crystal glasses but, rather, a leatherbound 125-page history of the Cressett family with the Cressett shield embossed in gilt on the dark-blue hide cover. It had been forty-five years in the making. After collecting the 'notes and jottings' he had made since 1970, he had finally written the book, *The De Uptons and Cressetts of Upton Cressett*, in 'total secrecy', as he described it, during our six-month engagement so that he could give it to us as a surprise wedding gift. It was privately printed, an edition of just five gilded leatherbound copies. Inside each is an *ex-libris* bookplate with our family motto.

In his preface, my father wrote:

> *Upton Cressett Hall is now fully restored and now is the time to publish this history of the distinguished Cressett family which has never been brought together before. I have written this book, weaving their history into the history of England. Although I dare say that there is more to be discovered, I decided that the time for me to set down my pen was the occasion of the marriage of my son, William, to Laura Cathcart on 28th February 2014.*

Because my marriage to Ilaria had been annulled, and my marriage to Vanessa had been a civil service, we could marry in a Catholic church, not far from the street where Laura had been partly brought up. The wedding service was co-celebrated by parish priest Canon Brockie, with whom we had our 'instruction', and Father Antony Sutch, former headmaster of Downside. He had married Laura's parents and christened Laura in 1984. He had also celebrated most of our family weddings. He was an old and dear friend of both our families. Having seen Antony himself buffeted by the winds of fortune, it was an honour to have him consecrate our marriage vows.

After reading St Mathew's Gospel about the man 'who built his house on rock', he gave an extraordinarily powerful sermon emphasising how marriage was a true sacrament of life – 'for *life*'.

My sister Laetitia read from the Old Testament's *Song of Songs*:

> For see, winter is past. The rains are over and gone.
> Flowers are appearing on the earth.
> The season of glad songs has come.

For too many years, I had lived my life on sand; now it was time to build a new life with Laura on new, more solid foundations. The Wheel had come full circle.

'Why are you packing that bottle of wine?' said Laura, as I stood before my open suitcase the day after our wedding, just as we headed off on our honeymoon.

'This is a special bottle,' I said, holding up a bottle of Château Pétrus 1985 that had been given to us as an engagement present by a financier friend. 'We'll have it at dinner on our first night in Jamaica. I'll wear my new cream linen suit.'

We went to Round Hill, near Montego Bay. JFK had taken his new wife Jacqueline there for their honeymoon in 1953, which meant it was old-school Jamaica. We stayed in the ground-floor suite of Cottage 16, which had been part of the Rothermere Villa. Thankfully, we weren't in the lower-ground suite below the swimming pool. When I dived in, I noticed a James Bond-style port-hole window built into the side of the pool that looked directly into the bedroom beneath it.

'Ah, yes,' said Josef Fortesmeyer, the hotel's manager, when I mentioned it. 'We don't usually give that room to honeymooners.'

Of course, I didn't get any writing done. I was too happy, even if I did look like the hotel's golf pro due to a wardrobe accident en route. On opening my suitcase, it transpired that the vintage bottle of Pétrus had exploded during the flight. My entire wardrobe was soaked in claret, so most of my honeymoon trousseau had to be thrown out or sent to the hotel laundry. Before dinner, I had to go down to the hotel boutique for a new outfit. I emerged wearing a banana-yellow polo shirt bearing the hotel logo and a bright pair of turquoise Bermuda-style checked pants. The cream suit was history. From that moment, for the rest of our honeymoon, I avoided red wine, preferring instead to stick to dark rum punch or piña coladas.

VI

30

A Studio of Her Own

As a wedding present, I had built Laura a new millinery studio at Upton Cressett in one of the old pig barns that my mother had once used as a pottery and painting shed. After many years of disuse, it had slowly become a junk repository room. Thanks to Martin, and Marcus, my cabinet maker, a new artisan studio was installed, with a wood-burning stove canopy forged by Shropshire blacksmith Archie Kennedy, with the Cressett sea-dragons along the edge. All Laura's ribbons, blocks, hat stretchers, pots of stiffener and rolls of straw had been moved up from London in wicker baskets.

The studio was where Laura created her dazzlingly beautiful new headpieces, all inspired by butterflies and flowers in her new 'millinery' garden at Upton Cressett. As she listened to Classic FM, with her little pug, Thimble, snorting in front of the fire, the new studio seemed to inspire her. When we met in the kitchen for a glass of wine at around 6.00 p.m. after a productive work day – when I was not in London

– she would often be wearing a new hat to show me, twirling around like a model ballerina. Most creations were conjured up in just a day. She was a true couture artist, using the finest of rare feathers, pins, braids, beads, sequins and silk flowers to create unique works of art.

It came as no surprise that orders started rolling in from royalty and various fashion icons. Then Laura was officially selected to be part of the Millinery Collective at Royal Ascot, alongside Britain's best-known milliners: Philip Treacy, Rachel Trevor-Morgan and Stephen Jones. There was an official milliners' lunch in a box on Ladies Day, along with a round of TV and press interviews. She also wrote a hilarious article for the *Sunday Times* about the social minefield of millinery etiquette. Her main advice was to stick to the golden rule that she had once been told by *Downton Abbey* creator Julian Fellowes: 'Ladies should only *ever* take off their hats in the bedroom.'

There was only one snag – the next Ladies Day at Royal Ascot was likely to be the day she might be giving birth. Yes, Laura was pregnant.

Scottish Thread

I was glad that Laura is half Scottish. She comes from an old Scottish family with a long and proud military history. That was one reason why she joined me in September 2014 as we headed up to Edinburgh on the train from Wolverhampton two days before the historic Scottish referendum vote. We both had Celtic ancestry, although my Cash clan ancestors of the Macbeth era cannot be looked up in *Burke's*. They do, however, appear in Nashville's Country Music Hall of Fame.

Back in April, not long after we'd got back from our honeymoon, my mother called me about a surprise invitation to a concert. My father had received an email at his House of Commons office from Rosanne Cash, eldest daughter of American country legend Johnny. She was an acclaimed singer-songwriter in her own right with fourteen albums and eleven Number 1 country singles to her name. Rosanne wrote that she knew about a William Cash who was a member of Parliament, and suspected we shared a genealogy.

Rosanne was touring Europe to perform her award-winning album, *The River & The Thread* – about our shared Cash family history, the Civil War and her family's relationship with the American south. She wanted to know if our family wanted to attend her concert at the Barbican on 30 April.

My father (who has always been proud of his singing 'voice') was delighted to learn that we were 'cousins' with America's greatest country legend and invited Rosanne to lunch. Alas, her tight touring schedule, with husband John, meant that she was going 'straight to Bremen the day after the Barbican show' but she would 'love to do lunch' at the House of Commons on another trip. As a post-script, she said she would send a photo of her Civil War ancestor William Cash.

'You are related to *Johnny Cash?*' said Laura, looking amazed. 'The legend?' She had seen *Walk The Line*, about his life, with Joaquin Phoenix.

Around halfway through the concert, a huge, thirty-foot-high, grainy, nineteenth-century, black-and-white photograph of a dashing soldier in grey battledress holding a rifle flashed up on the Barbican theatre screen.

'This is my ancestor William Cash who fought in the Civil War,' Rosanne told the audience. 'And I'm happy to have some members of my family here tonight.'

I saw Laura almost gasping with disbelief.

'He has the Cash *ears*', Laura whispered to me.

The Confederate Army officer looked strangely similar to both me and my father. The same Celtic features, prominent nose, high cheekbones and overall likeness were unmistakable.

Afterwards, we all went backstage to meet Rosanne and her husband John, bonding over beers and Scotch. In person, she was striking, with flowing Celtic dark auburn hair, Pre-Raphaelite shining eyes, and was warm and funny. A singer and writer who was very much the untamed and unflinching artist, like her father. Her soulful charisma gave her an almost ethereal quality. She looked like a beautiful folk singer, or Celtic poet, who could not escape her family history.

'The next time you are over please come and stay with us at Upton Cressett,' my father said before we left the back-stage area.

'Oh thank you,' Rosanne said. 'I'd love that.'

That my English family were directly related to the Cash family members who settled in New England in 1667 was only confirmed when my father subsequently dug around in the chest (at Upton Cressett) in which he keeps all the Cash family genealogy papers and 'family pedigree'. The chest contains a large file of detailed correspondence and family arms by family historian Don Cash, an genealogical 'obsessive' (yes, another family trait) who lived in San Diego, California. He had been in touch with our head of the English family, Sir William Cash, as far back as the early 1960s, well before Johnny Cash was even made aware of his noble Scottish roots.

Following our meeting at the Barbican, I was later to get to know Rosanne more as a 'friend and cousin,' as she was to inscribe a copy of her memoir, *Composed*. Meeting for lunch before she performed a concert in Atlanta, we explored our shared identity and what it was to be born with the Cash surname. Her direct line is through Reuben Cash (her great-grandfather, who fought for the Confederacy and survived the Civil War) but we all share a common Celtic Cash Scottish ancestry including blood ties to William Cash the New World pilgrim ship captain. I was fascinated by the extent to which family 'character' – and certain traits – could be determined by genes.

Also what it was like to grow up in the shadow of a famous and occasionally overbearing father. This was a sensitive subject for me as I approached fifty. With only two books and a play to my name, I felt as if I had not lived up to my hopes of myself. My brief attempt to follow my father into politics – after thirty years of being entirely apolitical – was to fail after I stood, aged forty-eight, on an idealistic 'Save Our English Countryside' and pro-heritage and tourism ticket after becoming so angered by what the Coalition government was doing to destroy our heritage and landscape with the new planning reforms.

The truth was, deep down, I agreed with Greene that writers shouldn't enter the political fray as their sympathies will always change. I should have been brave enough to stick with writing to have a voice. But for so many decades of of my life – as William Cash Jr – I felt an urge to step away from my father's public identity; one reason I wanted to be a writer. It didn't help that we had the same name. Maybe this was why Johnny Cash never voted. He was a populist without political loyalties. He was friends with both Republican and Democrat presidents.

So Rosanne was a welcome family role model, not the least as she was very much a *writer* and a singer. There is something in the often wayward Cash genes that strives to make order – or sense? – out of destruction and chaos. Light from darkness. Redemption from regret. Art from failure – or 'personal catastrophe', as Rosanne put it. She didn't just write her own songs (often collaborating with her husband John). Her fiction and essays appeared in the *New York Times*, *Rolling Stone* and *New York Magazine*. Her lyrical and disarming memoir was candid about the 'highs' and lows' of her often difficult personal journey as an artist, covering her complex relationship with her larger-than-life father. She is certainly as emotionally direct as her father was in his iconic songs of rebellion, remorse and spiritual questing and self-discovery.

Rosanne was fascinated to know that the Cash 'pilgrim' family from which she is descended were strict Quakers and radicals (such as the Liberal statesman John Bright) who took up various populist anti-Establishment causes including abolition of slavery and the Corn Laws. I asked if she felt there was something almost spiritually flagellating about the Cash 'line'?

'I think that the Cashes are full of longing,' Rosanne said. 'I think that that's definitive to our DNA and our nature, and that longing sometimes leads us down a rocky path.'

From our Celtic side?

'Yes. And I think it leads us also to some kind of spiritual, artistic, creative redemption, but some of them don't get off that path of longing that leads to self-destruction, and some do.'

As she has got older, she has come to the view that 'art is a more trustworthy expression of God than religion'.

When I mentioned our family's Quaker background, Rosanne said it didn't surprise her. 'My father's instincts were somewhat Quaker. His pacifism was absolute. He did not think there was a reason for any war at any time, even though he served in the Air Force. He was very much a pacifist, and tried to be temperate, his instincts were for that, but he couldn't.'

'I know the feeling,' I said before explaining how my Victorian ancestor William Cash was a fanatical teetotaller. 'Your father isn't the only Cash who has struggled to live temperately. In fact, I've struggled for most of my life.'

Rosanne smiled. She didn't have to say anything. She had come through the other side now. 'I think the fierceness of the longing is in the DNA, and for some people, it's led to religion, in some people it's led to destruction, and in some people it's led to art, but that kind of intensity of longing, I think it just finds an outlet in different ways. But I do think that intensity is part of our nature, very much.'

For somebody brought up in California, she had a surprisingly sixteenth- and seventeenth-century literary sensibility. She is a lifelong fan of the diaries of Samuel Pepys and had even been to see them at the Pepys Library of my old Cambridge college, Magdalene.

I guessed that she enjoyed Pepys's lacerating self-honesty, certainly a Cash family quirk.

Why did her father hang up the Cash coat of arms at home, I asked? 'He was very proud of his Cash and Scottish ancestry,' Rosanne said. Towards the end of his life, Johnny Cash was so proud of being able to trace a noble Scottish family connection back to Malcolm IV (known as the Maiden King) and a family castle that appears in Shakespeare's *Macbeth* that he checked himself in as 'Malcolm', not Cash, when he was admitted to hospital in his final days.

Rosanne's Scottish roots are at the heart of much of her song-writing. Her own son has William as a middle name. 'I hear the Celtic influences in my work all the time,' she said. '"The Good Intent" is about my first ancestor that sailed to America. That song is about 300 years of my ancestry.'

The song imagines William Cash as a narrative character not unlike the 'Ancient Mariner' of Coleridge's famous eighteenth-century poem of quest, sin and spiritual redemption. As we talked on, trying to fathom how to describe the Cash 'nature', Rosanne finally said: 'It's all about having an adventurous soul. There's a sense of quest to find the richness of the soul and everything that means. In my father's music, he was forever duelling between sin and redemption. This was a constant battle for him. But his longing for God was as intense as his art.'

Rosanne was brought up in a rambling hillside house in Casitas Springs, California, where she – and her sisters – attended St Bonaventure High School, a private Catholic convent school as her mother Vivian was of Italian (Sicilian) origin. But Rosanne told me her relationship with the church (her parents had been married in a Catholic church) became all but broken when her mother was effectively 'excommunicated' as a result of her divorce in 1967 due to his drugs, drinking and infidelity.

'My father wasn't an every Sunday kind of guy because he was on the road all the time,' Rosanne added. 'But he prayed daily. He even did Communion himself, in a little office.'

'"The Good Intent" says it all,' I said.

'Capitalism doesn't drive us!' Rosanne added, breaking into laughter. 'My father was terrible with money. Terrible. Oh, my God.'

At the Atlanta concert, I was very touched when Rosanne dedicated a very personal song to me (definitely a first in my life) called 'Long Black Veil'. This classic 1959 country ballad was a favourite of her father, who performed it on the first episode of *The Johnny Cash Show* in 1969.

When I texted her the day after to thank her, I said that it had a special resonance as 'being a Cash is often about embarking on a spiritual voyage of revelation.' To which she replied: 'Truer words were never said.' Her own memoir unsparingly describes her own heartbreaks, struggles and griefs to reveal how the 'power of art' – rather than religion – can transform and redeem a life. I only hope this memoir lives up to the family standard when it comes to emotional honesty.

When I was broken after my second divorce, and my world fell apart, I sometimes wondered who – without the social tinsel – I really was. Learning about my American Cash family was an intriguing lesson in how there is such a thing as family 'character'. While we have often been hard-working and pioneering, we also tend towards being mavericks and outsiders. There is also a missionary and radical streak in our genes (politics, journalism, publishing or religion). What is certain is that, as a family, we fall into two very different camps. On one side are the financially disciplined and temperate (the side that founded accounting firms and insurance companies and built railways); or else we are financially hopeless, impulsively creative, and intemperate often to the point of self-sabotage. Alas, I didn't have to read *Cash*, the autobiography ('money is not my God' Johnny wrote) to know which I fell into.

Strange, I've Seen That Face Before

Following my Barbican encounter with Civil War soldier William Cash, it wasn't long before Laura had her own double-take. On the day of the Scottish referendum vote, I took her to the National Gallery of Scotland. We soon found ourselves in a crowded room full of Japanese students standing in front of Gainsborough's full-length portrait of *The Honourable Mrs Thomas Graham*. It was the gallery's most famous painting.

'Exhibited to great acclaim at the Royal Academy in 1777, this famous painting is regarded as one of Gainsborough's masterpieces – a study in timeless beauty,' said the gallery lecturer.

'That's my ancestor, Mary Cathcart,' whispered Laura. 'I've always wanted to see the original. We have some other pictures of her hanging at home. And her sister Louisa.'

We leaned forward as the lecturer continued, 'As Mrs Graham leans with her elbow on a classical column, she looks at us with a glance that is starting to turn away from us. We admire her timeless beauty but she does not want to acknowledge that it is her beauty that she is being admired for.'

Laura turned towards me in a mock imitation of Mary's diffident bearing and we both smiled. Unlike her ancestor, she was wearing one of her own red berets, which made her look more like a 1930s art student in Paris than a fashionable Georgian beauty. But the resemblance was still uncanny.

Gainsborough's sitter was born the Hon Mary Cathcart, the beautiful daughter of Charles Cathcart, a swashbuckling military aristocrat, who wore a black silk patch on his face to hide a war scar received at the Battle of Fontenoy. He became ambassador to the Russian court of Catherine the Great in St Petersburg where Mary was brought up. Wearing a chic plumed feather hat, beaded with silver pearls, and a silk cream masquerade dress, the sitter is a celebration of Georgian fashion and beauty.

After the Japanese students had shuffled off to the next room, I took a photo of Laura standing in front of her famous eighteenth-century relation wearing her beret. As I did so, I suddenly remembered what had flooded through my head when I had first sat next to her at dinner in the Italian restaurant in Belgravia some five years earlier. I had thought that she resembled a half-familiar Gainsborough beauty. Now I knew why.

We had dinner on the night of the referendum vote in Edinburgh with my finance-world friend David Yarrow. With his tousled curly hair and *Miami Vice*-style black T-shirt, worn under a suit, David had the look of somebody who had survived a difficult divorce. He had a restless intensity about him and looked at you with an almost evangelical directness. I could see why people trusted him with their money.

He had been brought up in Glasgow, where his family had built ships for the Royal Navy and Scottish business owners for over a hundred years. Although still running his London hedge fund, he was spending more time in far-flung corners of the world pursuing his passion for wildlife photography. He was one of the few members of my Moneyman generation to jump career.

Before dinner, Laura and I had met David in a New Town basement bar, with a hundred different brands of whisky decorating the shelves. It was around 9.30 p.m., and the voting had just closed, when David sat on a stool and started scanning the choices before him. He ordered some obscure twenty-year-old malt.

With his wind-burned face and sure grip of the whisky glass, he reminded me of Saul Bellow's millionaire American narrator in *Henderson the Rain King*. While the hard-drinking tycoon seeks salvation in the African jungle, to escape from the 'tears and thunder' of his mid-life divorce crisis, David had sought out remote jungles, deserts and the Artic, as a form of creative redemption. In many ways, we were both looking for the same thing during our divorces – a means of escape. What I didn't realise until Laura became my wife was that the best way of divorcing the past was not exotic travel, but English love at home.

The mood in the restaurant was subdued. Even the pubs, which had been granted special licences to stay open all night, were mostly empty.

When Laura went to the ladies' room, David turned to me. 'You're lucky to have remarried so soon. She looks a lovely girl. I'm nearly fifty. The biggest failure of my life has been my divorce.'

'But your photography is going well,' I said. 'How long will you keep the fund going? Why not become a full-time photographer and rove the world?'

'My mother often looks at me and says, "Why do you do it, David? You seem so unhappy as a banker." When I travel as a photographer, I feel free, I feel happy. I don't know how long the fund will stay open. That's the one good thing about divorce. I can travel where I like, when I like. When I'm up in a plane looking over the desert, or alone in the Antarctic, I'm doing what I only ever really wanted to do. But I'm not a quitter.'

'So, how's the vote going to go?'

'The Scots are no fools,' said David. 'We have one of the best education systems in the world. Economic fear and currency will clearly be a major factor for Scottish businesses, along with the fact that many Scots tend to be private about what they really think. I reckon the Union will be saved.'

His eye met the barman's, whose glare left me in no doubt as to how he was voting.

'What are you drinking, Cash?'

David had a way of using surnames.

'Piña colada, please.'

The barman's eyes suddenly filled with disgust. Poncy English fucker, in *my* whisky bar, on Scottish referendum night, of all nights.

David looked at me as if to say, 'Funny one, William. You are *joking*, aren't you?'

I hadn't been. But I came to my senses. 'Macallan – a large one, please.'

The Reckoning

I began this memoir with the image of a man sitting in a pig shed in the weeks before his fiftieth birthday, trawling through his love letters and scrapbooks, trying to make sense of a life. Writing of the lost art of what he calls 'The Magic of Letters' in his book, *To the Letter,* Simon Garfield says: 'It must have seemed impossible that their worth would ever be taken for granted or swept aside. A world without letters would surely be a world without oxygen.'

Certainly revisiting my Binder Box letters has been like visiting an old pump room of the heart. 'How will we be able to tell our history without letters?' Garfield asks. He is clear that emails cannot substitute for handwritten letters, and he is right.

But if our lives and letters teach us who we are, can we learn anything from trawling through the written or faxed flotsam of our past lives? Or are such boxes best left gathering dust in the attic, only to end up after our death on a family bonfire?

Perhaps that is why I kept all my letters over thirty years, even the self-lacerating or self-incriminating ones. Letters are agents of hope and change. Our imaginations and memories allow our words to remain spiritually alive, just as the cosmos of a house or building can survive demolition.

Since without them I would not be able to remember much of my life, including many key events, the answer must be that they are worth keeping. I'm glad I've had my trawl. It was only marrying Laura that finally cured me of being a letter-writing addict.

One thing I have learned about personal happiness is that, as a general rule, the larger the love-letter file, the unhappier the relationship. It also occurred to me, after reading through hundreds of scrawled notes, letters and love faxes, that had I spent half as much energy and time channelling my writing creatively as opposed to writing to the women of my Binder Boxes, I might have written more books. Much of the letter-writing was a quest for meaning and an attempt to create order. Restoring Upton Cressett doubtless came from the same impulse.

That August before my fiftieth, after a dawn or evening walk with my dog, I would often end up in the Norman church that stands less than a hundred yards from the house. Despite not having regular services any more, our family was always glad that St Michael's remained consecrated. Its most recent service? The christening of our daughter Cosima.

I was forty-eight when Cosima arrived. She could easily have been born at Royal Ascot racecourse. Since Laura had been so heavily pregnant, the car-parking attendants turned a blind eye as we drove as close as possible to the entrance. I had made enquiries as to the nearest maternity hospitals in case her waters broke during the day. I had a printed map to the Royal Berkshire Hospital, along with emergency phone numbers.

As Laura sat happily in the Royal Ascot Millinery Collective's box overlooking the racecourse, chatting to Rachel Trevor-Morgan, milliner to the Queen, and Stephen Jones, who made hats for Dior, I felt hugely proud of her.

It was around midnight a few days later – after the preview party for the Masterpiece London art fair – when I was woken at 3 a.m. with a text from Laura saying her waters were breaking. I needed to get to Shropshire – fast.

I was on the 5.15 a.m. train to Birmingham, praying I would get to Bridgnorth hospital in time. After some hairy driving from Sasha, our new housekeeper who collected me, I got to our local hospital by around 9.30 a.m. Just as I knocked on the door, a woman slammed it shut. 'Do not enter,' she said loudly. It was made clear that Laura was in the final stages of delivery and that this wasn't the moment for an entrance.

Around twenty minutes later, I was handed my first-born child, Cosima, wrapped in a towel, as I sat in an armchair in the hospital kitchen and TV room. The maternity nurse then went back to Laura and I was left alone with the little sleeping bundle. I hadn't got a clue what I was meant to be doing, but it felt surreal to be a father for the first time. I was old enough to be a grandfather.

I knew the summer of 2016 was ending when our white peacock, York, started losing his tail feathers. They lay scattered around the garden like giant white quills. The last weeks of a wet August fell away and our tea-and-tours season at Upton Cressett wound up on the bank-holiday weekend. I was about to turn fifty.

The season had been a wash-out despite an exhibition of recently discovered black-and-white photographs in the Tate's archives that the artist John Piper had taken on his visit with John Betjeman to Upton Cressett in 1938. There was just one last 2.30 p.m. house tour to go.

Then our 'Bosworth' tent, a replica of a field tent from the Battle of Bosworth, would be packed up for another year. I had lost count of the number of times I tipped away the rain and leaves that pooled and collected on the tent's sagging canopy, secured by drooping ropes pegged to the grass. Once striped in a deep Lancastrian red, with a pair of Tudor sea-dragons painted by Adam Dant on each side of the entrance, the heraldic colours had now faded to an earthy brown. When the tent went up at the beginning of the summer, the ropes and canvas were pingingly taut. Now it looked like part of a travelling circus, its striped canopy sagging, like a deck chair left out in a thunderstorm.

The tent had been made by George Mudford & Son in Nottingham (established 1832) as a drinks pavilion for Laura's thirtieth 'Tudor' birthday party in June 2014. Laura's birthday party had offered a chance for some cosmic time travel. Dressed in doublet and tights, I dressed as a troubadour court minstrel whom I called 'John Cash'. I had donned a sixteenth-century black velvet cap with a feather that had once belonged to Thomas Seymour, 1st Baron Sudeley, and fourth husband of Catherine Parr, sixth and last wife of Henry VIII.

'I've borrowed the cap from our costume exhibition,' my old pal Henry Dent-Brocklehurst told me, when he handed over the heirloom before dinner. 'For God's sake, don't burn a cigar hole in it.'

We were meant to be using our knightly pavilion for drinks before my fiftieth birthday dinner, but the forecast was for rain. The costumed dancers I had booked to perform a few sixteenth-century jigs on the lawn were going to be drenched. Portable gas heaters and dozens of beeswax altar candles – the type that don't drip – from the ecclesiastical supplier in Much Wenlock would be badly needed, as the church still had no electricity.

The only power was coming from an extension cord that stretched like a coil of liquorice across the lawn from the house. This would provide sockets for a microphone for my speech and the début performance of a Johnny Cash-inspired 'cowboy ballad' by my musician, broadcaster and author friend Mike Read, who used to host the Radio 1 *Breakfast Show* in the Eighties. My friend had no shortage of raw material to draw on for his country song.

One thing was certain – my rickety life was made for some Johnny Cash-style songs of remorse and regret. The Man in Black was known for his troubled and soulful lyrics of wrong turnings, moral tribulations and the longing for redemption – all of which I could identify with. But this birthday ballad was the least of my worries; I had my own speech to think about.

To be fair, I wasn't dreading my fiftieth birthday. In the days running up to it my main emotion was relief. At least I had no plane to catch back to London and I wasn't eating alone in a diner on the wrong side of the LA Valley.

But in the weeks before I turned fifty, I began to measure my life against others. In his portrait in the Great Hall dining room, my father is dressed in a navy suit with thick greying hair and looks like the political Establishment figure he isn't. He is wearing his pink-and-green Garrick club tie and clasping a copy of the Lisbon Treaty, not unlike the way in which Sir Francis Cressett, wearing a giant wig, beside him, is clutching his helmet. Like Sir Francis, my father's life has mostly been one of public service, or parliamentary 'duty' as he prefers to see it. Both my father and Sir Francis earned their honours through their own achievements.

I knew there was not the slightest chance of opening *The Times* – my former paper – on 1 September to see 'William Cash, author and magazine publisher, 50' in the 'Today's Birthdays' section. Nor was there any *'aetatis suae* 50' portrait being painted by some society artist to mark the occasion.

My birthday was an irrelevance, although no doubt with several of the party guests being former newspaper diary editors or veteran *Private Eye* hacks, I could expect some waspish and colourful paragraph about my birthday weekend in one of the tabloid gossip columns where the personal vicissitudes and romantic failures of my last twenty years had so often appeared. I was not confident my birthday weekend would be an exception.

The gossip-columnists would be joined at the dinner by a motley troupe of friends collected over the years: wealthy ex-bankers; decaying aristos; lawyers; politicos; PRs; a Mayfair club owner; a semi-professional backgammon player-turned-currency trader; actress/models of varying levels of stardom; démodé It girls; a Condé Nast magazine mogul; various hacks; authors; an MEP; and various unemployables, alcoholics and family members. Elizabeth was in the Thatcher Suite, and actress Georgina Rylance was a floor above in the Prince Rupert Bedroom with her husband. I was also pleased that my old school friend Ben Marsh (grandson of Colonel Marsh) was coming, along with his Italian wife Speronella, who now lived at Monkhopton House.

The Norman church dinner and the Sunday steam-train journey would be hosting a cross-section of a generation whose combined baggage was very much a mixture of first-, second- and third-class, in terms of success and achievement. And happiness. Ah, yes, it had been quite some voyage. I would come to that theme, briefly, in my speech.

Even in the last week before the big day, I was chasing various old friends I hadn't been able to reach. Uncle Jonathan had said he was going to come but we weren't holding out much hope.

There were others who had 'saved' 27 August in their diary but never made it. Three weeks before my birthday, I sat in a pew with Laura at the Norman church of St Mary's in the idyllic village of Denham in Buckinghamshire for the funeral of my dear friend Christina Knudsen. She had moved back from LA to London, like me, at the end of the 1990s. There was a moving and touching tribute from her stepfather Sir Roger Moore and hardly a dry eye as 'The Swan' from *The Carnival of the Animals* by Camille Saint-Saëns was played at the end. At her funeral wake afterwards at the Buckinghamshire Golf Club, I spoke with another expat from LA who had moved back to England – actor Rupert Everett. He had been with Christina in hospital when she was dying.

'What brought you back to Shropshire?' Rupert asked. 'I've moved back to my family place in Wiltshire.'

'Restoring my old house.'

'Was it therapeutic?'

'It saved me.'

'I must try that.'

Christina had visited Upton Cressett several times. She had emailed to say that she hoped to come but was too ill to accept. She died of cancer on 26 July, aged just forty-seven, having been married (and divorced) but never having had children. Before her death, she had stoically kept friends updated with chatty emails of her treatment and news of her eventing horses. Having had my first child at forty-eight made me realise how lucky I was. My daughter was another form of salvation.

Three Generations

To see Cosima smiling as she had holy water splashed on her face while being held above the Norman font where I had proposed to Laura did seem something of a miracle. Modern christening services are often a more hurried affair with a photocopied template down-loaded from the Internet for the Order of Service and a blank or X for the child's name. Our service was the opposite of this. Instead of being baptism-lite, we went the other way, embracing a service that cele-brated religious ritual, mystery, symbolism and meaning.

Our priest, again, was Father Antony Sutch, who arrived with a tiny suitcase (containing just his robes), hobbling on a walking stick (he'd had a hip operation) after a six-hour train journey involving four changes. Disappearing to bed before supper the night before the service, refusing any food – as well as the offer of a cigar – he looked as if he had rowed to Bridgnorth up the River Severn from Bristol in a one-man boat. He drank water, not wine. He had lost his paunch and carried himself with humility.

The service began with our troupe of Elizabethan costume dancers, Courtesie, to perform a fifteenth-century Italian baptismal dance wearing velvet costumes and bizarre medieval headgear with stars and angels. This took place after a formal procession – formed of the family and godparents – progressed from the front door of the house through the garden and into the church.

Back in the Middle Ages, such was the seriousness of purpose attached to baptism that the mother was often not even present (she was still recovering in bed) as the child was usually baptised on the day of their birth or the following day. Part of the medieval service took place outside the church door so that the priest could check the godparents knew the Latin words to the Pater Noster and the Credo. Once they had passed this examination, the child then had salt put in their mouth to symbolise wisdom and any demons were exorcised. Only then did the party enter the church. Thankfully, our service did not include a formal quiz on the Norman porch. But what it did retain was a sense of the seriousness of the miracle of life.

As Father Antony turned towards the six godparents, including my old housemate Elizabeth, and Charles Dean, founder member of my Best Man Club, he ended his homily by saying that Cosima needed the example of parents and godparents because the world was not always a welcoming place.

'Some people say that they don't believe in God,' he said. 'But God cannot be described. In describing Him, we limit Him. God is there and we are calling upon God, through all of us here, to welcome Cosima into our community. A community that is full of gratitude for life itself. A community that believes that all has purpose. If Cosima learns from us how to be loved, she will be able to love, and that will give her the strength to live life to the full, whatever it may throw at her.'

As he finished, and turned towards the choir, the small congregation fell silent.

It was like the moment in *The Rime of the Ancient Mariner*, Coleridge's poem about the celebration of human life, and our original sin, when a wedding party is 'stunned' by some unexpected words from an old bearded mariner 'whose eye is bright' just before the feast is set. Now, as the old monk turned towards the choir, I was more than glad to hear John Rutter's valediction of life, 'Look at the World'.

Around the time of Cosima's christening, I became a director (and later chairman) of the *Catholic Herald*, founded in 1888 with writers of the pedigree of G. K. Chesterton, Graham Greene (who defended *The Power and The Glory* in its pages in 1940) and Evelyn Waugh. This appointment was something of an irony since it had always been the arch-rival to the left-wing *The Tablet*, founded in 1840 by my Quaker-turned-Catholic cousin Frederick Lucas.

My experience of finally becoming a father, aged forty-eight, had given me a renewed sense of purpose in life. After not having children in my first two marriages I felt especially blessed. I started to take more spiritual comfort from the irrational than the rational. I began leaning towards Evelyn Waugh's view on Catholics in England, where our numbers are so small. As Waugh once wrote in the *Herald*: 'There is a danger that we look on ourselves as the exceptions, instead of in the true perspective of ourselves as normal and the irreligious as freaks.'

After the service, we all gathered on the Moat Lawn, which runs down towards the churchyard, to plant my father's christening present to Cosima – a sweet chestnut sapling of a tree from the battlefield of Waterloo.

Ever since two of our Waterloo Spanish chestnuts had been felled due to disease, I had wanted to replant. The christening of Cosima seemed the perfect moment, a symbol of rebirth after a long battle.

Fittingly, the tree to mark the day of Cosima's christening was planted by Laura's father Charles, whose military family had served with such distinction at Waterloo. George Cathcart had his horse shot down three times and his younger brother was ADC to Wellington. The seeds of time were also symbolised by the presence of Laura's wonderful grandparents, Desmond and Susan, even though Des was in his early nineties. They had given us beautiful David Austin Roses as a wedding present.

We were three generations at lunch. When I mentioned the story of the exploding honeymoon bottle of wine, Laura's grandfather entertained us with another 'suitcase' story of how he had brought back some Gorgonzola from Italy, where he had been serving in the army at the end of the war. 'I knew that cheese was almost unobtainable in Norfolk,' he said, 'so I wrapped this giant wheel in muslin and put it in my case. When I opened it back home, it had melted and stank so badly that I had to throw the suitcase out.'

With the christening of Cosima, the replanting of the Waterloo tree and the presence of Father Antony, I felt that I had reached the end of my restoration journey.

While Upton Cressett survived the wrecker's ball and became my family home, Adam was on the point of packing up his nineteenth-century Shoreditch studio. It was being demolished by a developer wanting to build an expensive new block of flats. But Adam was not despondent. Much of his cartography is inspired by drawing on the 'spots of time' where famous buildings once stood, such as standing in front of the multi-storey car park in Shoreditch, which was once Shakespeare's theatre at New Inn Yard, and communing with its Spirit of Place.

His point is that our buildings, like good books, do not really die. Their spirit and voices live on, whether in bricks or words. 'Even when they are razed to the ground, all the places where we walk and live are essentially constant,' said Adam. 'In the widest and most profound sense, they are part of a cosmic cartography that is eternal, infinite and immutable.' So it is with our private maps of the heart that we store in our memories, imaginations and Binder Boxes.

* * *

'Is there a paddock to land a helicopter?' I was asked over the phone. 'Have you got the GPS landing coordinates? And latitude and longitude?'

It was the wife of an Italian financier friend. Her husband was planning to fly on to the birthday dinner after a day's grouse shooting in Yorkshire.

The impending arrival on Saturday of my friends had certainly focused the mind on questions of net- and self-worth, success and failure, private and public. One guest, my dear friend Philip Kerr, had written around thirty books. Another, Nicholas Coleridge, president of Condé Nast Europe, had written several bestsellers and had been a chronicler of the Moneyman generation for more than thirty years. Art dealer Philip Mould had a hugely successful BBC art detective show and an O.B.E. I was looking forward to showing him the restored (by my Uncle Mark) Prince Rupert 'studio' portrait by Peter Lely that he had sold me.

As I brooded in my pig shed about what most of us had achieved at fifty, personally and professionally, there was some silver lining to report. After thirty years of friendship with a lot of clever friends, I had found it was not only political careers that often ended in failure (David Cameron, my contemporary, had resigned as prime minister just a month before). The same rule applied to many of the most promising financial careers. Many of my financial friends failed to make the multi-millions they had set out to acquire when they decided to become Masters of the Universe in the late 1980s.

The unlikely friend who had made probably the most money – several billion dollars from 'crypto-currency' – was my pal Matthew Mellon, descendant of the great nineteenth-century American banker Thomas Mellon. While others had been getting to their desks at Goldman Sachs or Salomon Brothers by 7 a.m., he had spent much of the mid-1990s floating around the swimming-pool moat of his mock-Tudor manor with a giant Gekko-style mobile phone clamped to his head, organising pool parties.

As I looked at the guest list for my fiftieth, if I'd thought the hedgies and bankers were those with the happiest lives, I'd have been wrong. Of those who had gone into finance thirty years ago, few still had jobs. Proper jobs. Most had either personally or professionally burned out. Two of my oldest friends I hadn't even been able to track down. They were 'missing in financial action'. Were they on the run? They had certainly gone to ground. I had no idea where to send invitations.

The best examination of the theme of self-worth I knew was a little-seen play by William Nicholson (co-writer of *Gladiator*) called *Crash*, which I saw during its short run at the West Yorkshire Playhouse in Leeds in October 2010. Nicholson thought despairingly that the new world order, in which bankers paid themselves so many multiple times more than average professionals, was destroying his own (as an Oscar-winning writer) and others' sense of self-worth. 'How come these people were worth so much more than everyone else?' he asked.

Even for the brightest and best of a generation, the City and Wall Street turned out to be a blood-spattered career battleground. One birthday guest, Piers, worked for more than twenty years as a successful commodities trader with billionaire clients, including Sir James Goldsmith: 'I remember Jimmy once taking me to lunch and saying, "When I talk to a doctor, lawyer or a politician, they say they want to be at the top of their profession. But when I talk to anybody in the City, they say, "I want to make enough money and get out."'

Other than David Yarrow – who finally closed his fund to reinvent himself as a rock star-style wildlife photographer – I sensed that most of my Moneyman-generation friends who went into banking or finance never pursued the lives they truly wanted. In many ways, we were a 'Lost Generation', as so few ended up doing what they were most suited to doing with their well-educated lives. Most would have risen to the top of any profession they had chosen and become top QCs, headmasters, newspaper editors, brain surgeons, ambassadors or MPs.

In one of my slim Smythson notebooks (which my friend Dominick Dunne told me to buy as they looked 'like diaries rather than reporter's note-pads'), I described a conversation in November 2005 at a dinner party with a rich hedgie friend called Edmund (known as Ed) at the height of London's pre-crash financial golden age. He had already started giving large sums to the Tory party.

Ed had been staying at a stately home for a shoot and had been given a room whose bed turned out to be Empress Napoleon's 'cot' bed for her son Napoleon II. 'It was the most uncomfortable bed I had ever slept in,' he said. 'I had to take the mattress off and sleep on the floor.' He then predicted that by the time he was forty-five he would have made enough money 'never to work again'. And by fifty? 'A seat in the Cabinet and House of Lords.'

Things didn't go according to plan. His hedge fund blew up, and investors fled as the financial crisis hit. Divorce proceedings followed. Not even his closest friends knew where he was living. There had been sightings in New Jersey, St Moritz, Johannesburg and Wells-next-the-Sea. Yet I still loved him as a friend and sincerely hoped he would be coming to my party. He was one of the people I most wanted to see. I even had a dream about Ed suddenly showing up on the vintage steam train during the Sunday lunch journey as we chugged along the River Severn. I dreamed he had jumped on when it stopped at Highley, clutching a magnum of Pol Roger.

'Everybody had clapped as Ed sat down in the dining car,' I told Laura, when I woke. 'Then he opened the champagne and announced that life was "never better".'

But Ed never made it. Nor did Uncle Jonathan show up.

If you went into finance, how much money you made was your way of keeping the score. The great thing about not going into finance is that success at fifty is not defined by the millions you have made, or most likely lost. You look at the scoreboard and rate success differently.

So what exactly have I learned? The most important change in my life now was that Upton Cressett wasn't my 'safe house' any more. For as long as I could remember, my home was my most dependable of relationships. But the core of my life was now built on my love for Laura, and our family.

My missing friend Ed was the brightest of the bright young things at Oxford, where he took a first. When I first set up my publishing business, we were up against it with mounting bills and rent — and I remember him sitting at his enormous partner's desk in his eighteenth-century Mayfair office and writing me a cheque for £20,000 without a question. He got the money back, but never mentioned it. He was always a good friend. One thing I've learned over the years is that the most generous people are often those under the most pressure. Moneyman lives can have many acts.

I never wanted to be a banker. My luck was not landing a job with a bank, but being incredibly lucky with my third marriage. At fifty, I had an entirely different view of what constitutes family happiness.

As I sat in my pig shed sifting through my letters and debris of the past, I took hope from the career of *Downton Abbey* creator Julian Fellowes (a guest at my second wedding to Vanessa), who came to commercial success and an Oscar post-fifty. When once asked the secret of this success, Julian replied, 'Marriage.' As somebody who had failed twice on the marital front in my forties, I reflected that maybe a certain amount of failure is not only good for writers but perhaps *essential*.

So . . . fifty.

I may not have run a hedge fund but writers are fund managers of a different type. My converted pig shed, with its shelves of Binder Box love letters, was like the vault of my own private bank – a memory bank with its own forgotten valuables, even a form of buried treasure. One whose heavy bolted door leads to a maze of rooms of the heart.

Instead of Other People's Money, we invest our lives in the cargo hold of our memory and imagination – a life of writing, memorabilia and letters. In my vault is the material of half a century of this 'human-being business' of experience, as I had written to Catherine in 1996 after my thirtieth.

After the romances, affairs, weddings, honeymoons and divorces, and witnessing some of the most important events of modern times – from the fall of the Berlin Wall to the LA riots – I have certainly invested enough of my own human and emotional capital. It was what Ruskin (we were talking again) called the 'wealth of life' in *The Stones of Venice*.

When I lived in LA, I had the sort of ringside seat at the social circus of modern America that any writer would appreciate. I covered the trial of O. J. Simpson, the LA riots, notorious executions, and even got to ask Tom Wolfe during a conversation in his East 79th Street apartment if I could have a tour of his wardrobe. I wanted to know if he only had white suits, or owned any jeans or sneakers, having seen him the night before walking around Upper East Side holding an umbrella and wearing what looked like a tracksuit. 'My closet is not available for interview,' he drawled, as he signed my copy of *The Bonfire of the Vanities*, his first novel, which was not published until he was fifty-six. One dared to hope.

Epilogue

For the last Wednesday 2.30 p.m. tour of the season, I peered through the window in the drizzling rain to see if any punters were gathered under the Gatehouse archway. There were five, most with umbrellas.

Each paid their £12.50 and there was nothing unusual. I told my usual collection of anecdotes about the house: how Margaret and Denis Thatcher had stayed up until 3 a.m. in the drawing room drinking whisky; how the gardener Darren had nearly dropped a breakfast tray when he had been greeted at the door of the Prince Rupert Bedroom in the Gatehouse by Elizabeth Hurley in white silk pyjamas; and how my father had spent years attempting to locate the house's famed 'secret tunnel' using a pair of rusting metal water diviners until a tour guest had revealed where the entrance lay.

As the tour ended, I picked up my father's bulky leatherbound album – dark-blue with 'Upton Cressett Hall, 1971' in gilt on the cover. It would be handed around with the home-made cake and tea.

'Any questions?' I asked. 'Tea will now be served in the Great Hall dining room due to the poor weather.'

The group wanted their cake and tea and started heading off to the dining room.

'Before you leave,' I said, 'do pay a visit to our little Norman church. There's a fine monumental brass hanging up, which was missing for over fifty years. It's worth a look – along with the Norman font. It depicts Jane and Richard Cressett surrounded by their five children and is a celebration of a Tudor marriage.'

The return of the Cressett Brass just before my birthday was a source of much satisfaction. After forty years of my father battling with diocesan bureaucracy, I had finally managed to get the necessary 'facility' approval letter from the Hereford Diocese to have the brass returned to its rightful home at St Michael's. This was largely thanks to the help of my friend Loyd Grossman, chairman of the Churches Conservation Trust, and Crispin Truman, his CEO. It took our builder Martin less than a morning to remove the brass from Monkhopton's church, wrap it in a blanket, and fix it back to the wall of the Cressett Chapel where it had first hung in 1640 to mark the death of Jane Cressett.

He seemed in a good mood. It turned out that his daughter Megan had achieved her required A-level grades and was going to read English at Cambridge.

On touching the engraved brass for the first time, I felt a deep sense of the old Elizabethan order being restored. Time reconsecrated. I had felt the same at Cosima's christening when my hands had touched the beaten leaded tub-font as I held her head above it.

The Last Punter

As the last tour group of the season sat down to tea, following my tour, I opened my father's album. It included the very first photos my parents had taken after falling in love with the house on that sultry June day in 1970. There are pictures of my mother in flares standing by our white Citroën Safari, yellow JCB-style bulldozers at work clearing the moat – which had been so overgrown that its ramparts had been impossible to see – cement mixers and piles of sand, which I had used to build sandcastles and play with my Action Man.

As I handed the album around, I noticed a man in his sixties – grey beard and glasses, wearing a waterproof – studying the book with close interest. Normally, people just flicked through the pages but this visitor was taking a long and studious look.

'Where are the John Piper photos?' he asked.

'I'll bring them out,' I said.

This small exhibition ('The Summer Before the Storm') comprised just a few mounted boards. When I produced them, the bearded man began examining them with almost professional scrutiny. Piper's photos of Upton Cressett had been taken when he had visited the derelict Elizabethan house with John Betjeman to write their entry for *Shropshire: A Shell Guide*. The photos had been found in the newly digitised archives of Tate Britain. I'd been alerted to them by our guide Bridget Chappuis; she'd heard a BBC news item about the Tate asking the public to help identify hundreds of 'lost' John Piper architectural photos taken on his travels in Shropshire, Herefordshire and other counties.

The photos showed the Gatehouse with broken windows and a pre-war tractor parked under the archway, the twisted stacks of cut-brick chimneys still intact as the late-afternoon sun streamed down on the diaper brickwork. There were also photos of the neglected Norman church, its shabby grounds overgrown and long abandoned for worship.

The man waited until the other two couples had left before speaking to me. I sensed he wanted a private chat.

'The place has certainly changed,' he said, as I began to clear away tea. 'I can hardly recognise it from when I was last here.'

'When was that?' I asked.

'April 1970,' he replied.

There was a long pause.

'You see, I very nearly lived here,' he added. 'I nearly took the lease in 1970.'

I had seen and heard everything on my tours; I had been threatened with a 'report' to TripAdvisor by a punter after I once took a call from my lawyer in the middle of a tour; I'd had people running away down the stairs; and I'd dealt with unruly peacocks joining the tour. But I was not prepared for this.

The man introduced himself as Peter Lea. Back in May 1969, he had been a young freelance news and magazine photographer, based in Wolverhampton, and working for national papers. He had an interest in architectural photography. Part of his bread-and-butter work was photographing derelict historic houses – the worse their condition the better – and trying to sell them on to Fleet Street. He first visited the hamlet of Upton Cressett after seeing an article in the *Bridgnorth Journal*, which highlighted the old hall's recent vandalism.

His small Austin car struggled to get up Meadowley Bank, and then nearly couldn't cross the swirling ford at the end of the lane before the hall's tumbled chimneys and broken windows of the Gatehouse came into view, surrounded by ancient damson trees and thick brambles. 'It was love at first sight,' Peter said. 'The absolute desolation and tranquility was wonderful, I was hooked.'

Although he was intending to take only a few exterior photographs, he 'lingered for an hour or so' as he explored the overgrown grounds and stripped out interiors. He took a series of photographs of the abandoned house, with its pig and chicken inhabitants in the panelled rooms – or what was left of the panelling. He returned in April 1970 to take more pictures and also to have another look around.

'There were so many abandoned country houses that the picture story didn't run,' Peter told me.

Still, intrigued by the dilapidated magic of Upton Cressett, he had enquired to the land agent about taking over the lease as he was looking for a romantic wreck to restore. He was subsequently offered a caretaker five-year lease, just a month or so before my parents first visited in the summer of 1970.

Peter had different plans from my father's. 'It was the age of hippie communes,' he said. 'My imagination was fired up by the decayed beauty of the place. But the remote location didn't really fit in with my work style.'

After negotiating with Colonel Marsh, he finally pulled out. 'It was just a young man's romantic dream,' he told me, nearly half a century later.

Peter then produced a USB stick that contained the black-and-white photos he had taken on those two visits in 1969 and 1970. After loading them on to my laptop in the kitchen, I gazed aghast at the haunting images, which showed the house's medieval stone fireplaces bricked up, the front door with a corrugated iron 'portico' entrance, the twisting chimneys half broken and an outdoor brick WC in the middle of the Moat Lawn where our sagging Bosworth tent now stood. They closely mirrored the more amateur photos taken by my father with his Prinz camera just a few months later.

So much of life is a patchwork of arbitrary coincidence and chance. How different the circumstances of my fiftieth birthday might have been! Had Peter leased the Gatehouse, and my parents would probably never have known about the house.

Just a young man's dream.

Dressing for Dinner

As I closed the door behind me after the last tour of the season, I felt a strange rush of emotions. How would my life have turned out had I not been brought up at Upton Cressett? Would I ever have married Laura if the house had remained a derelict wreck?

I stand at the end of the final corridor of this memoir. This theatre of memory has only a single scene left.

It had drizzled most of the day on the Saturday of my fiftieth party. But at around 5 p.m., the rain stopped. The August sun broke through the clouds and the skies turned a pale and misty blue. It was going to be possible to have drinks in the Bosworth tent after all. As the bar staff started putting out glasses on the makeshift bar, I put a broom handle to the sagging puddle of rain water that had gathered on the front entrance canopy. It cascaded on to the lawn, drenching the two pugs that were scampering below.

It was time to put the lute and broom away. The chase was done, the old leaves and petals swept away. It was time to go inside ('Let's in,' as Marvell ends 'Upon Appleton House'). It was time to dress before dinner in our panelled bedroom as the evening sun flooded through the windows. As Laura put on her dress, I scrawled a few notes on a correspondence card and folded the card into the breast pocket of my velvet jacket before tying my bow-tie.

It was now time to descend the oak newel stairs and enter the millinery garden where the flowers, dewy with rain, stood up like the bright uniforms of soldiers on each border. Several of York's white feathers dressed the lawn.

'The lawns are looking good,' said Laura, as we walked down the steps towards the Bosworth tent.

We had around eighty people for dinner in the old Norman church. No electric lights, just candles stuck in old decanters.

It was time for Mike Read to sing his Johnny Cash song. This turned out to be a hilariously bumpy road trip through my life with Mike plucking away at the guitar. The twelfth-century church had certainly never heard the like before. But that is what such old buildings were made for. To be used, not preserved or left to decay or treated like a museum. I'd learned on my journey that our restorations – of houses and hearts – were not just about the past; they were as much about the future, and deciding what was worth preserving, or letting go.

Adopting his best bone-gravel Nashville drawl, Mike said, 'Hi folks, I've put together a little birthday ballad . . .'

> *The sat-nav doesn't register so one simply has to guess it,*
> *And you cruise through the gate an hour late for drinks at*
>   *Upton Cressett,*
> *It's an architectural gem says William, there's no need to*
>   *assess it,*
> *An Elizabethan jewel in the crown of Upton Cressett.*
> *Familial ties to Johnny Cash, hear William Cash finesse it,*
> *He reckons he's the man in black, who walks the line at*
>   *Upton Cressett.*
> *There's history within these walls from the Civil War to Brexit*
> *Even Edward V and Charles the First have stayed at*
>   *Upton Cressett . . .*

The guests were loving it. Mike went on for a few more verses before winding up with some unlikely fellow fiftieth birthday comparisons.

> *Cantona's fifty, Cameron too, it's easy to assess it*
> *So's Mike Tyson, Gordon Ramsay and the lad from*
>   *Upton Cressett.*
> *So here's a toast to William and may Spear's mag hot press it*
> *He's an eighth of the age of the Hall itself here at*
>   *Upton Cressett . . .*

There was a roar of laughter.

In my speech, I began by assuring any friends who had given me wine as a present (which was most of them) that, following the episode of the exploding bottle on my honeymoon, I had learned my lesson. 'All bottles will be drunk swiftly,' I said.

I thanked my parents for everything, then explained how Upton

Cressett had narrowly avoided being turned into a Seventies hippie commune. I also thanked photographer Peter Lea for *not* taking the Upton Cressett lease in 1970 a few months before my parents had arrived with me in the back seat.

'Had that Citroën Safari journey not taken place, the curtain would never have been raised on the stage set upon which so much of my life has taken place,' I said. 'One thing I do know,' I added, as the altar candle burning next to me just about lit my face in the church. 'If I had been brought up in Islington, we would not be sitting here tonight . . . What I also know is that, had it not been for my beautiful and wonderful wife Laura, I wouldn't be so happy. Thank you, Laura, and for our daughter Cosima . . .'

I paused.

'And I'm delighted to say that we have another baby on the way, which is the best birthday present one could ever imagine.'

This was to be our son Rex.

There was plenty of clapping.

'And can I ask one favour?' I said. 'Please don't write us a thank-you letter. We'd prefer if you wrote a TripAdvisor review of Upton Cressett instead.'

Outside the church, the sky had cleared. It was now a fine summer's evening with the moon glowing above the twisted chimneys, like a golden coin, as the glittering stars winked down on us. I took Laura's hand as we headed up towards the house, and when she smiled at me, I felt it was finally time to think about our future – to stop looking back. To let the past go. It was time, as W. H. Auden wrote, to 'dance while you can' and to 'dance till the stars come down from the rafters'.

Laura had booked 'Tina Turner' for the evening to help us do this in the house. That is, a Tina Turner tribute singer from Redditch called Kerry Whip. She wore the full Tina outfit including fishnet tights and killer heels. As she belted out classic Tina Turner songs in the dining room, in front of the portrait of Sir Francis Cressett in full court dress as a Groom of the Bedchamber, it was difficult to know whose wig looked more preposterous.

I had also asked my old jazz singer friend Christopher Silvester to sing a few numbers, including the song 'Laura'. Except Laura was no longer only a dream – she was the woman I loved, living in the Elizabethan brick house that was now our family home; and it was my wife's initials, LRC, that were to be carved on the panelling above our bed. They were also the initials of my restored heart.

Afterword

So what happened to my Binder Box girlfriends and ex-wives, and the other dramatis personae in my story?

I have remained friends, or so I hope, with all of my Binder Box correspondents. Until I contacted her in July 2016 to tell her of Christina Knudsen's death, I had not seen, or spoken with, Catherine Jordan since I left LA in 1999, some eighteen years before. She was now an award-winning film producer whose last film had premiered at the Venice Film Festival. Could she remember my thirtieth?

'I did all the cooking,' she replied by email, 'and Hugh Grant complimented my custard tart.' Shocked by the news of Christina, she added, 'I seem to be surrounded by death these days,' as both her parents had died recently. 'Your wife looks lovely,' she added.

Louise King married a lawyer, an Oxford 'Bullingdon' friend of David Cameron, and has four children.

Neither of my ex-wives has remarried to date. While on the King's

Road in Chelsea a few years ago, I recognised Ilaria's walk ahead of me – at fifty yards. We remain on good terms, despite the technical condition that we communicate only through her lawyers.

Vanessa was appointed as Ambassador to the United Kingdom in March 2019 by Venezuela's interim president Juan Guaidó (as recognised by the British and US governments). She has also been to stay at Upton Cressett.

I have not seen Helen for a long while but she has not married (as far as I know). She moved on to an aristocratic French art dealer and lives between Paris, London and Kent.

Anna married the scion of a shipping family and lives in a country house with two children and extensive stables, close to her mother in Hampshire. The only news I hear from her relates to when she has a new horse. Her most recent is called Boris.

Christina Knudsen was not the only one of my good friends to die far too young. Matthew Mellon died a billionaire the day before checking into a New Mexico rehab clinic not long after his fifty-fourth birthday in April 2018. He had been haunted for much of his life by the expectations of his American-banking-royalty name.

I couldn't attend Matthew's memorial in Florida as I was best man at my friend Charlie Dean's wedding in London (his second). He married the senior staff writer of *Spear's*, from a noble Scottish family, some twenty-two years his junior. He quickly became a member of the Old Dads Club. I am godfather to their first child, Ophelia.

Another friend who has gone is novelist Philip Kerr, who gave me a memorable bottle of vintage wine at my fiftieth. We had been working on a project set in 1930s Germany when he was diagnosed with cancer. The last time I saw him was in December 2017 at a Christmas lunch I hosted with Adam Dant. He took a sip of champagne and said, 'I always love coming to this event but I'm sorry to say this will be my last.' He was just sixty-one.

My wonderful art conservationist uncle Mark died in 2017 in

his late sixties. Our dear friend Lucy Birley, dog and rare-pig lover, horsewoman and beloved neighbour, died in July 2018 and is much missed in Shropshire. Nic Roeg died in November 2018, aged ninety, with the *Guardian* describing him as Britain's 'leading director' of the Seventies. Clem Franckenstein died after a heart-attack in May 2019, aged seventy-four. At his memorial service at Great Tew, a recording was played of him singing as a tenor at Eton.

Darren, my gardener and handyman, left to take up a factory job near Dudley. Then I had a text from him asking if he could return at weekends with Nathan. After the first day he texted: 'It felt like I was home. I've always loved your place.' Pedro and Luiza left shortly after Laura and I were married. I occasionally see Pedro selling the *Big Issue* on the King's Road.

Uncle Jonathan has not been to Upton Cressett for around fifteen years. When he finally arrives, I look forward to showing him the restoration and the library of his five thousand books, and tramping out to his newly designated Roman settlement.

Under Laura's management, we have now have a TripAdvisor 'Excellence' award certificate for our holiday lets. Martin Reidy has converted a new property called the Moat House. We now offer luxury B & B for romantic couples in our historic suites; or can host groups of up to sixteen for family or group occasions. I continue to perform the duties of head tour guide, as well as often cooking breakfast for our holiday guests.

Upton Cressett remains unchanged, as ever, with its time-worn Elizabethan bricks a little more in need of repointing each year.

Acknowledgements and
Author's Note

This is not a memoir in which real people have been turned into composites or semi-fictionalised. All names are real. I have only changed the identity of one person, and they only have a cameo appearance. The Binder Box letters are also all real, and the quotations are just as written or scrawled.

I have stuck with my journalistic habit of including real names and places rather than deracinating my story with phrases such as 'a pub in central London' or a 'hotel in Venice'. I have used real names again to help the reader picture the scene; and if any of the places described are followed up by the reader on their travels, I hope they still exist.

The book went through many drafts and I have many people to thank, not least my lawyer Melissa Lesson at Mishcon de Reya who insisted that any 'confidentiality' issues with my first marriage expired in 2017. So I couldn't properly start until then.

Thank you to my dear old friend Clare Reihill, executor of the T. S. Eliot literary estate, who read the first draft and offered some very useful notes. She also passed me on to the brilliant 'cutter' and copy-editor Hazel Orme, who honed the manuscript into shape before submission.

Others who edited and gave notes at the draft stage included the peerless Steve King, formerly of *Spear's* and *Vanity Fair*, Christopher Silvester and Patrick Keogh. Encouragement and advice also came from my dear friend Deirdre Brennan, Tom Bower, Chris Jackson and Emma Cole, Charlie Hart, Charlotte Radford, Toby Guise, Willa Greenock and Celia Weinstock; and my lawyer and friend Charlotte Harris and others who know who they are. Thanks also to Dr Vanessa Neumann ('Her Excellency') for bearing to read the pages about our marriage and saying she even enjoyed them. Also thank you to my screenwriting partner and good friend Tony Macnabb, who has put up with my romantic vicissitudes for nearly twenty years.

My agent Matthew Hamilton read several drafts, offered excellent advice and did a brilliant job of securing such a wonderful publisher for the book, Andreas Campomar at Constable.

Thanks to all the building team, especially Martin Reidy, a true craftsman builder. I was also lucky with my architects Trevor Edwards and Tony Craig and project manager Belinda Edwards, who somehow always found time for Upton Cressett between training her horses. Peter Welford helped with the architectural history, and I would also like to thank all at SPAB and Historic Houses (formerly Historic Houses Association), especially James Birch, for all their support over the years. Also Jeremy Musson, John Goodall, Harry Mount and Simon Jenkins for their architectural articles and/or book entries and also Norman Hudson, Simon Thurley, Historic England, English Heritage and the Churches Conservation Trust. All their words came to the rescue when Upton Cressett was under attack, as did the photos of Mike Wootton.

On the house front, thanks to Bridget Chappuis for her guided tours and detective work; Richard Harvey for being such a popular guide (even playing guitar to tour groups), and the wonderful Louise Pickard, our very own Mary Poppins, without whom life at Upton Cressett would be impossible. Darren and Nathan are also invaluable to keep the show going on, from mowing to logs. Thanks also to my genius wood carver Andrew Pearson.

Parts of the book previously appeared in very different forms in various publications. Thanks to Eleanor Mills at the *Sunday Times* magazine, Jason Cowley at the *New Statesman*, Sasha Slater at *ES* magazine and *Telegraph* magazine, Paul Clements at the *Daily Telegraph*, Luke Coppen at the *Catholic Herald*, various editors at the *Daily Mail* and *Country Life*, Neil Thomas at *Shropshire Magazine*, Claire Sargent at the CPRE's magazine and, of course, Alec Marsh at *Spear's*. Thanks also to Josh Spero, our former editor. Also to Richard and Christina at Bridgnorth Print for all their efforts and help over the years. And Dan Smith my website man.

As a memoir of double divorce, I must thank the members of my best man club: Charles Dean, William Dartmouth and Gus Hochschild. Also the members of my veteran ushers club who include Mowbray Jackson, Hugh Warrender, Jonathan Bailey, Patrick Paines, Harry Tyser, Tom Faure, Rupert Phelps, Piers, Porky, Bobby, James B, Ant Haden-Guest, Ant Rufus-Isaacs and the rest of the gang. Henry D-B for his hospitality over the years. And Dom Antony Sutch for marrying me – twice – and christening Cosima.

One of the most enjoyable aspects of researching our family history was becoming acquainted properly with my New York based 'cousin' (however distant) Rosanne Cash. Also thanks to Ben and Speronella Marsh who helped with the history of Upton Cressett.

Others who have been great friends and supporters include Robin Birley, Brooks Newmark, Rocco Forte, Elizabeth Hurley, Philip and Catherine Mould, Charles Macdowell, Allan Scott, Paul Flynn,

Constance Watson, Corinna Sayn-Wittgenstein, Caitlin Rankin-McCabe and, of course, our house artist Adam Dant who also designed the book jacket, illustrations and endpapers. Also thanks to Sandy Loder for carrying the final proofs in his rucksack along the West Highland Way in July 2019 as we tried to find a post office.

A special thanks to my parents who have been long-suffering about the manuscript for many years and these pages, of course, could never have been written if they hadn't decided to go restore-a-wreck hunting in the late 1960s. A special thanks also to other family members Laetitia, Sam and Uncle Jonathan for being part of the journey. Thank you also to my parents-in-law, Viv and Charles, for all your kindness and letting me write in the Brew House in Norfolk.

Above all, thanks to Laura for everything.

Upton Cressett, July 2019